BAPTISM IN EARLY METHODISM

BERNARD G. HOLLAND

*Baptism in
Early Methodism*

LONDON
EPWORTH PRESS

© BERNARD G. HOLLAND
FIRST PUBLISHED IN 1970
All Rights Reserved

No part of this publication may be reproduced, stored in a retrieval system, or transmitted, in any form or by any means, electronic, mechanical, photocopying, recording or otherwise, without the prior permission of the Epworth Press, 27 Marylebone Road, London, NW1

265.127
H719

180194

Printed and bound in Great Britain by
The Garden City Press Limited,
Letchworth, Hertfordshire

TO MY MOTHER AND THE MEMORY
OF MY FATHER
who down the years
have surrounded their children
'with such things as are pure and true,
lovely and of good report'

Acknowledgements

The research undertaken in the preparation of this book would not have been possible without help from many people.

Superintendent ministers stationed at the historic centres of Methodism have kindly given time to searching in the dark corners of circuit safes for old baptismal registers. I received most useful information about the New Room, Bristol, from the late Warden, the Rev. A. J. Gedye, B.A.; and regarding the Ogden Chapel registers from the Rev. C. Robertshaw, B.A., B.D. The Rectors of Epworth and Wroot, the Revs. W. B. Harvey, B.A., and H. D. Speakman, have most generously made available to me the registers of their churches; and the Methodist Connexional Archivist, the Rev. Dr. J. C. Bowmer, M.A., B.D., has, over a period of seven years, frequently given invaluable advice and information. Mr. J. D. Walsh, M.A., of Jesus College, Oxford, not only provided help with references for Chapter 10, but was kind enough to read that chapter in manuscript and comment most helpfully upon it. Both my father (the Rev. B. Holland) and the Rev. A. Raymond George, M.A., B.D., have greatly assisted me by reading through and criticising the first complete typescript of this study, and I have been glad to follow their suggestions at many points. Above all, I am indebted to the Rev. Dr. A. Marcus Ward, M.A., who, for many years, first as Lecturer, then as Tutor, and always as friend, has prompted and guided my studies and encouraged me in them. For all this help and interest, extended by so many people and always so readily given, I proffer my warmest thanks.

Reference must be made to my thesis, *Baptism in Wesleyan Methodism: Practice and Doctrine to 1882* (London University, 1966), some of the findings of which are incorporated in these pages along with much new material. Finally, I am grateful to the Fernley-Hartley Lecture Trustees whose invitation to deliver the Lecture during the 1970 Conference, at the Barrington Road Methodist Church, Altrincham, has enabled the results of these researches to be made more generally available.

Pinner
November 1969

BERNARD G HOLLAND

* * *

Thanks are due to the following for permission to quote from copyright sources:

Lutterworth Press: *Christian Baptism* (1959), edited by A. Gilmore.

Oxford University Press: *Baptism and Conversion* (1964), by J. Baillie.

S.P.C.K.: *The New Testament Doctrine of Baptism* (1948), by W. F. Flemington.

Contents

		Page
Introductory Note		1

Chapter

1.	The Riddle of Wesley's Baptismal Beliefs	3
2.	Wesley Learns Baptismal Regeneration, and begins to Baptise	14
3.	Ministry on Board Ship and in Georgia	27
4.	Wesley Learns to Equate Adult Regeneration with Conversion	35
5.	Wesley's Doctrine: 1. Adult Baptism and Regeneration	43
6.	2. Infant Baptism and the Two Regenerations	53
7.	3. An Assessment	72
8.	Baptism in the Ministry of the Wesleys	84
9.	Baptism and the Early Methodists: Practice	104
10.	Baptismal Regeneration: the Climate of Evangelical Opinion	117
11.	Baptismal Regeneration and the 'Sunday Service of the Methodists'	131
12.	Wesley and the Methodist Baptismal Tradition	140

Appendices

1.	Notes on Wesley's Baptismal Writings; and the Text of his Essay, 'Water Baptism is the Baptism of Christ'	152
2.	Baptism in Charles Wesley's Hymns and Verse	163
3.	Wesleyan Methodist Registers of Births and Baptisms begun before 1791	170
4.	The Baptismal Material in the 'Sunday Service' and the 'Book of Common Prayer' Compared	177
5.	Bibliography	189
Index		199

Abbreviations

Journal	The *Journal of John Wesley*, standard edition, 8 vols., edited by Nehemiah Curnock.
Letters	The *Letters of John Wesley*, standard edition, 8 vols., edited by John Telford.
Works	The *Works of John Wesley*, 3rd edition, 14 vols., edited by Thomas Jackson.
Sermons	The *Standard Sermons of John Wesley*, 2 vols., edited by E. H. Sugden.
Diary	The transliteration of Wesley's shorthand Diaries, as found in chronologically arranged footnotes in the *Journal*.
Thoughts	*Thoughts Upon Infant-Baptism, Extracted from a late Writer*, Bristol, 1751. By John Wesley.
Treatise	*A Treatise on Baptism*, By John Wesley, found in *Works* x. pp. 188ff.
Discourse	*A Short Discourse of Baptism*. By Samuel Wesley. (Included in *The Pious Communicant Rightly Prepar'd*, 1700.)
Charles' Journal	The *Journal of Charles Wesley*, 2 vols., edited by Thomas Jackson.
Poetical Works	The *Poetical Works of John and Charles Wesley*, 13 vols., edited by George Osborn.
Notes	*Explanatory Notes Upon the New Testament*, 1754, By John Wesley, 1950 edition.
Minutes	*Minutes of Conference*.
W.H.S.	The *Preceedings of the Wesley Historical Society*.
L.Q.H.R.	The *London Quarterly and Holborn Review*.
H.M.C.	*A History of the Methodist Church in Great Britain*, vol. 1. 1965. Editors: Rupert Davies and Gordon Rupp.

Introductory Note

It may be a help towards clarity if definitions are given at the outset of the main terms to be used in this study. In the first place, *regeneration* requires some comment. While bearing the general sense of *new birth*, it has from time to time been used by Christians in two specific ways: first, to refer to a gift received either by infants or adults in baptism; and second, to indicate a non-sacramental adult experience of *conversion*.

We will find that Wesley used the term in both of these particular senses, to denote the re-birth of infants in baptism and the conversion of adults. In order to compare the new birth at these two stages of life, we will refer to them as *infant regeneration* and *adult regeneration*[1] respectively.

Furthermore, in spite of the fact that Wesley himself rarely employed the term in this evangelical sense,[2] we will (in conformity with traditional Methodist usage) use *conversion* as a synonym for *adult regeneration* as John Wesley[3] understood it.

Normally, infant regeneration has been considered to be essentially a baptismal gift, and when so regarded it is termed *baptismal regeneration*.[4] It is to be observed, however, that there is no one doctrine of baptismal regeneration but rather that the expression has been used in a variety of ways at different times within diverse Christian traditions. Within this wide spectrum of usage one important distinction stands out. On the one hand, some have considered baptismal regeneration to be a matter of reconciliation to God, so that

---

[1] The expression is a little misleading in that children from about nine years of age were said to require 'adult' regeneration.

[2] v. *Letters*, iii., p. 266.

[3] For the differences between John and Charles Wesley in their understanding of conversion, v. J. E. Rattenbury, *The Evangelical Doctrines of Charles Wesley's Hymns* (1941) pp. 260 ff.

[4] Usually this term will be taken to refer only to infants, and when it is applied to adults this is made explicit.

its benefits are only *relative*—that is, while no real change is brought about in the character of the recipient his standing before God is adjusted; he is restored to God's favour, he is justified. On the other hand, others have argued that baptismal regeneration includes not only such a relative, but also some *real* change. This means that in baptism some change for good is made in the personality of the recipient, which is explained as being either the gift of the Holy Spirit, or the infusion of some principle of grace or of actual habits of virtue and goodness.

Finally, the term *evangelicals* will be used of those connected with the revival broadly considered, while *Evangelicals* will be reserved to indicate those who came to form the Evangelical party within the Church of England.

CHAPTER I

The Riddle of Wesley's Baptismal Beliefs

On being recalled to his Oxford College in 1729, John Wesley joined a little group which his brother had recently formed. It was not long before its members attracted ridicule because of their systematic life of study and worship, and they were given various nicknames: by some they were called Methodists, by others the Holy Club or the Godly Club, and by others again Sacramentarians.

The immediate reason for this last name was the frequency with which the members of the Club went to communion, and careful attention has been paid to the importance of this sacrament in the life and devotion of the early Methodists.[1] But what of the other sacrament? No full account has as yet been given of the attitude of the Wesleys and the first Methodists to baptism. Such an examination therefore is now attempted, and it will be seen, so high was their regard both for infant and adult baptism, that at Oxford and for many years afterwards, the Methodists for this reason also, were Sacramentarians indeed.

On approaching the subject of Wesley's beliefs about baptism, the enquirer may very well be made to think that here is something of a riddle. He is likely to be bewildered by varying and sometimes flatly contradictory claims about Wesley's opinions, and he may be told, not only that Wesley's own statements are inconsistent, but also that there is considerable uncertainty as to whether in his later years he changed his mind about the efficacy of the sacrament.

It is important, therefore, before we turn to the events and writings of the eighteenth century, to trace the changing attitude of Methodists to Wesley's baptismal beliefs, and to

[1] J. E. Rattenbury, *The Eucharistic Hymns of John and Charles Wesley* (1948); J. C. Bowmer, *The Sacrament of the Lord's Supper in Early Methodism* (1951).

explain how the tradition has grown up that these are perplexing and obscure.

During the period up to 1833, Wesley's teaching about baptism was virtually ignored. Until the rise of the Oxford Movement there was no cause for Methodists to examine their beliefs about this sacrament, nor therefore was there any reason for them to discover and explain what their late founder had said about it. Where baptism is mentioned in Methodist literature of this period, no reference is made to John Wesley.[1] This is particularly noticeable in the three most influential Wesleyan publications of these years, the commentaries by Thomas Coke (1801–3) and Adam Clarke (1810–25), and Richard Watson's *Theological Institutions* (1823), all of which ignore Wesley altogether in their articles on this ordinance.[2]

The one exception to this rule of silence appeared in 1824, in a letter to the editor of the *Methodist Magazine* from T.J.—presumably Thomas Jackson. This was occasioned by the publication in the previous year of the collected works of Daniel Waterland, in which, in an editorial comment, Dr. Van Mildert had argued that the form of regeneration preached by Whitefield and Wesley 'rendered Baptism, in effect, a nugatory and unavailing ordinance'.[3] In reply, T.J. quoted Wesley's writings to good effect, and provided a summary of his teaching about baptism and regeneration which, for a brief statement, can hardly be bettered. He wrote:

(Wesley) not only acknowledged that a gracious communication is made to the minds of children in baptism, but to the effect of that communication he gave the name of the New Birth. . . . Mr. Wesley, nevertheless, denied that the same effect is invariably

---

[1] e.g. *Articles of Religion Prepared by order of the Conference of 1806*, W. H. S. Publication (1897) pp. 22 f (in spite of the request that each Article should be supported by references to Wesley's Works); J. Crowther, *The Methodist Manual* (1810) pp. 115 f, and *A Portraiture of Methodism* (1810) 2nd ed. 1815, pp. 228 f; *Catechism* (1821); William Beal, *Remarks on Luke xviii, 15, 16, 17* (1824) *passim*; G. Jackson, *A Series of Letters, on the Subjects and Mode of Christian Baptism* (1828) *passim*.

[2] Coke's *Commentary on the New Testament* under John iii. 5, 1 John v. 8, 1 Peter iii. 21; Clarke's *Commentary*, v, pp. 361 ff; Watson's *Works*, xii, pp. 222 ff.

[3] Waterland's *Works*, i. pp. 180 ff. Richard Mant has made a similar point in his Bampton Lectures of 1812 (*An Appeal to the Gospel, or an Inquiry into the Justice of the Charge, alleged by Methodists and other Objectors, that The Gospel is not preached by the National Clergy*, Sermons VI and VII), but at that time no Methodist reply was forthcoming.

produced in cases of adult baptism; and believed that those children who receive that blessing in their infancy, generally lose it as they grow in years, and mix with the world. He also believed that when they are brought under the power of sinful affections and habits, the renewal of their minds in righteousness and true holiness, after the image of God, becomes again a matter of indispensable necessity; and to that renewal, whenever it is effected, and how often soever it may be repeated, he used to give the name of REGENERATION, or of the NEW BIRTH.[1]

Here it is plainly shown that Wesley taught the need for regeneration at two distinct and successive stages of life, in infancy and adulthood. However, before such a balanced assessment of his position could become widely known and accepted, the Oxford Movement began to dominate Church life in England. The teaching of the Tracts caused Methodists to consider the meaning and efficacy of this sacrament, the use of which was so firmly established in their Churches, and their immediate reaction was to protest that regeneration is not the invariable accompaniment of baptism. Thus when Pusey stated 'that "regeneration" is the gift of GOD, bestowed by Him, in this life, in Baptism only',[2] it was increasingly felt that here was a doctrine irreconcilable with the conception of regeneration as conversion: that the two regenerations (infant and adult) could not both be accepted by anyone of true evangelical persuasion.

It was against this background that Methodists began to study what Wesley had said about baptism, and so it came about that the first widespread Methodist awareness of his baptismal theology was an embarrassed awakening to the fact that in some places he had expressed a belief in the baptismal regeneration of infants. The author of the *Wesleyan Tracts for the Times* (1842), for example, examined Wesley's 'whole doctrine at large', and summed up:

From the whole of this it may be confidently concluded, that although Mr. Wesley acknowledged a blessing in baptism, even in infant baptism, and used the language of the Church in describing it, yet he carefully distinguished it from that great salvation from the guilt and power of sin which the Scriptures call justification and

[1] *Wesleyan–Methodist Magazine*, 1824, pp. 238 f.
[2] Tract 67, *Scriptural Views of Holy Baptism* (3rd ed. 1840) p. 42.

regeneration. And thus he left out of the Service Book expressions which might only tend to perplex and agitate the minds of those who, to say the least, were less committed to the Church liturgy as a whole than he was himself. He regarded baptism as a λομτρον, the bath or washing of regeneration, the outward sign; attended with such degrees of grace as the recipient could at the time receive, according to his maturity of nature, and obedience to the terms of the evangelical covenant: but the spiritual blessing just described he alone regarded as 'the renewing of the Holy Ghost', the inward part of regeneration. And hence, Mr. Wesley, as it is well known, preached regeneration as jealously and fervently to those ungodly individuals who had been baptized at the Church in infancy, as he did to any other sinner whatever.[1]

In this way, during the middle years of the last century, Wesley's references to baptismal regeneration were commonly regarded by Methodists as unfortunate lapses to be hushed up or explained away as best may be.

Such evasion, however, did not for long go unchallenged. A flurry of books written by high churchmen within a few years of each other later in the nineteenth century, laid bare the full extent of Wesley's belief in baptismal re-birth. Such authors as R. D. Urlin (*John Wesley's Place in Church History*,[2] 1870; and *A Churchman's Life of Wesley*,[3] 1880), W. H. Holden (*John Wesley in Company with High Churchmen*,[4] 1870), and F. Hockin (*John Wesley and Modern Methodism*,[5] 1887) claimed that Wesley had been himself very much of a high churchman, and that his followers ought to have departed neither from his doctrine nor from his Church.[6]

In regard to baptism, their argument ran as follows:

Here then we have Wesley's uniform Teaching on this subject throughout his life. He proclaims that 'in the waters of Baptism' as

---

[1] Tract 9, p. 11. This passage appears also in Alfred Barrett's *Catholic and Evangelical Principles* (1843) pp. 124 f. cf. Jabez Bunting (President) in the 1844 Conference (v. B. Gregory, *Side Lights on the Conflicts of Methodism* (1899 ed.) pp. 358 f); H. M. Luckock and E. T. Carrier, *John Wesley's Churchmanship* (1891) pp. 38 f. [2] pp. 215 ff. [3] pp. 60 f, 298 ff.
[4] pp. 6 ff.
[5] pp. 85 f. This is a reply to J. H. Rigg, *The Churchmanship of John Wesley* (1878). cf. J. H. Overton, *John Wesley* (1891) Ch. VI.
[6] This argument is found first in a pamphlet of 1842, *Remarks upon the 'Wesleyan Tracts for the Times'*, pp. 13 ff, by a 'Layman of the Church of England'. cf. H. M. Luckock and E. T. Carrier, *op. cit.* pp. 17 ff; Anon, *Wesley and Modern Methodism* (n.d.) pp. 9 ff; E. G. Harvey, *John Wesley, his Principles and his Practice* (n.d.) pp. 4 f.

a means we are regenerated or born again—infants absolutely so, adults 'where the outward sign is duly received'. That in Baptism, 'original sin is washed away', and the baptized 'engrafted into Christ'. That Baptism 'is the ordinary instrument of our justification', and that 'there is no other means in the ordinary way of entering Heaven', inasmuch as John iii. 5. is spoken of nothing more or less than Baptism.[1]

The most prominent champion who came forward from the Wesleyan ranks to rebut these charges was Dr. James H. Rigg. He replied by claiming that long before the end of his life Wesley had ceased to believe in baptismal regeneration. Rigg agreed that Wesley had indeed been a ritualistic high churchman, but only between the years 1725 to 1738; and he goes on:

> Though for some time yet he retained his rubrical scruples and punctilios as to the necessity of episcopalian baptism, and even went so far, on at least one occasion . . . as to re-baptize Dissenters, yet henceforth the sacraments, according to his teaching, were to be regarded only as means and seals of grace, not as fountains of supernatural power.[2]

Rigg notices, with a strong suggestion of regret, that along with his 'rubrical scruples' Wesley retained a belief in the baptismal regeneration of infants after 1738: and yet he softens this by explaining, first, that Wesley did not demand this belief in his preachers and people;[3] second, that he did not allow past baptism to serve as an excuse for continuing ungodliness;[4] and third, that by his emendations to the *Book of Common Prayer* in 1784, Wesley had shown that he 'must, in his later years, have ceased to hold, or at least have come to doubt of, the doctrine of baptismal regeneration'.[5]

During this same period (towards the end of the nineteenth century) there was discussion within the Wesleyan Connexion following a demand for a new and authoritative service book. The provision of acceptable Offices of baptism proved to be most difficult, and part of the trouble was to know what changes in the *Sunday Service* could be made without doing violence to Wesley's baptismal convictions. This dilemma called for an exposition of those convictions—and the account

---

[1] Hockin, *op. cit.* pp. 85 f.   [2] *Op. cit.* pp. 39 f.
[3] *Ibid.* p. 42.   [4] *Ibid.* p. 41.   [5] *Ibid.* p. 43.

given by James Rigg found wide acceptance. To the Connexion at large,[1] and in the Conference itself,[2] Rigg explained that while in some places Wesley had allowed baptismal regeneration, this was a blemish in his doctrines, inconsistent with the broad tenor of his evangelical teaching, and in any case renounced by him in his later years. The Conference of 1882 (which finally approved the new Wesleyan liturgy) and Methodism generally were satisfied with this assessment, and so Rigg's view of Wesley's baptismal thinking had now become normative.

We find it set out at length in a booklet produced in 1881, entitled *Baptism and the Wesleyan Conference*,[3] which takes the form of a series of conversations between two Wesleyan ministers, Lovetruth and Goode. Together they agree to study the Methodist doctrinal standards, and find: that Wesley nowhere 'in these works defined clearly the doctrine of the sacrament of baptism'; that when in his sermons he allowed the baptismal regeneration of infants, it was upon the authority of his Church and as 'the ground of appeal to the unregenerate'; and they finally agree that, 'though Mr. Wesley may occasionally use an expression which characterized the Baptismal Regeneration School in which he was educated, the general drift of his writings is in a contrary direction'.[4] Thus viewed, Wesley provided no stumbling-block to hinder the Wesleyans in removing the last vestigial hints of sacramental regeneration from their baptismal Offices; which, in 1882, they proceeded to do.

By the end of the last century, therefore, the riddle of Wesley's baptismal theology had been propounded. It arose because no appraisal of his baptismal views was made until after the rise of the Oxford Movement, and by then an objective study was no longer possible. The unbalanced presentation of Wesley's opinions, for which James Rigg was principally responsible, inevitably suggested that here is a mystery, for it assumed that over most of his life Wesley, normally so

---

[1] *Was John Wesley a High Churchman?* (1881. Written by Rigg at the request of the Wesleyan Book Committee) pp. 9, 21.
[2] *Sermons* i. pp. 281 f; *The Methodist* (newspaper), 4 August 1882, pp. 516 ff.
[3] A note in pencil in the Methodist Archives' copy gives the author's name as F. W. Briggs. cf. John Harris, *Wesleyan Infant Baptism* (1886) *passim*.
[4] pp. 8–14.

clear-minded, had held contradictory beliefs about the efficacy of baptism; and that when finally he abandoned his belief in baptismal regeneration he was secretive about it.

During the present century, widely differing opinions have been expressed about Wesley's attitude to baptism, which serve to deepen rather than to dispel perplexity. In the first place, some commentators have continued to put forward Rigg's hypothesis, arguing that before the end of his life Wesley relinquished his former belief in baptismal regeneration. E. H. Sugden gave prominence to this view-point in an editorial note in the *Standard Sermons of John Wesley* (1921), where he says: 'it may fairly be argued that Wesley's revision of the (baptismal) service in 1784 proves that in his later life he altered his earlier opinion'.[1] Among others who have taken this line,[2] J. Baillie has spoken most categorically:

> Wesley altogether dissociated regeneration from baptism, being the first clearly to do so. Unlike the Anabaptists, he held to baptism in infancy, yet would not allow that infants could be regenerated. Regeneration for him must be a conscious experience.[3]

On the other hand the larger number of commentators have disagreed with this estimate, but, while concluding that Wesley at no time repudiated the doctrine of baptismal regeneration, they nevertheless differ among themselves as to the importance which he attached to it. Some say that he held it simply as a formal principle which was (to his mind) barren and unedifying, but retained because of its place in the authoritative doctrinal standards of his Church. W. R. Cannon writes:

> It must be understood, it seems to me, that Wesley's acceptance of the efficacy of infant baptism is just an acceptance, and nothing more. He affirms it as a teaching of the Church. Nowhere does he stress it as a fundamental tenet of his own doctrine.[4]

---

[1] i, p. 282.
[2] R. Green, *John Wesley Evangelist* (1904) p. 216; J. Telford, *The Life of John Wesley* (1947 ed.) p. 307; H. Wheeler, *History and Exposition of the Twenty-five Articles of Religion of the Methodist Episcopal Church* (1908) pp. 28 f, 301 ff; J. S. Simon, *John Wesley and the Religious Societies* (1921) pp. 333 f; E. v. Eicken, *Rechtfertigung und Heiligung bei Wesley* (1934) p. 43; K. Grayston, L.Q.H.R., July, 1944, p. 217; F. Hunter, W.H.S. xxiii, p. 126; J. C. English, *Methodist History*, January 1967, pp. 11 ff. [3] *Baptism and Conversion* (1964) p. 84.
[4] *The Theology of John Wesley* (1946) p. 129. cf. Horton Davies, *Worship and Theology in England . . . 1690–1850* (1961) pp. 205 f; A. S. Wood, *The Burning Heart: John Wesley Evangelist* (1967) pp. 248 f.

Others give greater place to baptismal regeneration in Wesley's scheme of salvation, but consider that, while he believed in both regenerations, conversion loomed so large in his preaching and interest as to make him lose sight of infant regeneration—which doctrine, therefore, Wesley believed but virtually ignored. One exponent of this view is W. F. Flemington, who writes:

It is noticeable that John Wesley, in several of his published sermons and other writings, subscribed to the teaching of the Church that infants are regenerated in baptism; yet he seems to have dwelt so much on the fact that the gift could be and was frequently lost, and to have become so sure that the 'new birth' is a spiritual process by which 'our inmost souls are changed, so that of sinners we become saints', that towards the end of his life he published a revision of the *Sunday Service of the Methodists*, from which almost all references to the baptismal regeneration of infants were expunged.[1]

In other places, we find Wesley explained as setting greater store by baptismal regeneration, so that, while conversion is still of the two the more important, infant re-birth has nevertheless a definite place of its own among his convictions.[2] This view is expounded, in one form, in *A History of the Methodist Church in Great Britain* (Vol. 1, 1965), by R. E. Davies. He says there that Wesley believed in baptismal regeneration 'very wholeheartedly', and goes on:

But the whole tendency of the rest of Wesley's theology and method seems to go against the doctrine. ... Yet there is no actual contradiction. He believed that a child once baptized was cleansed from original sin, and if he did not commit actual sin would go to heaven. But every child who remained alive did commit actual sin and needed to be born again for the second time. ... He was very careful to say that for an adult Baptism did not wash away sin, and the only inconsistency in his teaching that remains is that he usually preaches

---

[1] *The New Testament Doctrine of Baptism* (1948) p. 140. cf. C. C. J. Webb, *Religious Thought in the Oxford Movement* (1927) p. 115; H. Lindström, *Wesley and Sanctification* (1950) pp. 108 f; E. Gallagher, *The Irish Christian Advocate*, 4–25 August 1950: 'The Methodist Doctrine of Baptism'; F. Hildebrandt, *From Luther to Wesley* (1951) pp. 68 f.

[2] v. N. B. Harmon, *The Rites and Ritual of Episcopal Methodism* (1926) pp. 160, 238; A. C. Outler, *John Wesley* (1964) pp. 317 f; R. T. Beckwith, *Priesthood and Sacraments* (1964) pp. 54 f.

as if his audience were steeped in original sin, as well as actual sin, whereas many of them must have been cleansed from the former by Baptism in infancy.[1]

While Rupert Davies here suggests that Wesley related the two regenerations by giving them separate and successive relevance in the course of each life, others regard him as having allied the two by making them aspects of one progressive process—so that the regeneration given in baptism is the beginning of a re-birth which (Wesley believed) was furthered and fulfilled in adult conversion. R. E. Cushman takes up this position.

While justifying grace tends to depress the role of infant baptism in the economy of salvation, yet it is pervasively plain that Wesley viewed infant baptism as the inaugural influence of grace upon the life of the child, incorporating it within the community of faith and nurture. The tenor of Wesley's utterances reveals, then, that infant baptism entails a first work of grace, a 'means' God himself enjoins by the institution of Christ. As a work of grace it is effectual, but not necessarily or invariably unto salvation. . . . Accordingly 'the circumcision of the heart', or 'new birth', or justifying grace, must complete what is begun in baptismal regeneration. All this was for Wesley, quite objectively, the work of God.[2]

F. E. Stoeffler, in a similar manner, argues that Wesley related the two regenerations by regarding them, in the Puritan tradition, as being in the one case the making of a covenant, and in the other the adult ratification of that agreement with God:

Thus the objective grace that began its work in infant baptism fulfills its work in conversion and commitment of riper years. Regeneration is a process.[3]

---

[1] pp. 160 f. cf. *Ibid.* pp. 268 f; C. Ryder Smith, 'Methodism and Baptism', *The Baptist Quarterly*, July 1934, Vol. VII, No. 3, pp. 97 ff; R. E. Davies, *Methodism* (1963) p. 77.
[2] *The Doctrine of the Church* Ed. Dow Kirkpatrick (1964) pp. 87 f. cf. *Ibid* pp. 83 ff; C. W. Williams, *John Wesley's Theology Today* (1960) pp. 119 f; J. R. Parris, *John Wesley's Doctrine of the Sacraments* (1963) pp. 50, 54; V. H. H. Green, *John Wesley* (1964) p. 109; H. A. Hodges and A. M. Allchin, *A Rapture of Praise* (1966) p. 41; B. J. N. Galliers, W.H.S. xxxii, p. 124.
[3] As summarized by R. E. Cushman in *The Doctrine of the Church*, p. 81. cf. D. Tripp, *The Renewal of the Covenant in the Methodist Tradition* (1969) p. 12.

Others again—for example, C. W. Williams and J. R. Parris—consider that Wesley accepted both regenerations but was unable to establish any reconciliation between them since they are essentially incompatible, and in consequence they detect an unresolved conflict in his theology. Williams defines this as 'an inescapable tension between the ecclesiastical and evangelical';[1] and Parris as a conflict between 'Catholic and Protestant' elements which were 'present in Wesley from the Epworth rectory days to the end of his long life'.[2]

In the face of so many varied assessments of Wesley's baptismal position, it comes as no surprise, finally, to discover that some scholars believe that he was simply muddled and confused at this point, so that it is a useless task to look in his works for a clear and consistent baptismal theology.[3]

However, the aim of this book is, along with a study of the practice and understanding of this sacrament among the early Methodists generally, to undertake just such a search, so as, if possible, to dispel the mystery which has come to surround Wesley's baptismal thought. To anticipate our findings, it will be seen that our conclusion will stand in close agreement with the analysis of R. E. Davies quoted above.

In coming to this conclusion it has been necessary to extend the scope of the enquiry beyond the limits of Wesley's own published works. When his baptismal statements are examined in isolation, it remains something of an open question whether or not he retained his belief in baptismal regeneration up to the close of his life. This internal evidence led me rather hesitantly to conclude, some years ago, that in his later years Wesley did come to reject this doctrine.[4] But a consequent investigation into the baptismal beliefs of the early Methodist preachers and other evangelicals of the period has tilted the balance of likelihood very firmly down on the other side. This wider

---

[1] *Op. cit.* p. 116.
[2] *Op. cit.* p. 100. cf. W. R. Cannon, *op. cit.* p. 129; L.Q.H.R. January 1968, p. 59.
[3] v. L. F. Church, *More about the Early Methodist People* (1949) p. 250; H. Carter, *The Methodist Heritage* (1951) p. 159; P. S. Sanders, *Church History*, December 1957, pp. 355 ff.
[4] In a thesis, *Baptism in Wesleyan Methodism: Practice and Doctrine to 1882*, London University, 1966.

evidence is therefore also presented in these pages: and against the background of the almost unanimous acceptance by evangelicals of baptismal regeneration (in one form or another), the only possible conclusion seems to be that Wesley, all his life, considered regeneration to be given to infants in baptism as well as to adults at conversion.

CHAPTER 2

Wesley Learns Baptismal Regeneration, and Begins to Baptise

On 17 June 1703, the incumbent of Epworth in Lincolnshire baptised his eleventh child, a weakly boy, a few hours after his birth and named him John. The boy was brought up in the High Church tradition of his parents and absorbed their views on many matters—not least as to the importance and efficacy of the sacraments.

Samuel Wesley[1] gave an account of his understanding of baptism in *A Short Discourse of Baptism*, published in 1700 as a kind of appendix to his work, *The Pious Communicant Rightly Prepar'd*.[2] On this *Discourse* Dr. Outler has commented that 'such importance as it had lay in its square-toed summary of what was already essentially commonplace in central Anglican sacramental theology',[3] so that, as we should expect, Samuel Wesley reveals a steadfast belief in baptismal regeneration. 'By water then, as a means', he wrote, 'the water of baptism, we are regenerated or born again';[4] and in the preceding pages he has set out in detail the nature of that regeneration which he considered to be effected in the sacrament.

In part, Samuel Wesley understood baptismal regeneration as the relative adjustment of the candidate's standing with God, through His forgiveness given sacramentally. Thus he listed the benefits of baptism as being, the *'Washing* away the

---

[1] A clue to Susanna Wesley's beliefs is found in a letter she wrote in January 1710. '(God) hath appointed in His Church *Baptism* for the first remission (of sin), and *Repentance* for the constant forgiveness of all following trespasses.' v. A. Clarke, *Memoirs of the Wesley Family* (1823) p. 308.

[2] *The Pious Communicant Rightly Prepar'd; or, A Discourse Concerning the Blessed Sacrament: . . . To which is added, A Short Discourse of Baptism.* v. also the *Athenian Oracle*, i, p. 457. Cit. Tyerman, *Samuel Wesley* (1866) p. 238 f.

[3] *John Wesley*, p. 317. For studies in Anglican baptismal doctrine, v. W. Goode, *The Doctrine of the Church of England as to the Effects of Baptism in the Case of Infants* (1849); J. B. Mozley, *A Review of the Baptismal Controversy* (1862) 3rd ed. 1895, pp. 170 ff. [4] *Discourse*, p. 204.

damning Guilt of original sin' (since the merits of Christ's death are applied to us in baptism 'as an Instrument of our Justification'), admission into the covenant and into the Church, and being made children of God and heirs of the kingdom of heaven.[1] All this is true for adults (who must, however, have faith and be repentant to be eligible for baptism[2]), but it is argued that infants were also included by Jesus when he commanded His disciples, and through them His Church, to baptise all nations;[3] and, in the case of children, the general implication is that regeneration is given in the sacrament unconditionally—that is, irrespective of any response on their part or on their behalf by sponsors or parents.[4]

Yet occasionally Samuel Wesley reflected the attitude of the Puritans in this matter. There had been no one clear baptismal position common to them all, but in general the Puritans had been inclined to describe the regenerative gift of baptism as relative only, and to view this pre-eminently in the light of admission into the new covenant. Thus Richard Baxter had written:

> I had read Dr. Burges and (some years later) Mr. Bedford for Baptismal Regeneration, and heard it in the Common Prayer that God would bless Baptism to the infant's Regeneration (which I thought to be meant of a Real and not a Relative change). I soon discovered the error of this doctrine, when I found in Scripture that Repentance and Faith in the aged were ever prerequisite, and that no Word of God did make the end to infants which was prerequisite in others: and that signs cannot, by moral operations, be the instruments of a Real change on infants, but only of a Relative.

Baptism is administered to infants, said Baxter:

> that it might be a sign to enter them Church-members, and solemnize their Dedication to Christ, and to engage them to his people, and to take Him for their Lord and Saviour, and to confer on them remission of sins, and what Christ by the Covenant promised to the Baptized.[5]

The consequence of this approach was that many Puritans

---

[1] *Ibid.* pp. 199 ff.   [2] *Ibid.* pp. 241 ff.   [3] *Ibid.* pp. 213 ff.
[4] *Ibid.* pp. 242 ff.
[5] *Plain Scripture Proof of Infants Church—Membership and Baptism* (1656), cited in *Christian Baptism* (1959) ed. A. Gilmore, pp. 279 f.

had wanted to restrict infant baptism to the children of Christian parents only. Edmund Calamy reported that one of the 'Grounds of the Nonconformity of the Ministers who were Ejected' in 1662 had been their refusal (in obedience to the Sixty-eighth Canon) to baptise all-comers, for

> Tho' some of the Silenc'd Ministers were much straiter in their Notions about the *qualified Subjects of Baptism* than others, yet they were generally against Submission to this Canon, because not convinc'd that the Children of all Comers, (as of Atheists suppose, Infidels, Jews, Hereticks or Blasphemers; who might upon occasion, be offer'd as well as others) were so far in the Covenant of Grace, as to have a right to a Solemn Investiture in the Blessings of it.[1]

Occasionally Samuel Wesley inclined towards this Puritan attitude, as when, for example, he wrote of limiting baptism to believers and 'the *Children* also of *Believers*';[2] and of '*Baptizing* the *Infants*, (at least) of *believing Parents*'[3]: but the broad tenor of his argument is that in infant baptism all comers are regenerated.

In addition, Samuel Wesley held that there is a *real* as well as a relative benefit bestowed in the initiatory sacrament, and he expressed this in words which in their vagueness echo accurately the tone of the Anglican sacramental theology of his day.

> We say not that *Regeneration* is always *compleated* in this *Sacrament*, but that it is *begun* in it: a *Principle* of *Grace* is infused, which we lost by the *Fall*, which shall never be wholly withdrawn, unless we *quench* God's *Holy Spirit* by obstinate *habits* of *Wickedness*. . . . A Christian's Life is *progressive*, as is our *natural life*; and tho' the *Seeds* of *Grace*, should like the *reasonable Soul*, the *Principle* of *Life*, and of all *Action*, be infused in a *Moment*, yet there requires *time* to produce *strong habits* of *Grace*, as well as of *Reason*.[4]

Such was the doctrine of baptism which John Wesley

---

[1] E. Calamy, *Abridgement of Mr. Baxter's History of His Life and Times* (1702), p. 529. cf. *Ibid.* pp. 164, 505; A. Gilmore (ed.) *op. cit.* pp. 281 f; *Directory for the Public Worship of God* (1644), 'Of the Administration of Baptism'; Westminster Confession (1643), Art. xxviii, 'Of Baptism'.
[2] *The Pious Communicant* . . . , p. 213.   [3] *Ibid.* p. 214.
[4] *Ibid.* p. 205. J. B. Mozley said that among Anglicans the real aspect of infant regeneration was most typically thought of as 'an implanted *faculty* for the attainment of goodness and holiness—a capacity to be improved, a power to be cultivated, an assisting grace to be used'. *Op. cit.* p. 170.

learned in his early years, and so satisfied was he to be with his father's statement of it that when later on he wished to publish his own baptismal views, he was content to issue an abridged version of the *Short Discourse* as his own *Treatise on Baptism*.[1]

However, if Samuel Wesley's doctrine in this matter was unexceptional, he demanded a proper dignity and care in the manner of his administration of baptism which contrasted very strongly with the laxity and abuse of it general in his Church at that time; and his family must have learned, through their father's costly concern, to regard baptism as a serious and significant sacrament.

The rubrics of the *Book of Common Prayer* state, and the clear implication of the order for the 'Ministration of Publick Baptism of Infants' is, that infant baptism should take place in church, during public worship, and by immersion. Christening by pouring is allowed only if it is certified that 'the Child is weak'; sprinkling is not mentioned at all. Private baptism is to be procured only where there is 'great cause and necessity'. Yet William Wall reported that, by the beginning of the eighteenth century, custom had moved a long way from what was officially prescribed.

'Public' baptism was usually administered at home, where, as Wall said, 'the regard is commonly given to the preparation for eating and drinking; very little to the sacrament'.[2] Sponsors were often ill-chosen and unaware of their duties either in the ceremony or thereafter.[3] Wall adds:

I know that if any curate of a parish do insist upon having all children of rich and poor, that are in health, brought to church, and do refuse to shew the respect . . . of bringing the sacrament to their houses, and do plead the rubric and order of the church in his own vindication; he shall in some parishes of haughty, rude, and ill-bred people, meet with a great deal of obloquy.[4]

Samuel Wesley was one who suffered for so doing. Having

[1] v. *Infra* Appendix 1.
[2] *History of Infant Baptism* (1705) 1862 ed. ii. pp. 645–7. cf. Horton Davies, *Worship and Theology in England* . . . *1690–1850*, p. 64. J. Wickham Legg gives examples to show how, during this period, baptism normally followed closely upon birth. v. *English Church Life from the Restoration to the Tractarian Movement* (1914) pp. 164 f.
[3] Wall, *Op. cit.* ii. pp. 645 ff. [4] *Ibid.* ii. p. 647.

admitted his failure to persuade godparents to repeat their responses, he goes on, in his *Letter to a Curate,*

> And yet something I have done, nor have the least apprehension that you should let them break through that good order which has cost me the biggest struggle I ever had since I came to the parish, in prevailing with the people to bring their children to Church for public baptism, as their wives to be churched; whereas both were commonly done before in their houses, where they had godfathers and godmothers, and the whole baptismal office, as they generally have it still in the Levels; though I would never administer it there in that manner. But in case of real necessity, . . . God forbid they should ever want private baptism, whether it be day or night, that they send for you. But then you will do what you can, and take the best vouchers you are able, for their bringing them to Church to be received there soon afterwards, at the farthest when the mother is churched; because, some will keep them an enormous while before they will do it, sometimes a year, or near, or more: as they also will commonly do before they get their children christened at all, either publicly or privately, and will bring such monsters of men-children to the font, as will almost break your arms, and with their manful voices disturb and alarm the whole congregation. . . . As for churchings, you will find many, especially of the poorer sort, will be for getting this over before the child is baptized; and when the woman is once at liberty, notwithstanding their fair promises before, will drive the other sometimes world without end; for their children have died unbaptized. I wish with all my heart you could break this bad custom.[1]

Yet in one matter Samuel Wesley (along with his fellow-clergymen generally) made no effort to follow the due order of the Anglican Church—he did not encourage baptism by immersion.

The practice of baptising even healthy people by pouring seems to have come to Britain after the death of Queen Mary, when refugees from her regime returned from the Continent bringing with them a regard for the customs of those Protestant Churches in which they had been worshipping.[2] In particular they had learned a freedom in the manner of baptising which went back to Calvin himself, who had argued in his *Institutes*:

> Whether a person baptized is to be wholly immersed, and that

---

[1] T. Jackson, *The Life of the Rev. Charles Wesley* (1841) ii, pp. 530 f. v. Tyerman, *Samuel Wesley*, p. 387.   [2] Wall, *op. cit.* i. pp. 576–583; ii. pp. 463 f.

whether once or thrice, or whether he is only to be sprinkled with water, is not of the least consequence: churches should be at liberty to adopt either, according to the diversity of climates, although it is evident that the term baptism means to immerse.[1]

Wall explained that baptism by affusion had become customary in England by 1645:[2] and he said that from that time sprinkling began to be commonly used—a few drops replacing the more thoroughgoing pouring of water.[3] Wall claimed that responsibility for this change also lay with the Puritans,[4] for the *Directory for the Public Worship of God* (which superseded the Prayer Book from 1645-62) reads:

That baptizing, or sprinkling and washing with water, signifieth the cleansing from sin by the blood and for the merit of Christ.

Similarly the Westminster Confession states that

Dipping of the person into the water is not necessary; but baptism is rightly administered by pouring or sprinkling water upon the person.

Wall reported that by the beginning of the eighteenth century it had become the established Anglican practice to baptise by sprinkling,[5] and he wrote that he knew of only

one clergyman now living, that has baptized some infants (by immersion): but am not certain. P.S. I have since heard of several. And I myself have had one opportunity of administering baptism so, by the parents' consent.[6]

So firmly was the custom established, that midwives and mothers everywhere dressed babies for the ceremony in such

---

[1] (Beveridge's translation) iv. 15. 19. cf. *Tract. Theolog. Catechismus* (Ed. Bezae, 1576) p. 57. v. L.Q.H.R. January 1966, p. 51.
[2] This is to be expected in the light of Canon 30 (1604) which allows that baptism is valid if it is by 'dipping ... or laying water upon the face of the infant'. There is no reference to sprinkling.
[3] Daniel Featley's widely influential book, *The Dipper Dipt*, was published in 1644, giving six arguments for regarding sprinkling as a valid mode.
[4] v. his description of Puritan baptisms, *op. cit.* i. pp. 582 f. cf. C. Wheatly, *A Rational Illustration of the Book of Common Prayer* (1710) 1852 ed., p. 334; N. Sykes, *Church and State in England in the Eighteenth Century* (1934) p. 22; C. J. Abbey and J. H. Overton, *The English Church in the Eighteenth Century* (2nd ed. 1896) p. 468.
[5] *Ibid.* ii. pp. 463 ff; cf. Wheatly, *op. cit.* pp. 337 f. 350; Abbey and Overton, *op. cit.* p. 416. [6] *Op. cit.* i. p. 581.

elaborate finery that anything other than a token sprinkling was impossible—upon all of which Wall wrote with scathing wit,[1] for he hoped to bring about a return to the earlier and statutory practice of baptism by immersion, or at least to encourage affusion.[2]

Samuel Wesley would have earned Wall's praise for trying to insist on baptising whenever possible in church and for attempting to make the sponsors play their proper part, but he would have fallen under his condemnation for being content with sprinkling only; and the christening gown worn by the Wesley children (which is still preserved[3]) is of the kind for which Wall had so much scorn.

The practice of confirmation was also unsatisfactory at this time, although by reason in this case of the practical difficulties in the way of its effective administration. Even where bishops were conscientious in this duty and made the necessary long and arduous tours of their dioceses, the confirmation services were commonly so large as to reduce solemnity to a minimum and to turn the ordinance into a formal and sometimes farcical ritual. A thousand confirmations at one place and on one day were not uncommon.[4] Yet, in spite of such gigantic ceremonies, Richard Baxter said

> That as far as I can learn, there is not one of an hundred confirmed at all. All the thousands that are unconfirmed live in the parishes as reputed Christians, and may come to the sacrament when they will.[5]

John Wesley would have seen the hopelessness of the situation when, during the bishop's tour of his Lincoln Diocese in 1712, eight hundred people were confirmed at Epworth on 15 July.[6] His father later wrote to the Bishop saying that the ceremony would have been more edifying

> if according to his lordship's directions, a way could have been found for every parish to have come by themselves and none to have been confirmed but those whose names had been given in by the minister; for want of which great numbers were confirmed who

---

[1] *Ibid.* i. pp. 583 f; ii. pp. 462 f.   [2] *Ibid.* i. pp. 585 ff; ii. pp. 642 ff.
[3] v. F. C. Gill, *In the Steps of John Wesley* (1962) illustration opp. p. 72.
[4] v. Sykes, *op. cit.* pp. 115 ff, 429 ff.
[5] *The English Nonconformity . . . Truly Stated and Argued*, pp. 100 f. Cit. Sykes, *op. cit.* p. 131. v. also Abbey and Overton, *op. cit.* pp. 470 f.
[6] Sykes, *op. cit.* pp. 123, 430.

ought not to have been; ... and many who had been confirmed before, some of them twice or thrice over.[1]

It is not known when John Wesley was confirmed—Dr. Bowmer suggests that it may have been on this very occasion[2] —but it seems probable that, before confirmation, his father had already given him communion when he was eight years old.[3] This irregularity (for the Prayer Book requires that only those confirmed or desirous of it be admitted to the Lord's supper) would have been in line with Samuel Wesley's view of baptism as expressed in his *Discourse*, where he presents baptism, unaccompanied by this later ceremony, as giving admission into the Church. It is likely, therefore, that John Wesley's apparent disregard for confirmation in years to come was grounded in his father's attitude observed during his boyhood.

The years passed by. John became gownboy at Charterhouse, and at the age of seventeen went up to Oxford University, which for the next fifteen years (1720–35) became the true centre of his life. It is to the development of his baptismal thinking during this time that we now turn.

Dr. V. H. H. Green has depicted the climate of religious opinion at Oxford when Wesley was there in these words:

The majority of its dons would have subscribed to learned but somewhat controversial High-Churchmanship. This did not mean that they would have identified themselves with the Non-jurors, though some ... greatly sympathized with their theology. It does suggest, however, that the contemporary religious feeling at Oxford was equally unsympathetic towards Latitudinarianism and Erastianism, Enthusiasm and Pietism. It drew its spiritual nourishment from the patristic studies which had been its principal contribution to research in the seventeenth century.[4]

From what we know of his home background we would expect Wesley to have been very much at ease in such an environment, and so he was. His High Church views were generally encouraged and strengthened, and we find, in particular, that his belief in baptismal regeneration was given a greater stability.

[1] *Ibid.* p. 133.
[2] *The Sacrament of the Lord's Supper in Early Methodism*, p. 11.
[3] R. Green, *The Conversion of John Wesley* (1937) p. 15. i.e. in 1711.
[4] *The Young Mr. Wesley* (1961) p. 34.

Thus in 1725 he prepared the 1549 Prayer Book for examination,[1] and if Wesley believed (as he did) that the 1661 order 'supposes that all who are baptised in their infancy are at the same time born again',[2] he must have been the more conscious of this implication in the earlier baptismal service, which, with its elaborate and strongly symbolical regenerative ritual, was prescribed for all baptisms, infant as well as adult. Nor did this pointer to the faith of the early Church stand alone. In 1731 he read Charles Wheatly's *Rational Illustration of the Book of Common Prayer*,[3] in which it is said that

in the Christian Church, by our Saviour's institution and appointment, those who are dead to God through sin, are born again by the *washing of regeneration, and renewing of the Holy Ghost*.[4]

In the following year he read William Cave's book, *Primitive Christianity*, where the same view is expressed. Speaking of the acceptance by the early Church of baptism by laymen, Cave says:

This, without question, arose from an Opinion they had of the absolute and indispensable *necessity* of Baptism, without which they scarce thought a man's future Condition could be safe, and that therefore 'twas better it should be had from *any*, than to depart this life without it; for excepting the Case of *Martyrs* . . . they reckoned no man could be saved without being baptized.[5]

More important still, in 1734 he read *The History of Infant Baptism* (1720 edition) by William Wall. This book (which was generally regarded by Anglicans as a definitive work) has as one of its main conclusions that

all the ancient Christians, not one man excepted, do take the word *regeneration*, or *new birth*, to signify *baptism*; and *regenerate, baptized*.[6]

Wesley held all these books in high esteem. They were

---

[1] *Journal*, i. p. 167 n.
[2] *Sermons*, ii. p. 238.
[3] For Wesley's reading list, 1725–34, v. V. H. H. Green, *op. cit.* pp. 289 ff. Other relevant books read during these years are: 1730: *Case of Infant Baptism*; 1732: Robert Nelson, *On the Sacraments*; Samuel Clark, *Practical Essays on Baptism, Confirmation and Repentance*; 1733: William Wogan, *Letter on Baptism*.
[4] 1852 ed. p. 326. cf. 324–44, 360–2.   [5] 1676 ed. p. 299.
[6] i. p. 639. cf. i. pp. 19, 43, 175, 443.

among those which he selected to take with him to Georgia,¹ and in later years he was to include Cave's *Primitive Christianity* in the *Christian Library*,² and to use Wall's *History* as a source for one of his own publications.³

In his reading at Oxford, therefore, Wesley found that baptismal regeneration, which he had learned from his own father, had the sanction and authority of the early Church Fathers behind it, and he was thereby confirmed in his acceptance of that doctrine.

Wesley began to write and to preach sermons during these years and, as we should expect, this conviction found its place in what he had to say. A contributor to the *London Quarterly Review* for January 1868 wrote:

We have before us a number of unpublished sermons written by Wesley at Oxford, during the ten years which followed his ordination.... Frequent communion is insisted on as a source of spiritual quickening; regeneration by baptism is assumed as the true doctrine of the Church; but Christ is nowhere.... Church formalism and strict morality, ceremonies and ethics, are all in all.⁴

An interesting sidelight on the conviction of another member of the Holy Club is provided by a letter from Benjamin Ingham to Wesley when he was in Georgia. The letter (dated 19 October 1737) gives news of friends in England, and includes this item:

Your friend Mr. Morgan (I hear) either has, or is about publishing a book, to prove that every one baptized with water is regenerate.⁵

In maintaining this himself it is probable that Wesley did not go beyond what his father had believed, but now he came under the influence of the Non-jurors, and they were to teach him to make demands in the administration of this sacrament even more severe than those made by his father upon the perplexed and unwilling parishioners of Epworth.

---

¹ J. C. Bowmer, *op. cit.* pp. 30 f.
² Vol. xxxi. v. *Journal*, i. pp. 264–8; iii. pp. 392, 499. By 1750 his opinion of the book as a whole was rather less enthusiastic.
³ i.e. *Thoughts upon Infant Baptism*. v. *Infra* Appendix 1.
⁴ R. Green, *John Wesley Evangelist*, p. 134.
⁵ L. Tyerman, *The Life and Times of the Rev. John Wesley* (1890) i. p. 137. Presumably this was Richard Morgan.

Wesley's association with the Non-jurors began when John Clayton joined the Methodists in 1732. Clayton was a close friend of the widely influential Thomas Deacon, and it was now that, under their tutelage, the period of the Wesleys' narrow-minded Non-juring churchmanship began.[1]

The Non-jurors (as their name suggests) were in origin a political group who felt themselves to be so bound by their oath of allegiance to James II and his successors that they were unable to swear loyalty to William and Mary.[2] Susanna Wesley shared these sympathies to some extent,[3] and John and Charles, while not taking up this political standpoint, were nevertheless swayed by the Non-jurors' ritualism. These distinctive practices were based upon what the Non-jurors believed had been the procedures in the primitive Church. The *Apostolic Constitutions* (which John and Charles studied under Dr. Deacon's guidance[4]) held a definitive place for them, and they were drawn to the 1549 Prayer Book which, they believed, adhered more closely to the liturgical practices of the early Church than did the Prayer Book of 1661.

The Non-jurors regarded baptism by persons not episcopally ordained as invalid, and they advocated the use of triple immersion as conforming to the usage of the first Christians.[5] This was not new within the Anglican Church, since it had been prescribed as the ordinary mode of baptising in the 1549 Prayer Book. The Non-jurors found it there (and in older liturgies) and, taking it to be the ancient manner of administering the sacrament, wished to re-introduce it.[6]

But the belief that none except those ordained within the episcopal line of Apostolic Succession could validly administer the sacraments, was less well attested in the Church of England. The disputed consequence of this view, in regard to baptism,

---

[1] v. L. Tyerman, *The Oxford Methodists* (1873) pp. 32 ff; J. C. Bowmer, *op. cit.* pp. 26–36; F. Hunter, *John Wesley and the Coming Comprehensive Church* (1968) pp. 12 ff.

[2] e.g. F. Proctor and W. H. Frere, *A New History of the Book of Common Prayer* (1920) 3rd impression 1951, pp. 226 ff. F. Lathbury, *History of the Nonjurors* (1845) *passim*.

[3] v. Tyerman, *Life of Samuel Wesley*, pp. 252 f.

[4] J. S. Simon, *John Wesley and the Religious Societies*, p. 103.

[5] V. H. H. Green, *op. cit.* p. 259; Proctor and Frere, *op. cit.* p. 607; Tyerman, *The Oxford Methodists*, pp. v f.

[6] v. Thomas Deacon, *Compleat Collection of Devotions* (1734), order for baptism.

was the Non-jurors' insistence that those baptised by Dissenting ministers should be re-baptised. This matter was discussed in the Convocation of 1711–12, of which Samuel Wesley was a member. Bishop Burnet, in the *History of His Own Times*,[1] spoke of the issues involved and of the outcome of the debates in Convocation.

At this time there appeared an inclination in many of the clergy to a nearer approach to the Church of Rome. . . . (One) conceit was the invalidity of lay baptism, and that, as dissenting teachers were laymen, they and their congregations ought to be rebaptized. Dodwell[2] left all who died without the sacraments to the uncovenanted mercies of God; and maintained that none had a right to give the sacraments except the apostles, and, after them, bishops and priests ordained by them. The bishops thought it necessary to put a stop to such doctrines, and agreed to a declaration against the irregularity of all baptism by persons not in holy orders; but yet allowing that, according to the practice of the primitive Church, and the constant usage of the Church of England, no baptism ought to be reiterated. Archbishop Sharpe (the friend of Samuel Wesley) refused to sign the declaration, pretending that it would encourage irregular baptisms. The Archbishop of Canterbury, with most of the bishops of his province, submitted the matter to the convocation. It was agreed to in the Upper House, but the Lower House refused even to consider it, because it would encourage those who struck at the dignity of the priesthood.

Whether Samuel Wesley was swayed by the Non-jurors' arguments is uncertain, but there is no doubt that, at Oxford, his sons accepted readily enough their views as to the use of triple immersion and the necessity of the apostolic succession for valid sacraments, so that in Georgia they were eager to put them into effect.

Wesley was ordained deacon on 19 September 1725, and the first discovered instance of his administering this sacrament was five weeks later, on 24 October, at Shipton-under-Wychwood, near Oxford.[3] From August 1727 to November 1729 he

---

[1] Cit. Tyerman, *Samuel Wesley*, p. 345 n.
[2] i.e. Henry Dodwell (1641–1711), a Non-juror.
[3] Wesley's Oxford Diary reads: 'Preached, Read Prayers, Baptized a child and married a couple.'

served as his father's curate at Epworth and Wroot, being ordained priest on 22 September 1728. The prayer book which he used at Wroot is still kept at the Church there, and there are no markings in it to suggest that at this time he deviated at all from the prescribed order.[1]

On his recall to Oxford we find Wesley engaging in the enterprises of the Holy Club and, among other activities, in making arrangements for prisoners and their children to be baptised when this was required. In the case of William Irwin, we notice the scrupulous correctness with which he proceeded.

Wesley was particularly interested in a prisoner called Irwin. . . . On 15th June, 1732, he rode out to Cuddesdon to see the Bishop of Oxford and evidently secured from him permission to baptize Irwin; though the Bishop was reluctant to give Wesley a general commission.[2] Irwin was christened the next morning and subsequently prepared for confirmation.[3]

Although by this time Clayton (the Non-juror) had joined the Methodists—so that Wesley may have wanted to use triple immersion—there is no suggestion that this baptism was other than by sprinkling or affusion. Indeed, it may be presumed that prison conditions would have made anything other than the simplest ceremony impossible. But there were no such restraints in Georgia, and our next task is to consider the manner in which Wesley carried out his baptismal duties in the New World.

[1] The register at Epworth contains the record of twenty-three baptisms in John Wesley's handwriting over the period 12 July 1727 to 19 May 1729, although it is not stated whether he officiated. The Wroot register reveals no baptismal entries in Wesley's hand, and very few baptisms are there recorded—only three in 1728—but these may have been performed by him.

[2] The Diary reads: 'He ō giv an Commission.'

[3] V. H. H. Green, *op. cit.* p. 176. Wesley baptised 'young John Stewart' in 1733. v. *Ibid.* p. 179.

CHAPTER 3

Ministry on Board Ship and in Georgia

On 14 October 1735, a little group of Oxford Methodists—Benjamin Ingham, Charles Delamotte, and John and Charles Wesley—embarked for Georgia, and from now onwards Wesley's *Journal* and published diaries provide us with a fascinating record of his life day by day.

On board the *Simmonds* Wesley acted as a kind of unofficial chaplain to the ship's company and passengers until their arrival at the Colony where he took up his post under the Society for the Propagation of the Gospel in Foreign Parts—and all this time we find that he was acting upon those extreme principles which he had embraced at Oxford.

In some things it was enough for him to follow the example of his father. As was the custom in England, so also in Georgia, Wesley evidently found indiscriminate private baptism to be usual, and as the father had insisted at Epworth, so now the son demanded in America that all infants who were strong enough should be christened during public worship. So much can be inferred from the following *Journal* entry.

Many complaints being made of what had been done in my absence by Mr. Dison, chaplain of the Independent Company,[1] who had now been at Savannah several weeks, I went to his lodgings, and taxed him, (1) with baptizing several strong, healthy children in private houses, which was what I had entirely broke through; (2) marrying several couples without first publishing the banns . . .; and (3) with endeavouring to make a division between my parishioners and me. . . . The last two charges he denied; but owned the first, promised never to do it again, and did the very same thing the next day. O Discipline! where art thou to be found? Not in England, nor (as yet) in America.[2]

Like his father also—although with good reason in those

[1] A Dissenting minister. v. M. Schmidt, *John Wesley* (1962) p. 204.
[2] i. pp. 270 f.

isolated circumstances—Wesley accepted baptism, without consequent confirmation, as being the complete act of initiation into the life of the Church. It is true of course that on the high seas and in the Colony no bishop was available, yet Wesley showed no qualms now at allowing people to take communion immediately after their baptism, and even when back again in England (where confirmation was obtainable) he seems never to have put either himself or his people to the trouble of asking for it.

Ambrosius Tackner (thirty years of age, and Wesley's German tutor on the *Simmonds*) was the first of his converts, and Wesley baptised him, apparently at the Falcon Inn, Gravesend, during a shore trip made while the ship lay off the land waiting for fair winds.[1] On the next day he records:

> We then celebrated the Holy Eucharist, Ambrosius Tackner and two more communicating with us.[2]

In the following month:

> Thomas Hird, and Grace his wife, with their children, Mark, aged twenty-one, and Phoebe, about seventeen, who had been educated among the Quakers, were, at their own often-repeated desire, and after frequent and careful instruction, received into the Church by Baptism, whereby we gained four more serious and constant communicants.[3]

Wesley's position is quite plain, and in this regard we will find him consistently maintaining his standpoint to the end of his life: the faithful are 'received into the Church by Baptism'.

In the above instances there is no record of the manner in which the sacrament was administered,[4] but during these years both John and Charles Wesley normally baptised, not only by dipping, but by triple immersion. John tells how he christened the infant Mary Welch, eleven days after her birth, 'according to the custom of the first Church, and the rule of the Church of England, by immersion'. His diary fills in the details: '9.30

---

[1] *Journal*, i. p. iii. The diary reads: '9 Clayton; 10 Falcon with Tackner; baptized him!' Ingham was a witness. v. Tyerman *Oxford Methodists*, p. 68.

[2] *Journal*, i. p. iii.

[3] *Journal*, i. p. 117. Ingham again was a witness. v. Tyerman, *op. cit.* pp. 70 f.

[4] It is likely, at any rate in the case of Tackner, that triple immersion was used. The facilities of the inn would permit this, and the presence of John Clayton (the Non-juror) would encourage it.

MINISTRY ON BOARD SHIP AND IN GEORGIA

baptized Mary Welch by Trine Immersion!'[1] A Mr. and Mrs. Parker, however, were not so accommodating, and a spirited interview was the consequence. Wesley wrote:

I was asked to baptize a child of Mr. Parker's, second Bailiff of Savannah; but Mrs. Parker told me, 'Neither Mr. Parker nor I will consent to its being dipped.' I answered, 'If you "certify that" your "child is weak, it will suffice" (the rubric says) "to pour water upon it".' She replied, 'Nay, the child is not weak; but I am resolved it shall not be dipped.' This argument I could not confute. So I went home, and the child was baptized by another person.[2]

Parker afterwards figured prominently in the trial of Wesley, and the seeds of his antipathy to the over-exacting priest may have been sown by this incident.

Here was an obstacle, also, in the path of Wesley's mission to the Indians. It was his intention to baptise any converts among them by immersion, and he was concerned about the propriety of this ceremony, in the case of women, in isolated places where he might be the only administrator. The diary of Spangenberg (the leader of the Herrnhut settlement) reveals that, so great was this anxiety, Wesley consulted him over the possibility of ordaining some women of the Moravian community as deaconesses to assist in this task.[3] In view of Wesley's almost total failure, in the event, to establish effective missionary contact with the Indians, this remarkable suggestion was not pursued very far.[4]

Charles Wesley was also having a mixed reception to his insistence upon baptism by immersion. His *Journal* for Wednesday, 10 March 1736[5] reads:

After dinner I began talking with M. Germain, about baptizing her child by immersion. She was much averse to it, though she owned it

---

[1] *Journal*, i. pp. 166 f.
[2] *Ibid*. i. pp. 210 f. Five months later the Diary contains the unexplained entry, 'christened Parker'. i. p. 278.
[3] Schmidt, *op. cit.* p. 152.
[4] *The True Narrative of the State of Georgia* (1741) says that one reason why Wesley had angered the Colonists was 'by appointing deaconesses' (*Journal*, viii. p. 305). Deaconesses appear in the *Apostolic Constitutions* (iii. 15), and Thomas Deacon (in his *Compleat Devotions*) had provided a 'Form ... of ... Ordaining Deaconesses.' cf. F. Hunter *op. cit.* p. 39. N. Curnock suggested that Wesley may have been training the elder Miss Bovey as a deaconess. *Journal*, i. pp. 272, 276, 314 n.
[5] i. p. 2.

a strong, healthy child. I then spoke to her husband, who was soon satisfied, and brought his wife to be so too.

But by the following Sunday she had changed her mind.

M. Germain now retracted her consent for having her child baptized: however, M. Colwell's I did baptize by trine immersion, before a numerous congregation.[1]

Adult candidates for this sacrament found that they were not to be exempt from dipping. We read of John Bradley, a well-to-do colonist, being baptised by John Wesley 'by immersion' —presumably by threefold immersion, although the diary[2] does not specify this.

Just how strongly the people resented this regimen can be gathered from William Stephen's *Journal of the Proceedings in Georgia*. He tells of George Whitefield's arrival there, shortly after the departure of the Wesleys in 1738.

June 18. Mr. Whitefield went on moving the people with his captivating discourses. A child being brought to church to be baptized, he performed that office by *sprinkling*, which gave great content to many who had taken great distaste at the form of *dipping*, so strictly required and so obstinately withstood by some parents that they have suffered their children to go without the benefit of that sacrament, till a convenient opportunity could be found of another minister to do that office.[3]

All this caused resentment enough among the settlers: but even greater animosity was aroused by Wesley's narrowness in insisting upon the sole validity of episcopal baptism—that is, baptism by a deacon or priest episcopally ordained—and upon re-baptising those otherwise christened before permitting them to enjoy the full offices of the Church.

This demand (learned, of course, from the Non-jurors) Wesley had first made on the voyage. Ambrosius Tackner (whose baptism by immersion we have already noted) had received only 'lay-baptism' previously, and so Wesley insisted upon re-baptism before allowing him to take communion.[4] Wesley followed the same course in Georgia. Richard and

---

[1] *Ibid.* i. p. 4.
[2] *Journal*, i. p. 181.
[3] L. Tyerman, *The Life of the Rev. George Whitefield* (1876) i. p. 131 n.
[4] *Journal*, i. p. 111.

Thomas Turner were refused communion until they had submitted to re-baptism, because they were Dissenters. Among the reasons the settlers found for thinking Wesley to be a Roman Catholic, was that he

> unmercifully damned all Dissenters of whatever denomination, who were never admitted to communicate with him until they first gave up their faith and principles entirely to his moulding and direction, and, in confirmation thereof, declared their belief in the invalidity of their former baptism, and then to receive a new one from him. This was done publicly on the persons of Richard Turner, carpenter, and his son. Another instance was that of William Gaff, who had once communicated and always conformed to his regulations, but was at last found out by Mr. Wesley to have been baptized by a Presbyterian Dissenter. The same thing was proposed to him; but Mr. Gaff, not inclinable to go that length, was ever thereafter excluded from the communion.[1]

This insistence upon episcopal baptism is reflected in Wesley's ambivalent attitude to the Salzburgher community in Georgia. On the one hand he admired their faith and piety, but on the other he would not accept their Lutheran (and thus non-episcopal) ministry[2] as valid, nor therefore their baptism; and so it came about that he refused one of their pastors, Johann Martin Bolzius, admission to the Lord's table.[3] On receiving a letter from Bolzius several years later, Wesley showed that by then (1749) he regretted this action, and he also explained what his reasons for it had been at the time.

> What a truly Christian piety and simplicity breathe in these lines! And yet this very man, when I was at Savannah, did I refuse to admit to the Lord's Table, because he was not baptized—that is, not baptized by a minister who had been episcopally ordained.[4]

It is necessary for our understanding of Wesley to realize

---

[1] *Journal*, viii. p. 305, an extract from *A True Narrative of the State of Georgia*. Gaff must be the Gough of the indictment (v. *Journal*, i. p. 390), who professed himself satisfied with Wesley's explanation (p. 394).

[2] v. Schmidt, *op. cit.* pp. 169 f.

[3] *Journal*, i. p. 370. Bolzius disputed Wesley's appeal to apostolic succession, v. Schmidt, *op. cit.* pp. 180 f.

[4] *Journal*, iii. p. 434. Schmidt suggests (*op. cit.* p. 179) that the real reason for this refusal was adherence by Wesley to his instructions from the S.P.G. (*Journal*, i. p. 355); but it seems unnecessary to look beyond his own confession for another motive.

just how important these principles were to him; to see that they dominated his relationships with Christians of other Communions. Thus Wesley's friendliness with the Moravians became really close only after he had taken pains to assure himself of the episcopal validity of their ordination:[1] and it is of interest to note that Spangenberg, who met Wesley on his arrival in America, formed this impression of him:

He has ... several quite special principles, which he still holds strongly, since he drank them in with his mother's milk. He thinks that an ordination not performed by a bishop in the apostolic succession is invalid. Therefore he believes that neither Calvinists nor Lutherans have *legitimos doctores* and *pastores*. From this it follows that the sacraments administered by such teachers are not valid: this also he maintains. Therefore he thinks that anybody who has been baptized by a Calvinist or Lutheran pastor is not truly baptized. Further, nobody can partake of the holy meal without being first baptized: accordingly be baptizes all persons who come from other sects, although not those who have been baptized in Roman Catholicism. He considers Nitschmann's and Anton's[2] baptism valid. Reason: they have an episcopal order from the apostolic church. But he thinks it a great wrong in the Herrnhut community that they allow their children to be baptized by H. Rothe (the Lutheran pastor of the neighbouring congregation at Berthelsdorf, in whose jurisdiction Herrnhut came). He will therefore not share the Lord's Supper with anyone who is not baptized by a minister who has been ordained by a true bishop. All these doctrines derive from the view of the episcopacy which is held in the Papist and English churches and which rests upon the authority of the Fathers. Above all he believes that all references in Scripture of doubtful interpretation must be decided not by reason but from the writings of the first three centuries, e.g. infant baptism, footwashing, fast days, celibacy and many others.[3]

In addition to excluding from the Lord's table all who had not received (in his opinion) valid baptism, it is likely that Wesley also refused to bury all who had not received episco-

[1] Schmidt, *op. cit.* pp. 147, 162. In 1737, Archbishop Potter declared the validity of their orders to be beyond doubt (C. W. Towlson, *Moravian and Methodist*, 1957, p. 34); but cf. Schmidt, *op. cit.* p. 162 n.
[2] Moravian pastors.
[3] Spangenberg's handwritten diary, 30 June to 28 October 1736, cit. Schmidt, *op. cit.* p. 138 n.

palian baptism.¹ The facts in this matter, however, are not altogether clear. We read that the Grand Jury

present ... John Westley, for that he did, in the latter end of June 1736, refuse reading the Office of Burial of the Dead over the body of Nathanael Polhill, only because the said Nathanael Polhill was not of the said John Westley's opinion: by means of which refusal, the said Nathanael Polhill was interred without the appointed Office for the Burial of the Dead.²

On the other hand, the defence offered against this charge shows how uncertain the whole matter was. The accusation is unfounded, it was said,

for Nathanael Polhill was an Anabaptist, and desired in his lifetime that he might not be interred with the Office of the Church of England. And further, we have good reason to believe that Mr. Wesley was at Frederica, or on his return thence, when Polhill was buried.³

Yet if there is no unambiguous instance of Wesley refusing to bury for this reason, it is consistent with his views that he should have done so. The rubric of the Prayer Book says that the Burial Service 'is not to be used for any that die unbaptized', and this was commonly enforced when the deceased person had not been baptised at all.⁴ Moreover, Charles Wheatly (writing in 1710) suggests that the stricter interpretation of this rubric (i.e. to regard Dissenters as being 'unbaptised' and so to refuse to bury them) was fairly widely followed.⁵ It is probable, therefore, that Wesley would not at this time bury any except those who had been baptised at the hands of an episcopally ordained officiant; and even if in so doing he did not stand alone, yet in the exceptionally isolated circumstances of his Colonial ministry, such a rigid attitude was surely misplaced.

Looking back over his bearing in Georgia, we can see that Wesley was a little disingenuous in his description of it. He said that he and his companions were 'rigorous observers of

---

¹ v. J. H. Rigg, *The Churchmanship of John Wesley*, p. 29; J. Telford, *op. cit.* p. 303; R. Green, *op. cit.* p. 151; T. Dearing, *Wesleyan and Tractarian Worship* (1966) p. 109.
² *Journal*, i. p. 390.
³ *Ibid.* i. pp. 394 f.
⁴ e.g. Whitefield's *Journal*, p. 144.
⁵ *A Rational Illustration of the Book of Common Prayer*, 1852 ed., pp. 468 f.

every Rubric and Canon, as well as (to the best of our knowledge) every tenet of the Church'.[1] This was true, particularly of his refusal to baptise privately, his insistence upon using immersion where possible, and his demand that godparents be communicants[2] (as the Canon requires). Yet in some respects Wesley went beyond the discipline of his Church, striving first of all to follow the customs of the early Christians. For this reason he regarded baptism as valid only if it had been administered by one episcopally ordained—and this led to his refusal to allow Dissenters to take communion and (probably) to bury them: and, following this older and, for him, greater authority, he used triple immersion. Wesley's baptismal practice in America is thus found to conform to a consistent pattern—he was putting into effect the principles he had learned from the Non-jurors while at Oxford.

The sequel is well known. Suspecting him to be a Roman Catholic, his parishioners brought charges against Wesley, and it is interesting that out of the ten indictments, five are concerned with his administration of baptism: i.e. refusing to baptise the Parkers' baby except by immersion; refusing communion to William Gough on discovering him to have received Dissenters' baptism; refusing to bury Nathanael Polhill because he was an Anabaptist; refusing to accept William Aglionby as a sponsor since he was not a communicant; and finally, baptising a child with only two godparents.[3] We can see, in consequence, that it was not only 'over the administration of Holy Communion that Wesley came to grief' (as Dr. Bowmer has suggested[4]), but it was his scruples in dispensing both sacraments which so aroused the ire of the Colonists that, less than two years after arriving in the New World, Wesley was on his way back again to the Old.

[1] *Letters*, iv. p. 28. cf. *Works*, viii. pp. 32 ff; x. p. 394.
[2] The evidence for this is supplied by the indictment brought against Wesley, given below.
[3] *Journal* i. pp. 390 f. On this last Wesley commented: 'This, I own, was wrong; for I ought, at all hazards, to have refused baptizing it till he had procured a third.' *Works* i. p. 57.
[4] *Op. cit.* p. 33.

CHAPTER 4

Wesley Learns to Equate Adult Regeneration with Conversion

Wesley left Georgia ignominiously, and yet it cannot be said that the months he spent there were wasted. It is doubtful whether he was able to leave anything very lasting with those he had gone out to serve,[1] but what he himself received among the settlers was of tremendous value, for it was through his contacts with the Moravians in America that his feet were set upon the path which was to end at Aldersgate Street and his conversion experience of 1738. It was the Moravians, first in America and then back in England, who were to teach Wesley to regard the non-sacramental experience of conversion as being the regeneration of adults.

Before meeting with the Moravians, Wesley seems to have used the word regeneration only in close association with baptism,[2] but now he was to learn from them a new meaning of the term, so that 'adult regeneration', in all Wesley's later writing and preaching would be no longer essentially tied to baptism but would indicate conscious, instantaneous experiences of re-birth.

The idea that there could be some kind of immediate non-sacramental awareness of God's forgiveness and power, and that this should be called regeneration, was far from Wesley's mind when he set sail for America. When in 1735 his father was lying in his last illness, he said to him, 'The inward witness, son, the inward witness, that is the proof, the strongest proof of Christianity'; but whatever it was precisely that the dying man had meant by this, Wesley admitted that he himself 'understood him not'.[3] The certainty of his being forgiven by God and released from under His wrath he looked for in

---

[1] Whitefield was over-generous in his praise. v. Whitefield's *Journals* (1965) p. 157.
[2] For one ambiguous instance, however, v. *Letters*, i. p. 20 (1725).
[3] Tyerman, *Samuel Wesley*, p. 444.

receiving the Holy Communion, the graces of which (he wrote to his mother) 'are not of so little force, as that we can't perceive whether we have them or no'.[1] The authors who had been his devotional mentors at Oxford had opened various doors to him,[2] but they had not even distantly led him to see that an immediate experience of conversion was either desirable or possible. 'These convinced me, more than ever, of the absolute impossibility of being half a Christian', he later wrote of them,[3] 'and I determined ... to be all-devoted to God, to give him my soul, my body, and my substance'; and the disciplined, ascetic life of early rising, prayer, study, fasting and constant communion which he led, bears witness to the intensity of this self-devotion to God.

Yet, when Wesley was met on arriving in America by the Moravian pastor, A. G. Spangenberg, he did not understand the drift of the questions when he was asked—'Do you know yourself? Have you the witness within you? Does the Spirit of God bear witness with your spirit that you are a child of God?'[4] for these interrogatories were prompted by a view of regeneration commonplace among the Moravian Pietists, but as unknown to Wesley as to English churchmen generally.[5]

The account has been frequently given[6] of how the Moravians opened Wesley's eyes to the meaning of conversion, and how they helped him to reach the point at which he could experience it for himself. On board the *Simmonds*, and in Georgia, Wesley was impressed by the piety and fearlessness of the Moravians, and he longed to learn their inner secret. He asked them about regeneration as they understood it, and carefully recorded their answers.

What do you mean by conversion?
'The passing from darkness to light, and from the power of Satan unto God' (Acts xxvi. 25–33).
Is it commonly wrought at once, or by degrees?

---

[1] *Letters*, i. p. 20.
[2] v. esp. Schmidt, *John Wesley*, pp. 73–89, 106–12, for a full exposition.
[3] *Works*, xi. p. 367.
[4] *Journal*, i. p. 151.
[5] v. the important article by J. D. Walsh in *Essays in Modern English Church History*, Edds. G. V. Bennett and J. D. Walsh (1966) pp. 132 ff.
[6] Perhaps best by J. E. Rattenbury, *The Conversion of the Wesleys* (1938) pp. 60 ff; Schmidt, *op. cit.* Chapters. 6, 7.

'The design of passing thus from darkness unto light is sometimes wrought in a moment (Acts xvi. 25–34); but the passage itself is gradual' (Acts ii. 37, etc.).[1]

To all that they had to say, Wesley listened with anxious attention and with growing understanding, so that when he left the Colony for England, while he knew what it is, he knew the more certainly to his despair that he lacked this regeneration still. Pouring out his heart in his *Journal*, he wrote:

But what have I learned myself in the meantime? Why, what I the least of all suspected, that I, who went to America to convert others, was never myself converted to God. . . . This, then, have I learned in the ends of the earth,—that I 'am fallen short of the glory of God': that my whole heart is 'altogether corrupt and abominable'; . . . that 'having the sentence of death' in my heart, and having nothing in or of myself to plead, I have no hope, but that of being justified freely, 'through the redemption that is in Jesus' . . . I want that faith which none can have without knowing that he hath it (though many imagine they have it, who have it not); for whosoever hath it, is 'freed from sin, the whole body of sin is destroyed' in him: he is freed from fear, 'having peace with God through Christ, and rejoicing in hope of the glory of God.' And he is freed from doubt, 'having the love of God shed abroad in his heart, through the Holy Ghost which is given unto him'; which 'Spirit itself beareth witness with his spirit, that he is a child of God'.[2]

Back in England, Wesley almost immediately resumed his association with the Moravians through a friendship which sprang up between himself and Peter Böhler.[3] They were drawn together partly because Böhler was shortly to leave for the Colony which Wesley had just left. Yet the tenor of his *Journal* makes it plain that the Englishman eagerly sought Böhler's counsel and help in his search for the Moravians' regeneration—and he was not to be disappointed. Böhler proved to be the guide who brought Wesley to Christ as, step by step, the remaining difficulties and uncertainties were cleared away, until the Aldersgate Street experience was in view.

Having convinced himself from an examination of the New

[1] *Journal*, i. p. 372.
[2] *Journal*, i. pp. 422 ff.
[3] For biographical notes, v. Schmidt, *op. cit.* pp. 224 ff.

Testament that conversion can be instantaneous, Wesley came to Böhler arguing that, whatever may have been the way of God's working in the first ages of Christianity, times are so far changed that God no longer regenerates people in an instant. But Böhler had the answer to this—the living answer provided from the lips of four men (Moravians also) who 'testified God had thus wrought in themselves, giving them in a moment such a faith in the blood of His Son as translated them out of darkness into light'.[1] 'Here ended my disputing,' added Wesley. 'I could now only cry out, "Lord, help Thou my unbelief"'; and this prayer was, at last, answered on 24 May 1738. In his *Journal* account of that day, he wrote:

In the evening I went very unwillingly to a society in Aldersgate Street, where one was reading Luther's preface to the *Epistle to the Romans*. About a quarter before nine, while he was describing the change which God works in the heart through faith in Christ, I felt my heart strangely warmed. I felt I did trust in Christ, Christ alone for salvation; and an assurance was given me that He had taken away *my* sins, even *mine*, and saved *me* from the law of sin and death.[2]

Some months before leaving America, Wesley had written to his friend John Gambold apparently asking him: 'O, what is regeneration?' Gambold had not been able to answer this question with any precision;[3] but the Moravians first in America and then in England had given Wesley the answer, and its truth was now sealed for him as he experienced it for himself. The Methodists, he wrote in March 1738, call a person who experiences this work wrought by the Holy Ghost in the heart, 'regenerated, born again, a new creature'.[4]

This had been to Wesley 'a new doctrine'.[5] Böhler reported him as saying that 'he had never seen an Englishman ... who had experienced this'; that it was 'a completely new gospel, one which he had never heard of in the whole of his life.'[6] But it is important to see precisely where the novelty lay.

---

[1] *Journal*, i. p. 455; and again i. p. 457.
[2] *Ibid.* i. pp. 475 f. Charles had three days earlier known a similar experience (v. *Charles' Journal* i. pp. 90 ff) having also been convinced of his need of it by Böhler. v. *Journal*, i. p. 459.
[3] Tyerman, *Oxford Methodists*, pp. 165 ff.
[4] *Letters*, i. p. 235.
[5] *Journal*, i. p. 442.   [6] Schmidt, *op. cit.* p. 238.

The Moravians had taught Wesley that justification was by faith alone—but this was only opening his eyes to the traditional teaching of the Reformation which he could find readily enough in the Articles and Homilies of his Church.[1] What is of more note is that, beyond this, they taught him to regard Christ's victory not simply as an objective fact concerned with the sin of all mankind, but as a personal experience of forgiveness;[2] they showed him not only that we are justified by faith but that we can know, in a given moment, that we have faith and are forgiven;[3] they taught him to regard this experience as true re-birth or conversion, so that from now on, 'adult regeneration' will be defined for Wesley as 'justification personally experienced'[4]—and this was for him a new doctrine indeed. It is the teaching of the Reformation given a new, personal grounding in a conscious conversion experience of forgiveness and atonement, and here we have the contribution of the Moravians not only to Wesley's own religious development but through him to the Church at large.[5]

Here we have, then, the most important contribution made by the Moravians to Wesley's Christian understanding. They taught him to think of adult regeneration as conversion— a new doctrine. Yet, less noticeably, they influenced him in another way. They gave him confirmation of an already familiar doctrine—baptismal regeneration. This point needs to be stressed because it seems often to be assumed that the Moravians denied that infants were born again in baptism, and so caused Wesley to doubt this also. C. W. Towlson has said of the Moravian Brethren, that

they differed from Luther in their doctrine of infant baptism; they rejected any idea of baptismal regeneration. To them ... infant

---

[1] *Journal*, i. p. 454. cf. J. E. Rattenbury, *The Conversion of the Wesleys*, p. 74 n.
[2] v. W. R. Cannon, *The Theology of John Wesley*, p. 74; H. D. Rack, *The Future of John Wesley's Methodism* (1965) p. 8.
[3] v. Schmidt, *op. cit.* p. 238; C. W. Williams, *John Wesley's Theology Today*, pp. 101–4; C. W. Towlson, *Moravian and Methodist*, pp. 174, 221.
[4] v. Schmidt, *op. cit.* p. 307; H. A. Hodges and A. M. Allchin, *A Rapture of Praise*, p. 11.
[5] v. C. W. Towlson, *op. cit.* p. 67. Charles Wesley's doctrine differed from his brother's at this point, and he preferred to use the term 'regeneration' not of conversion but of 'Christian perfection' (v. J. E. Rattenbury, *The Evangelical Doctrines of Charles Wesley's Hymns*, 1941, pp. 260 ff). But John's usage was dominant both at the time and in later Methodism.

baptism was simply the outward and visible sign of admission to the Church.[1]

However, a study of the liturgies used by the *Unitas Fratrum* indicates that they were grafted much more surely on to the Lutheran stock[2] than Towlson allowed, and that they believed very firmly in baptismal regeneration. In their worship they used Luther's litany,[3] in which provision is made at different points for various ceremonies to be held when necessary; and infants are to be baptised at the words:

Regenerate our Children through Water and the Holy Spirit; And take them in thy Arms from the Mother's womb.

The hymns provided to accompany the sacrament are even more explicit. For example:

> *The eye sees Water, nothing more,*
> *How it is poured out by men;*
> *But faith alone conceives the pow'r*
> *Of Jesu's Blood to make us clean:*
> *Faith sees it as a purple flood,*
> *Colour'd with Jesu's Blood and Grace,*
> *Which heals each sore, and makes all good,*
> *What Adam brought on us his Race,*
> *And what we ourselves have done.*[4]

In the Moravian liturgy which was used at Herrnhut from 1770 onwards, we find two alternative orders for the baptism of children,[5] and it can immediately be seen that the earlier doctrine of baptismal regeneration had continued unchanged over these years. For example, in the first of these orders, the *Liturgus* asks:

What is baptism?

---

[1] *Op. cit.* p. 26.
[2] Luther believed that with infant baptism a relative reconciliation to God is effected, along with a real work involving the transforming of the whole character of the recipient, the granting of the Spirit, and an infusion of grace. This marks the beginning of a process of regeneration which must be worked out over the whole consequent life. v. e.g. J. B. Mozley, *A Review of the Baptismal Controversy*, pp. 295 f, 312 f; J. Baillie, *Baptism and Conversion*, pp. 22 ff.
[3] A. E. Peaston, *The Prayer Book Tradition in the Free Churches* (1964) pp. 98 ff.
[4] English trans. by J. Gambold, 1754, No. 303.
[5] English translation, *Liturgic Hymns of the United Brethern* (1793), Nos. 43, 44; pp. 105 ff.

and the children are to reply:

The answer of a good conscience towards God, the washing of regeneration and renewing of the Holy Ghost, which is shed on us abundantly thro' Jesus Christ our Savior (sic.).

Further on, this verse is sung:

> Be present with us, Lord our God,
> This water can't make clean,
> But whilst we pour it, cleanse by blood
> This infant from all sin.[1]

The baptismal regeneration here expressed includes both a relative and real work of God, for not only is the forgiveness of sin spoken of, but also it is stated that the Holy Spirit is bestowed on the child. In other words, the Moravians believed most wholeheartedly in the regeneration of infants in baptism, as well as in the need for the regeneration (or conversion) of adults.

Since this is so, it must not be assumed that the impact of Moravianism upon Wesley made him belittle infant regeneration in favour of adult conversion. In particular, we cannot agree with the often-quoted words of Miss Julia Wedgwood who, when commenting on the consequence of the Moravian stress upon conversion, wrote that, for evangelicals,

The birthday of a Christian was already shifted from his baptism to his conversion, and in that change the partition line of two great systems is crossed.[2]

The Moravians had not made such a shift, nor did they teach Wesley to do so. It is true that they believed the Christian birthday of an adult to be his conversion, but they were equally firmly convinced that the Christian birthday of an infant is his baptism. The Moravians held that regeneration

---

[1] v. also, *ibid.*, alternative order for baptism; 'Extract of the Twenty-one Doctrinal Articles of the . . . Augsburg Confession; for the use of the Brethren's Congregations', Art. ix; *A Collection of Hymns* (1754), Pt. i. nos. 595–7; Pt. ii. nos. 275, 276.

[2] *John Wesley and the Evangelical Reaction of the Eighteenth Century* (1870) p. 157. Cited by, e.g. J. H. Rigg, *The Churchmanship of John Wesley*, p. 35; R. Green, *John Wesley Evangelist*, p. 230; J. S. Simon, *John Wesley and the Religious Societies*, p. 334.

can be received twice—in infancy and in later life—and they encouraged Wesley to think in the same way.

At this point we may pause to look back over and reflect upon the ground that has been covered. We have followed Wesley as he learned to give a two-fold use to the term regeneration, for he became convinced that there is, by the grace of God, a re-birth offered to infants as well as to adults. It is important to see that he was led to believe in both kinds of regeneration without any suggestion that they might be mutually incompatible. He learned conversion from the Moravians, but he could find baptismal regeneration stated as plainly in their liturgy as it was in his own *Book of Common Prayer*. Thus from the start there was no thought that the preaching of conversion might involve any radical break with the Anglican understanding of the way to salvation in which he had been brought up.[1]

In fact, however, Wesley was making such a break. The early evangelicals believed that their doctrine of regeneration did accord with the doctrinal standards of the Church of England, but they were mistaken; and we must now turn to a consideration of this predicament as it is reflected in Wesley's baptismal beliefs.

[1] Wesley claimed to find conversion in the writings of the Primitive Church (*Works*, viii. pp. 97 ff), 'Luther, Melanchthon, and many other (if not all) of the Reformers' (*Letters*, iii. p. 159), the Puritans (*Letters*, iv. p. 126), as well as in the formularies of the Church of England (*Letters*, iv. pp. 376 ff; *Works*, viii. pp. 101 ff).

CHAPTER 5

Wesley's Doctrine: 1 Adult Baptism and Regeneration

At the beginning of the eighteenth century, Churchmen of all kinds agreed that the doctrine of adult baptism presented no problems. The protests of the Baptists stirred no controversy at this point, and it was generally taken for granted that adult baptism is scriptural, and that all who in penitence and faith wished to ally themselves with God in His Church should receive this sacrament.

Furthermore, the Anglican teaching,[1] following the tradition of the early and medieval Church, was that the essential benefit of baptism—infant and adult—is regeneration. It was believed not only that this re-birth is signified by the outward action of the sacramental washing but also that it is conveyed to infants and believing adults in and through the rite, for regeneration was defined as the inner spiritual re-birth which is signed and sealed by the outward ceremony of baptism. Baptism and regeneration were thus regarded as the inner and outer aspects of a unity, so that, strictly speaking, it would be incorrect to refer to any renewal as 'regeneration' other than that associated with baptism.

This attitude is to be found in Samuel Wesley's *Discourse of Baptism* (1700) in which, the benefits of baptism (including regeneration) having been set out, it is then enquired, 'Who are the proper subjects of baptism? grown persons only, or infants also?'[2]—and the answer given that both are called to receive the outward washing of the sacrament and its inward grace. A few years later, William Wall in his authoritative *History of Infant Baptism* had concluded that in the Early Church the

---

[1] v. J. B. Mozley, *The Primitive Doctrine of Baptismal Regeneration* (1856) *passim*, and *A Review of the Baptismal Controversy*, pp. 126 ff; P. E. Hughes, *Theology of the English Reformers* (1965) pp. 195 ff.
[2] *The Pious Communicant* . . . , pp. 213 f.

term 'regeneration' had been used synonymously for 'baptism',[1] and he deplored the custom, growing up among some 'modern writers', of using

the word *regeneration*, or *new-birth*, for repentance and conversion, whether it be accompanied with baptism at the time or not.[2]

Dr. Waterland had spoken squarely from the Anglican position when he said:

the new birth, in the general, means a spiritual change, wrought upon any person by the Holy Spirit, in the use of Baptism.[3]

In the case of adult baptism, the Church of England had for long made it plain that its efficacy is conditional: that is, only those candidates who have faith and are penitent receive the inward grace of the sacrament. Any who are baptised without satisfying these conditions do not receive regeneration at that time. Article XXV was understood as implying that baptism has a 'wholesome effect or operation' only on those adults who receive it 'worthily' in this manner; and those only who fulfil these conditions are, by baptism, 'regenerate, and grafted into the body of Christ's Church'.[4]

The consequence of this was that, in the case of adults, the sign and the signification—the outward ceremony and its inward counterpart—can be separated in point of time. A person may receive the inward spiritual renewal before being baptised, but it was held that he should not be termed 'regenerate' until this re-birth had been signed and sealed to him in the sacrament. Again, should a person be baptised without faith and penitence, then it was maintained that the sacrament remains ineffective unless or until he does fulfil these conditions, at which time his regeneration becomes complete. The inward significance and the outward sacrament of regeneration may thus be separated in time, but still, in Anglican eyes, they constituted one essential unity.

It is plain that in his early years Wesley believed in the baptismal regeneration of both infants and adults, maintaining

---

[1] v. *Supra* p. 22.
[2] *Op. cit.* i. p. 43; cf. p. 447.
[3] *Regeneration Stated and Explained* ... (1739). cit. Tyerman, *John Wesley*, i. p. 330.
[4] v. the prayer following the baptism in the *Book of Common Prayer* adult order. For Wesley, v. *Notes* for Acts ii. 38; *Works*, x. p. 149.

that in both cases the sacrament is an effective sign, by which means regeneration is imparted. This at any rate is the assumption which underlies his exposition in the *Treatise*, in which, following his father's *Discourse*, the same benefits are set down as being given in baptism to both infants and adults alike.[1] Yet when he had learned to equate adult regeneration with conversion, this straight-forward position was no longer tenable. No re-appraisal was necessary in regard to infant baptism, for the Moravians had taught Wesley nothing that conflicted with his earlier belief in the unconditional granting of infant re-birth in the sacrament, but some considerable re-adjustment was required in his understanding of adult baptism; for the fact is, quite simply, that conversion as he had learned it is not in any special way a baptismal experience.[2]

Wesley very soon found that conversion is not given in conjunction with any one particular means of grace, but that it may be received by the faithful, whether or not baptised, at any time and in the use of any of the means of grace. Should someone be converted before baptism, then Wesley regarded that work as complete—although, as we will notice, he was willing to baptise the regenerated person. Should someone be converted after baptism, then Wesley considered this to be an independent work of God, unrelated to the earlier administration of the sacrament. Should a person be converted during the administration of baptism, then Wesley held this to be an altogether fitting but coincidental concurrence. For him, conversion was the result of the free working of God's Spirit, signified indeed by baptism but bound up with the ordinance no more closely than that.

In other words, Wesley could not believe in the baptismal regeneration of adults, for his new understanding of adult regeneration allowed the reception of this re-birth to be tied to baptism no more than to any other of the means of grace.

It was soon after 1738 that the Wesleys saw that conversion can precede baptism. John would have shared the evident

---

[1] *Works*, x. pp. 190–2.
[2] Thus Wesley said that the test of regeneration is not whether a person has been baptised, but whether at the present moment he has assurance of being re-born and shows its fruit in holiness of life. *Sermons*, i. pp. 294 ff; ii. pp. 238 ff. Furthermore, he suggested that adult regeneration (unlike baptism) may be repeated whenever a converted person falls again into sin. *Sermons*, i. pp. 310 f.

surprise of his brother on discovering that this could be so. Commenting on the conversions of Susanna Trapman and Elizabeth Parsons in 1739, Charles Wesley wrote:

It is observable of the two last, that they have never been baptized. I now require no farther proof that one may be an *inward* Christian without baptism. They are both desirous of it; and who can forbid water?[1]

Those who, being unbaptised, were regenerated, Wesley christened if they wished for it. He took scripture for his pattern.

After sermon an elderly woman (Elizabeth Tyerman) asked me abruptly, 'Dost thou think water baptism an ordinance of Christ?' I said, 'What saith Peter? "Who can forbid water, that these should not be baptized, who have received the Holy Ghost even as we?"' I spoke but little more, before she cried out, ' 'Tis right! 'Tis right! I will be baptized'. And so she was, the same hour.[2]

Wesley saw in practice that conversion did not always accompany the administration of baptism. He wrote:

From the preceding reflections we may ... observe, that as the new birth is not the same thing with baptism, so it does not always accompany baptism; they do not constantly go together. A man may possibly be 'born of water', and yet not be 'born of the Spirit'. There may sometimes be the outward sign, where there is not the inward grace. I do not now speak with regard to infants: it is certain our Church supposes that all who are baptized in their infancy are at the same time born again. ... But whatever be the case with infants, it is sure all of riper years who are baptized are not at the same time born again. 'The tree is known by its fruits'. And hereby it appears too plain to be denied, that divers of those who were children of the devil before they were baptized continue the same after baptism.[3]

Yet there were occasions when regeneration did accompany adult baptism. In October 1758, Wesley

baptized a young woman, deeply convinced of sin. We all found the power of God was present to heal (he reports), and she herself felt what she had not words to express.[4]

---

[1] *Charles' Journal*, i. p. 180. cf. *ibid.* p. 318.
[2] *Journal*, iii. p. 171. cf. *Notes* for Acts x. 47.
[3] *Sermons*, ii. p. 238. e.g. *Journal*, iv. p. 540; v. pp. 3 f.
[4] *Journal*, iv. p. 286.

On another occasion, a young woman similarly

received a full assurance of His pardoning love and was filled with joy unspeakable.[1]

And again:

I baptized a young woman brought up an Anabaptist; and God bore witness to His ordinance, filling her heart, at the very time, with peace and joy unspeakable.[2]

Yet again, Sara Labbe (brought up a Baptist) and later 'a young woman (late a Quaker)' were both at their baptisms 'filled with the Holy Ghost'.[3]

Looking at these extracts, it can be seen that in some respects Wesley's conclusions agreed with the teaching of the Anglican Church. He accepted that baptism is a sign of regeneration; he baptised those who were born again prior to baptism; and he found that sometimes regeneration accompanied the administration of the sacrament. And yet these are superficial points of agreement, the last vestiges of that vital unity which in Anglican thought bound regeneration to baptism, but which Wesley (in the case of adults only) had almost totally destroyed. By defining adult regeneration as 'conversion' he had, at a stroke, severed it from its sacramental setting and lifted in into the realm of the free working of God's Spirit.

The consequence of this separation of regeneration from the sacrament is to be seen in the way in which Wesley came to view the efficiency of adult baptism. His Church taught that adult baptism is the means of one grace in particular—regeneration: Wesley found it to be a means of grace in general. Just as the Lord's supper, or prayer, or reading the Bible, or listening to preaching can convey the varied benefits of 'preventing, justifying, or sanctifying grace'[4] to people at different stages in their Christian experience, so Wesley found that baptism was equally an instrument used by God to give such blessing to the candidate as was warranted

---

[1] *Journal*, vi. p. 49. cf. *Letters*, iii. p. 159.
[2] *Journal*, vii. p. 132.
[3] *Letters*, i. p. 313 (cf. *Journal*, ii. p. 199 n); *Letters*, i. p. 317 (cf. *Journal*, ii. p. 206 n). cf. *The Christian Library*, Vol. xiii. p. 73.
[4] *Sermons*, i. p. 242.

by the level of his spiritual progress at the time. For some, as we have seen, this could be conversion, but to others, who were not at that particular stage of Christian development when they were baptised, some other benefit was often given. Baptism was received 'not without a blessing';[1] or, 'a deep sense of the presence of God' was felt 'in His ordinance'.[2] Indeed, whenever baptism was approached by the candidate in the proper spirit, Wesley came to expect that some grace would invariably be received. He said:

> I baptized a gentlewoman at the Foundery, and the peace she immediately found was a fresh proof that the outward sign, duly received, is always accompanied with the inward grace.[3]

As early as January 1739, Wesley was familiar with the variety of experience which may be found in the use of this ordinance. He wrote in his *Journal*:

> Of the adults I have known baptized lately, one only was at that time born again, in the full sense of the word; that is, found a thorough, inward change, by the love of God filling her heart. Most of them were only born again in a lower sense; that is, received the remission of their sins. And some (as it has since too plainly appeared) neither in one sense nor the other.[4]

Charles Wesley came to a similar conclusion about adult baptism as a means of grace, for he also found that sincere candidates 'received both the outward visible sign, and the inward spiritual grace',[5] and sometimes he described this transformation in some detail.

For Charles, the essence of conversion was the instantaneous inward realization of pardon,[6] and so, although he does once speak as though regeneration was received in baptism,[7] his

---

[1] *Journal*, iii. p. 342.   [2] *Ibid*. vi. p. 49.
[3] *Ibid*. iv. p. 365. cf. iv. p. 189 ('God, as usual, bore witness to this ordinance'); iv. p. 462; v. p. 195; *Notes* for Acts xxii. 16.
[4] ii. p. 135. (Wesley's terminology here is immature. v. Tyerman, *John Wesley*, i. pp. 229 f.). Note the frequent use of an exclamation mark in Wesley's Diaries to stress the spiritual efficacy of adult baptism. For examples, v. *infra*. p. 91.
[5] *Charles' Journal*, ii. p. 59.
[6] i.e. Justification. For the difference in emphasis in the thought of John and Charles at this point, v. J. E. Rattenbury, *The Evangelical Doctrines of Charles Wesley's Hymns* (1941) pp. 260 ff.
[7] *Charles' Journal*, i. p. 234. ' . . . knows that she is born of water and of the Spirit . . . ' The reference is to John iii. I ff.

descriptions normally are in terms of 'the justifying baptismal grace',[1] marked by the descent of the Holy Spirit.

Two instances may be given.

I prayed at Islington with Anne Gates, believing we had the petitions we asked. I then baptized a child and her. We all felt the descent of the Holy Ghost. Before, she was in the spirit of heaviness and bondage. The moment the water touched her, she declares she felt her load removed, and sensibly received forgiveness. Sorrow and sighing fled away. The Spirit bore witness with the water, and she longed to be with Christ. We gave glory to God, who so magnified his ordinance.[2]

I baptized a woman at the chapel, before the service. She was in the spirit of heaviness; but God magnified his ordinance, and she was therein enlightened to see her sins forgiven.[3]

In words reminiscent of those of his brother, Charles summed up his experience of adult baptism as a means of grace:

The Spirit infallibly bears witness on this occasion.[4]

All this means that, apparently without realizing it, the Wesleys had transformed adult baptism. In much the same way as they gave new life and purpose to the Lord's supper,[5] so they took adult baptism out of the rather austere and formal place allotted to it by the Church of their day, and made it into a living handmaid of evangelism. Of course, should a candidate come carelessly to the sacrament no grace would be given; but if he came with due faith then his baptism could prove to be a converting or sanctifying moment and, if so, he would look back to that occasion all his life and be grateful for what his baptism had meant to him. The evangelical fruitfulness of adult baptism must have charged it, in the minds of candidates and congregations alike, with a value that infant baptism could scarcely match.[6] The hymns that Charles Wesley wrote for such occasions show that the Methodists were encouraged to

---

[1] *Charles' Journal*, i. p. 396. [2] *Ibid.* i. p. 223.
[3] *Ibid.* i. p. 335. cf. i. pp. 151, 286, 358, 367 f, 396, 398, 415, 427; ii. pp. 13, 16, 71, 73, 75, 81. v. F. Baker, *Charles Wesley as Revealed in his Letters* (1948) pp. 121 f.
[4] *Charles' Journal*, i. p. 234. cf. ii. p. 71.
[5] v. J. C. Bowmer, *The Sacrament of the Lord's Supper in Early Methodism*, pp. 82 ff.
[6] Although Charles Wesley's hymns for infant baptism indicate that these were occasions for joy, thanksgiving and solemn prayer.

approach adult baptism with a sense of expectancy.[1] Verses such as these can never have been sung to accompany a merely formal ceremony. The people must always have been sure that here was an opportunity full of the promise of God's converting and perfecting action. Rapturously these hymns were sung ('For Believers Interceding' was their heading); and time and again these prayers were answered. The spirit of one such occasion is captured for us in this extract from the *Journal* of Charles Wesley:

> I baptized Sarah and Eliz., a Quaker and a Baptist, before a full congregation. All were moved by the descent of that Spirit: many wept, and trembled, and rejoiced. The persons baptized most of all.[2]

We can now see what it was that Wesley regarded as the necessary precondition which must be met if adult baptism was to convey grace to the candidate. When first in Georgia, the Wesleys evidently looked for 'sincerity' in those asking for this ordinance,[3] but they learned from the Moravians their practice—that of only baptising adults upon their conversion; on hearing which, Töltschig recalled, Wesley and Ingham 'became very quiet and sighed over the degeneracy of their own Church'.[4] Yet in fact the Wesleys did not adopt this standpoint. Those who, like Elizabeth Tyerman, were converted prior to baptism they christened; and yet more frequently it happened that people were baptised before their conversion, upon their confession of faith, their awareness of sin, and their desire for the sacrament:[5] and for some of these, as we have seen, the sacrament proved to be the effective means of their regeneration.

It is commonly noted that the evangelical conception of conversion came into conflict with the doctrine of infant baptismal regeneration. Our analysis, however, has shown that the immediate impact of evangelicalism was not upon infant but *adult* baptismal regeneration. The teaching of the Church

---

[1] v. Appendix 2. cf. The Moravian hymns for adult baptism, in which this same intercessory note is sounded. *Collection of Hymns* (1754) Pt. i. Nos. 595–7, Pt. ii. No. 275.   [2] ii. p. 81.

[3] *Charles' Journal*, i. p. 26. A Mr. Appee asked for baptism, but Charles 'thought he ought to have a longer trial of his sincerity'. cf. *Journal*, i. p. 117.

[4] Schmidt, *John Wesley*, i. p. 162.   [5] v. *Works*, viii. p. 52.

of England was that regeneration is the same for infants and adults, and that in both cases it is a baptismal gift. Wesley persisted in this belief with regard to infant re-birth: but his new understanding of adult regeneration (as conversion) meant that he now regarded adult re-birth in a different light, for he saw that it was not essentially a baptismal experience. This led him, in effect, to abandon his belief in the baptismal regeneration of adults, and enabled him to transform adult baptism into a means of general grace.

It is interesting to notice, however, that this incompatibility between adult regeneration evangelically defined and adult baptismal regeneration did not seem to have been observed by Wesley. When preaching on 'The Marks of the New Birth', he would introduce his theme by saying that the new birth is 'ordinarily annexed to baptism'[1]—and then go on to expound at length regeneration as a conversion experience ordinarily wholly divorced from this ordinance. In the same way, when speaking of baptism in general, Wesley says that 'the merits of Christ's life and death, are applied to us in baptism . . . (which is) the ordinary instrument of our justification';[2] and yet he could also preach a sermon setting out 'The Scripture Way of Salvation' in which baptism is not mentioned at all.[3]

If it seems surprising that Wesley did not realize the contradiction here involved, it must be pointed out that neither did anyone else at that time, whether friends of his or foes;[4] and various reasons may be given to account for this. The fact that most of those who were converted had been baptised in infancy, served to raise the issue of the relationship between conversion and infant baptism, while leaving aside as marginal the problem of relating conversion to adult baptism. Again, the fact that conversions happened at other times than during baptism seemed to conform to the Anglican view that adult baptism and regeneration may be separated in point of time. Perhaps it was for these reasons that neither Wesley nor his critics grasped that

---

[1] *Sermons*, i. p. 283.   [2] *Works*, x. p. 191.
[3] *Sermons*, ii. pp. 444 ff.
[4] R. Southey (writing in 1820) did so, and commented: 'I do not believe that an instance of equal blindness or disingenuity (whichever it may be thought) can be found in all the other parts of Wesley's works.' *Life of John Wesley* (1899 ed.) p. 321 n.

acceptance of the 'new doctrine' of conversion had brought him into conflict with the traditional teaching of the Church of England regarding adult baptism.

However, we have yet to see the full extent of Wesley's departure from the orthodoxy of his church, and we investigate this further as we turn to his doctrine of regeneration in relation to infant baptism.

CHAPTER 6

Wesley's Doctrine: 2 Infant Baptism and the Two Regenerations

An investigation into Wesley's convictions regarding infant baptism and regeneration will naturally begin with a study of his *Treatise on Baptism*,[1] but at the outset we must deal with two preliminary difficulties with which this treatise confronts us.

First, we must meet the suggestion that, since the treatise is derived wholly from Samuel Wesley's *Discourse of Baptism*, Wesley was here reproducing the opinions of another which he did not himself hold. The facts, however, are against this interpretation. It is possible that Wesley prepared the *Treatise* in answer to a request from his brother Charles and William Grimshaw that 'a small treatise be written' to provide material with which the Methodists could refute Baptist arguments[2]—and, if so, he would scarcely have set out views with which he disagreed. Whether or not this was the occasion of its composition, Wesley first published the *Treatise* in a volume called *A Preservative against Unsettled Notions in Religion*, and it is inconceivable that he would have included anything under such a title unless he was firmly convinced of its orthodoxy. Without a doubt Wesley thoroughly believed all that he set down in this *Treatise*.

The other difficulty is to account for the fact that in the *Treatise* adult as well as infant baptismal regeneration is assumed—whereas we have argued in the previous chapter that Wesley did not accept the baptismal regeneration of adults. Two reasons may be given to explain this apparent discrepancy. First, Wesley's purpose in preparing and publishing this tract was to defend and encourage the practice of infant baptism, and throughout its pages, while baptism in general is under review, it is plain that the author was thinking

[1] *Works*, x. pp. 188 ff.
[2] For full notes, v. *infra*, Appendix 1.

almost exclusively of its administration to children. Adult baptism, as such, is hardly considered at all. Second, we have suggested that Wesley seemed to be unaware that his belief in adult regeneration as conversion conflicted with the teaching of his Church that regeneration is always a baptismal benefit. It seems, therefore, that Wesley prepared the *Treatise* with his eye firmly fixed upon infant baptism, and was oblivious to the fact that at the same time he was making assertions about adult baptismal regeneration which are inconsistent with his general teaching elsewhere about conversion. If this is so, then we may take the *Treatise* to be a sure guide to Wesley's views about baptismal regeneration only in so far as infants are concerned —and, in so doing, we are probably reading no more and no less into this tract than the author intended.

In the *Treatise* Wesley listed the benefits of infant baptism as being six in number. These are:

1. *The 'washing away of the guilt of Original Sin'*. Wesley regarded original sin very seriously, believing that here was the grave and vicious cause of all those ills which made necessary the redeeming work of Christ. Were original sin to be denied, then Wesley felt that the need for Christ's atonement was being removed. Thus he said that a 'denial of original sin . . . renders baptism needless with regard to infants'.[1] Arguing from the command of Our Lord, he said:

by the appointment of Christ, (infants) are to be baptized; which shows they are unclean, and that there is no salvation for them, but 'by the washing of regeneration, and renewing of the Holy Ghost'.[2]

It is not surprising therefore that this, the principle benefit of baptism, should appear first in order in the *Treatise*. The removal of the guilt of original sin is

by the application of the merits of Christ's death. . . . This plainly includes infants; for they too die; therefore they have sinned: But not by actual sin; therefore by original; else what need have they of the death of Christ? . . . And the virtue of this free gift, the merits of Christ's life and death, are applied to us in baptism.[3]

---

[1] *Works*, ix. p. 429. Wesley is quoting from 'four several tracts professedly against Dr. Taylor', by Samuel Hebden.
[2] *Works*, ix. p. 438. Wesley here quoted from Boston's *Fourfold State of Man*.
[3] *Works*, x. pp. 190 f; cf. *Discourse*, p. 200.

In consequence, Wesley accepted the rubric at the end of the Common Prayer office for infant baptism:

It is certain, by God's word, that children who are baptized, dying before they commit actual sin are saved.[1]

2. *Entry into Covenant with God.*

As circumcision was then (i.e. under the old dispensation) the way of entering into this covenant, so baptism is now (i.e. under the new dispensation).[2]

F. E. Stoeffler has argued that 'John Wesley's views on infant baptism must be seen as lying within the tradition of Puritan "covenant theology" '; but Robert Cushman comments very fairly that

there is, perhaps insufficient evidence that Wesley shows direct dependence upon the elaborate covenantal theology of such representative Puritan divines as John Owen or William Strong. On the contrary, one has the impression that the covenantal theory is embraced within a composite of catholic ingredients of wider provenance.[3]

This is true, and it is to be noticed that Wesley put even less emphasis upon Puritan covenantalism than his father had done. Samuel Wesley (as we have seen[4]) was inclined to limit the sphere of infant baptismal efficacy to the children of believers, in the Puritan manner. John omitted these qualifying statements when preparing the *Discourse* for publication, and, while he did still hint at this limitation sometimes (particularly when arguing from Jewish circumcision to Christian baptism[5]), he generally rested infant baptism not so much upon a covenant made with believers and their families as upon the fact of universal sin, and the offer of universal pardon through the work of Christ available for all. Thus, applying his Arminian theology to baptism, he taught:

---

[1] *Works*, x. p. 191.   [2] *Works*, x, p. 191; cf. *Discourse*, p. 201.
[3] *The Doctrine of the Church* (Ed. Dow Kirkpatrick, 1964) pp. 80 f.
[4] v. *supra*, pp. 15 f.
[5] e.g. *Works*, x, pp. 191 f, 194 f; *Thoughts*, pp. 4 f. cp. the statement by B. J. N. Galliers (W.H.S. xxxii, p. 123) that 'the connexion between baptism and circumcision is important for Wesley, as it is a justification (perhaps *the* justification) for infant baptism'.

that the whole race of mankind are obnoxious both to the guilt and punishment of Adam's transgression. But 'as by the offence of one, judgment came upon all men to condemnation; so by the righteousness of one, the free gift came upon all men, to justification of life.' And the virtue of this free gift, the merits of Christ's life and death, are applied to us in baptism.[1]

And again:

Infants need to be washed from original sin; therefore they are proper subjects of baptism.[2]

3. *Admission into the Church.* It is noticeable that neither father nor son made any reference to confirmation at this point, even though the due order of their Church demanded that full communicant membership be given by baptism and confirmation together. Wesley said that baptism alone gives

union with the Church, a share in all its privileges, and in all the promises Christ has made to it.[3]

4. *Being made children of God.* Wesley wrote:

(Baptism) is more than barely being admitted into the Church...; being 'grafted into the body of Christ's Church, we are made the children of God by adoption and grace'.... By water then, as a means, the water of baptism, we are regenerated or born again.[4]

5. In consequence—*Being made heirs of the Kingdom of Heaven.*

... (For) as (baptism) admits us into the Church here, so into glory hereafter.[5]

6. *The bestowal of a 'principle of grace'.* So far, the benefits enumerated have been relative[6]—that is, have had to do with justification; with the reconciliation of the sinner to God. But now Wesley hints at the reception of a *real* benefit in the sacrament.

[1] *Works*, x. pp. 190 f.
[2] *Works*, x. p. 193; cf. *Discourse*, p. 207.
[3] *Works*, x. p. 191; cf. *Discourse*, p. 203. The note on Exodus xii. 48 reads: '... Neither may any now approach the Lord's supper who have not first submitted to baptism.' *Explanatory Notes Upon the Old Testament.*
[4] *Works*, x. pp. 191 f; cf. *Discourse*, p. 204.
[5] *Works*, x. p. 192; cf. *Discourse*, p. 207.
[6] With the exception of No. 3, Admission into the Church.

Herein a principle of grace is infused, which will not be wholly taken away, unless we quench the Holy Spirit of God by long-continuing wickedness.[1]

Yet it is plainly noticeable how unimportant this real benefit was to Wesley. In the *Treatise* he introduces it in this vague manner without any further explanation, and nowhere else in his *Works* does he allude to it at all—indeed, so completely is it ignored that sometimes Wesley speaks simply of 'baptismal justification'.[2] Almost his entire emphasis, therefore, was upon the relative benefits of baptism which are listed above.

In addition to these, B. J. N. Galliers has noted four other baptismal benefits which he has found mentioned by Wesley outside the *Treatise*.[3] These are: sharing in the death of Christ; the way to the Lord's table; the gift of the Holy Spirit; and physical healing. Of these, the first two are in fact implicitly contained in Wesley's list in the *Treatise*,[4] but the other two are lacking there.

Thus we find, in the first place, that Wesley does elsewhere associate the gift of the Spirit with baptism, and it may be at first surprising that he does not mention this in the *Treatise*. However, an examination of the places in Wesley's other writings cited by Mr. Galliers[5] shows that, in every case, Wesley was concerned with adult baptism: and while he indeed found that the Spirit was sometimes received by adults in the sacrament, he seems to have considered that infant baptism (with which he was principally concerned in the *Treatise*) conveys only the less eminent and ill-defined real benefit of a 'principle of grace'.

The other addition made by Mr. Galliers refers to the christening of Mary Welch at eleven days old, in Georgia. 'The child was ill then,' reported Wesley, 'but recovered from that hour.'[6] This is the only occasion in all his writings when any connection between baptism and healing is suggested[7]

---

[1] *Works*, x. p. 192; cf. *Discourse*, p. 205.
[2] *Works*, viii. pp. 52, 430. [3] W.H.S. xxxii, p. 123.
[4] 'Sharing in the death of Christ' in 1 above; and 'the way to the Lord's table' in 3.
[5] i.e. *Notes* for Acts ii. 38, 1 Cor. xii. 13; *Letters*, i. pp. 313, 317.
[6] *Journal*, i. pp. 166 f.
[7] Benjamin Ingham recorded such a consequence in 1736, also in Georgia. v. Tyerman, *Oxford Methodists*, pp. 73 f.

—nor is it clear even in this instance whether Wesley saw anything other than coincidence, or the answer to prayer, in the child's recovery. There is, therefore, no need for us to imagine that he shared any ignorant or superstitious faith in baptism as a remedy for sickness.

Having thus detailed the advantages which Wesley said are given in infant baptism, we may now summarize those benefits which together constitute infant regeneration as he understood it. These are, first, the relative benefits of forgiveness of original sin, entry into the new covenant, being made a child of God, and, in consequence, an heir of the Kingdom of Heaven. In addition there is the real benefit of regeneration which Wesley hinted at, calling it an infused 'principle of grace'.

Having arrived at this definition, it is of interest to compare infant with adult regeneration in Wesley's teaching,[1] and to notice that in his understanding of them he did not have in mind two re-births very different from one another. Both involve the relative blessings of justification—i.e. the forgiveness of prior sin (original only in one case, original and actual in the other), admission into the new covenant, being made a child of God and an heir of the Kingdom of Heaven; and also both include some real work done in the personality of the recipient. In other words, Wesley did not think so much of two distinct regenerations as of one re-birth which can be received at two stages of life; and the dissimilarities between them are thus created by the inability of infants to experience or to accept regeneration in the same mature way as can adults.

Two differences thus stand out.

Firstly, infant regeneration does not (for it cannot) involve that assurance of re-birth which Wesley had discovered was the normal accompaniment of conversion. This distinction was made explicitly by Wesley, after his conversion in 1738, in correspondence with his brother. Samuel had argued that the witness of the Spirit is not necessary to salvation (as John was now claiming), and he referred in proof of this to the case of baptised infants. John answered that

---

[1] Descriptions of conversion may be found, e.g. in *Sermons*, i. pp. 119 ff, 280 ff, 298 ff.

No kind of *assurance* (that I know), or of *faith*, or of *repentance*, is essential to their salvation who die *infants*.[1]

Secondly, adult regeneration differs from that of infants (according to Wesley) in that it involves the gift of the Spirit. Wesley spoke hesitantly of the real benefit of infant baptism as being 'a principle of grace', perhaps because he failed to find any virtue in baptised children which was lacking in those not christened. However, in adult re-birth, much greater stress is laid upon the real benefit bestowed in the giving of the Spirit,[2] which can be an effective power in the future for the progressive sanctification of the believer.

Having compared infant and adult regeneration as they appear in Wesley's works, we turn now to the question of how he viewed these re-births in relation to infant baptism: and, in the first place, we will consider the way in which Wesley considered infant regeneration to be associated with infant baptism.

In several places Wesley asserted quite plainly that infant regeneration is the invariable and unconditional accompaniment of infant baptism. Not that he believed it to be given *ex opere operato*—that doctrine he condemned strongly as being Roman and superstitious.

The virtue in the sacraments doth not proceed from the mere elements and words, but from the blessing of God in consequence of his promise to such only as rightly partake of them,[3]

said Wesley; and he similarly condemned those of his own Church who 'speak of the new birth as an outward thing—as if it were no more than baptism'.[4] Writing to Mr. Potter about the scriptural use of regeneration, he said that it is always the 'inward work of the Spirit whereof baptism is the outward sign';[5] and having examined certain of their doctrinal

[1] A. Clarke, *Memoirs of the Wesley Family* (1823) p. 418. cp. J. Baillie, *Baptism and Conversion* (1964) p. 85. '... the evangelicals emphasized the conscious experience (of conversion) and therefore came to hold ... that babies cannot be regenerated.'
[2] e.g. *Sermons*, ii. p. 446. '... there is a *real* as well as a *relative* change ... We feel 'the love of God shed abroad in our heart by the Holy Ghost which is given unto us' ...'
[3] *A Roman Catechism ... with a Reply Thereto, Works*, x. p. 113.
[4] *Journal*, ii. pp. 275 f.
[5] *Works*, ix. pp. 89 f.

standards, Wesley concluded that for both the Nonconformists and the Church of England, 'baptism is not the new birth'.[1] But while the sign (baptism) is not to be confused with the thing signified (regeneration), nevertheless Wesley believed that, for infants, the two invariably accompany one another; that it is God's free and gracious will to give regeneration to infants when they are baptised.

That this is so seems to have been a point constantly made in Wesley's sermons. Expounding the new birth, he says:

> With regard to infants: it is certain our Church supposes that all who are baptized in their infancy are at the same time born again; and it is allowed that the whole office for the Baptism of Infants proceeds upon this supposition. Nor is it an objection of any weight against this, that we cannot comprehend how this work is wrought in infants. For neither can we comprehend how it is wrought in a person of riper years.[2]

Again, referring to his hearers' baptism in their infancy, he said:

> Who denies that ye were then made children of God, and heirs of the kingdom of heaven?[3]

While explaining and defending Methodism to 'Men of Reason and Religion', he asserted the same thing:

> Baptism is the outward sign of this inward grace, which is supposed by our Church to be given with and through that sign to all infants.[4]

Infant regeneration is therefore taught to be a free gift, invariably and unconditionally given to children in baptism.

Yet Wesley did not go further than this, and claim that infant regeneration is given in baptism exclusively: that baptism is necessary for infant re-birth. It is true that his thinking at this point is not altogether clear. In particular, it is not wholly plain what it is that God was considered to give to all unbaptised infants.[5] But Wesley seems to have been con-

---

[1] *Sermons*, ii. p. 238. v. also *Sermons*, i. pp. 267, 300; ii. pp. 237 ff; *Notes* for John iii. 5; Eph. v. 26; Col. ii. 12; 1 Pet. iii. 21; *Works*, ix. p. 90.
[2] *Sermons*, ii. p. 238.
[3] *Ibid.* i. p. 296.   [4] *Works*, viii. p. 48.
[5] Judging by the quotation from the letter to John Mason which follows, it may have been the relative benefits only as given in infant baptism—i.e. justification—excluding the 'principle of grace', and admission into the Church.

vinced that, irrespective of baptism, all babies are reconciled to God through the work of Christ. In an important passage in a letter to John Mason, Wesley wrote:

That, 'by the offence of one, judgment came upon all men' (all born into the world) 'unto condemnation', is an undoubted truth, and affects every infant as well as every adult person. But it is equally true that, 'by the righteousness of one, the free gift came upon all men' (all born into the world, infants and adults) 'unto justification'. Therefore no infant ever was or ever will be 'sent to hell for the guilt of Adam's sin', seeing it is cancelled by the righteousness of Christ as soon as they are sent into the world.[1]

Wesley's view seems to be that the normal channel for this cancellation is baptism, but that should this be withheld or be unobtainable, God will give regeneration apart from it. This benefit, he wrote:

is to be received through the means which he hath appointed; through baptism in particular, which is the ordinary means he hath appointed for that purpose; and to which God hath tied us, though he may not have tied himself. Indeed, where it cannot be had, the case is different, but extraordinary cases do not make void a standing rule.[2]

It appears to be the case therefore, that while Wesley did not consider infant baptism to be necessary for infant regeneration, he nevertheless regarded it as the normal means by which God gives re-birth, unconditionally, to infants; and this is so because of the universal applicability of Christ's redeeming work.[3]

The next step in our enquiry is to discover how Wesley regarded the two regenerations in relation to one another. This is made the more difficult because he never dealt specifically with this issue, but there is no need to feel that he was unaware of the problem, or (with H. A. Hodges and A. M.

---

[1] *Letters*, vi. pp. 239 f (1776). cf. *Minutes* for 1774 (which state the universality of Christ's atonement but with no reference to baptism); *Works*, viii. p. 277; ix. p. 332 ('Not one child of man finally loses [by the fall of Adam], unless by his own choice'). cf. the first of John Fletcher's Four Degrees of Justification, viz. 'that which belongs to all infants, without any action on their part', cit. H.M.C. p. 178; *Letters*, iii. pp. 36, 186; Charles Wesley's verse on Mark xvi. 16, cit. *infra* Appendix 2. [2] *Works*, x. p. 193.
[3] v. W. R. Cannon, *The Theology of John Wesley*, p. 200 n; H. Lindström, *Wesley and Sanctification*, p. 107 n. cf. pp. 30 and 106 f.

Allchin[1]) to think that he had not resolved it clearly in his own mind. In fact, from comments made in many places, it is plain that he regarded the two regenerations as re-births that are offered to people successively at different stages in life.

In this matter Wesley was following the course already marked out by the Pietists.[2] John Baillie has summed up the teaching of Spener ('the father of Pietism') in this way:

> True to his Lutheran background, he continued to believe that regeneration takes place at baptism in infancy; but what is significant is that he insisted also on the necessity for true Christians of a second regeneration, and it is this latter that came to be spoken of among the pietists as conversion. ... Further, Spener taught that even after the second regeneration, a man may lapse again and yet again from the state of grace, so requiring further conversions.[3]

Such a treatment Wesley had learned from the Moravians, who stated that they did not 'account any man a brother, unless he had either preserved inviolate the covenant he made with God in baptism, or, if he has broken it, been born again of God'.[4] This seems to indicate that the *Unitas Fratrum* regarded infant and adult regenerations as having successive validity: that is, they considered the covenant of baptism to be valid only until it is broken, when a new and separate re-birth becomes necessary—and this is how Wesley came to consider the matter. We can see that he was already of this mind at the time of his conversion. A few days after the Aldersgate Street experience, Wesley claimed that 'Five days before I was not a Christian'. His brother Samuel, writing about this outburst, said:

---

[1] *A Rapture of Praise*, p. 41.
[2] And not that suggested by his father, who had written in his *Discourse*: 'We say not that *Regeneration* is always *compleated* in this *Sacrament*, but that it is *begun* in it ...' (v. *supra* p. 16). Wesley omitted these words from his *Treatise*.
[3] *Baptism and Conversion*, pp. 83 f.
[4] *Journal*, ii. p. 32. This kind of terminology was sometimes loosely used by the Puritans. e.g. 'This said Reference to all Comers ... gives ground to all concern'd to think themselves sufficiently Regenerated already, and to apprehend that the Church doth not think their aiming at any farther Regeneration needful, when once they are Baptiz'd and Confirm'd'. E. Calamy, *Abridgmen of Mr. Baxter's History of his Life and Times* (1702) pp. 506 f. The evangelicals, however, defined conversion more clearly than this, as a distinct adult experience.

What Jack means by his not being a Christian till last month, I understand not. Had he never been in covenant with God? Then ... baptism was nothing. Had he totally apostatized from it? I dare say not: and yet he must either be unbaptized, or an apostate to make his words true.[1]

Wesley accepted his brother's alternatives, and his claim was that, for all his disciplined and devoted endeavour to please God, and in the absence from his life of any apparent apostasy, yet nevertheless the onset of actual sin had been sufficient of itself to cancel the benefits received in his baptism and so to put him out of covenant with God; and he believed, further, that he had not been restored to God's favour until he had received adult regeneration at Aldersgate Street.[2]

Indeed, Wesley was specific about this. Reflecting upon his life up to that time as he prepared to set down the momentous events of 24 May 1738, he says:

I believe, till I was about ten years old I had not sinned away that 'washing of the Holy Ghost' which was given me in baptism.[3]

Moreover, his *Journal* shows that Wesley found in other people generally that conscious sin vitiated infant regeneration at about the age of nine to ten years. It is true that much younger children are mentioned as being faithful—for example, 'one who had soon finished her course, going to God in the full assurance of faith when she was little more than four years old'[4] —but although many features of adult experience are noted in such very young children, a sense of pardoned sin is not. Wesley saw this in children from about nine years upwards,[5] and he marked this as the stage at which baptismal regeneration ceases to ensure a state of salvation. From now onwards, conscious sin must be covered by conscious faith and conscious adult regeneration.

It would, logically, be possible for someone to pass from baptismal into adult regeneration without succumbing to sin

---

[1] R. Green, *John Wesley Evangelist*, p. 216. v. *Journal*, i. pp. 479 f.n.
[2] He claimed to have had the faith of a servant before, now the faith of a Son of God. v. marginal note, *Journal*, i. p. 423.
[3] *Ibid.* i. p. 465. cf. *Works*, ix. pp. 294 f, 365.
[4] *Journal*, iii. p. 150. cf. *ibid.* iii. pp. 244, 527, etc.
[5] *Ibid.* iii. pp. 236, 256, 477; iv. pp. 27, 208, 523; v. pp. 49, 357.

at all,¹ but no such instances are recorded,² and Wesley's conviction was that everyone will in fact invariably commit actual sin, and will thus need to be born again.³

This is to be seen plainly in Wesley's preaching. Baptism was not one of the great themes of his sermons—that he did not stress it more heavily was due, partly, to the fact that, since almost all of his hearers from the most godly to the most vicious had been already baptised, the preacher was inviting them not to 'repent and be baptised' but to 'repent and believe'. The washing he called them to was not with water but with blood. 'Delay not,' he cried, 'all things are now ready. "Arise, and wash away thy sins." The fountain is open. Now is the time to wash thee white in the blood of the Lamb.'⁴

In addition, Wesley regarded baptism, at least in the practical aspects of its administration, as being a controversial matter on which public utterances lead only to unedifying disputation. Thus, writing to Gilbert Boyce (a Baptist), he summed up his attitude in this way:

I wish your zeal was better employed than in persuading men to be either dipped or sprinkled ... and it might be worth while for another man to dispute these points with you. But for me it is not. I am called to other work; not to make Church of England men, or Baptists, but Christians, men of faith and love.⁵

Nevertheless, while it is true that baptism was not among the great fundamentals of Wesley's preaching, it was frequently mentioned in his sermons in a non-controversial manner. Most

---

[1] In any case, a person baptised in infancy would still, on coming to maturity, need to receive those features of conversion lacking in infant re-birth, viz. the Holy Spirit, and assurance of forgiveness.

[2] Those approximating most closely to this were John Dudly (*Journal*, iii. p. 480) and Elizabeth Walcam (*ibid*. iii. p. 527).

[3] v. *Works*, ix. p. 295. The denial of baptism is in itself an additional wrong which adds to the sinner's guilt. v. *Sermons*, ii. pp. 241 f; *Works*, viii. pp. 48 f; xi. p. 172. Paul Sangster (in his study, *Pity my Simplicity*, 1963) says: 'Wesley promulgated it as a theory' that it is possible for a child to be so brought up as to retain its baptismal innocence (pp. 26, 28, 178 f); but he gives inadequate references to support this view. We are in agreement when he adds: 'the ideal was never realized, nor was it expected' (p. 178).

[4] *Sermons*, i. p. 144. cf. Acts xxii, 16 (here quoted) where the washing is that of baptism.

[5] *Letters*, iii. p. 37. cf. *Sermons*, ii. pp. 135 f; *Journal*, iii. p. 360; iv. p. 229.

commonly he dismissed past baptism when this was offered as an excuse for ignoring the present need to be born again by faith; so that baptism became a weapon in the armoury of the evangelist as he drove home his plea. We can almost hear the preacher as we read:

> The question is not, what you was made in baptism (do not evade); but, what you are now? ... I ask not, whether you *was* born of water and of the Spirit; but are you *now* the temple of the Holy Ghost which dwelleth in you? I allow you was 'circumcised with the circumcision of Christ' (as St. Paul emphatically terms baptism); but does the Spirit of Christ and of glory *now* rest upon you? Else, 'your circumcision is become uncircumcision'. Say not then in your heart, 'I *was once* baptized, therefore I *am now* a child of God'. Alas, that consequence will by no means hold. How many are the baptized gluttons and drunkards, the baptized liars and common swearers, the baptized railers and evil-speakers, the baptized whoremongers, thieves, extortioners? What think you? Are these now the children of God? ... Lean no more on the staff of that broken reed, that ye *were* born again in baptism. Who denies that ye were then made children of God, and heirs of the kingdom of heaven? But, notwithstanding this, ye are now children of the devil. Therefore, ye must be born again. And let not Satan put it into your heart to cavil at a word, when the thing is clear. Ye have heard what are the marks of the children of God: all ye who have them not on your souls, baptized or unbaptized, must needs receive them, or without doubt ye will perish everlastingly.[1]

This sermon ('The Marks of the New Birth') Wesley preached at least eight times between January 1747 and December 1761,[2] but he gave his discourse on 'The New Birth' (in which he makes the same point[3]) on at least fifty occasions during the same period, so that this effective appeal was driven home from one end of the country to the other, and it must have been Wesley's most characteristic spoken utterance about this sacrament.

In so saying the preacher was indicating that, however effective infant baptism may have been in covering past sin, present faults have made regeneration necessary once more.

---

[1] *Sermons*, i. pp. 295 f. cf. *Ibid*. i. p. 300; *Journal* ii. p. 276; *Works*, viii. pp. 48 f, 430.
[2] Sermon Register, *Journal*, viii. pp. 171 ff.
[3] *Sermons*, ii. p. 242.

Sometimes Wesley expressed this dissipation of the former baptismal salvation in terms of a 'denial' of baptism.

But perhaps the sinner himself, to whom in real charity we say, 'You must be born again', has been taught to say, 'I defy your new doctrine: I need not be born again; I was born again when I was baptized. What! would you have me deny my baptism?'[1] I answer ... you have already denied your baptism; and that in the most effectual manner. You have denied it a thousand and a thousand times; and you do so still, day by day. For in your baptism you renounced the devil and all his works. Whenever, therefore, you give place to him again, whenever you do any of the works of the devil, then you deny your baptism. Therefore you deny it by every wilful sin; by every act of uncleanness, drunkenness, or revenge; by every obscene or profane word; by every oath that comes out of your mouth. Every time you profane the day of the Lord, you thereby deny your baptism; yea, every time you do anything to another which you would not he should do to you.[2]

It thus seems certain that Wesley considered infant regeneration to be applicable only to the first years of life, prior to the beginning of actual sin (at about nine or ten years of age) at which stage adult re-birth becomes necessary. The two regenerations are placed in separate compartments of life, and the dividing wall between them is the onset of conscious sin. In baptism, infant regeneration restores the child to favour with God, but his first acts of conscious sin break this relationship so that a new atonement is now required, and this is effected when (and if) conversion occurs. Commenting on Wesley's teaching about the effect of sin in general, E. H. Sugden said:

Wesley seems to regard a single lapse into outward sin as a complete forfeiture of the favour of God, and a loss of all that we have gained by conversion.[3]

We have now found that this attitude extended, likewise, to the effect of sin after baptismal re-birth.

---

[1] After his conversion, Christopher Hopper found that 'all agreed I had renounced my baptism'. *Wesley's Veterans*. Ed. J. Telford (n.d.) i. p. 119.

[2] *Sermons*, ii. pp. 241 f. The more fervently Wesley claimed that *all* need to be converted, the more clearly he implied that infant regeneration has no lasting consequences for the adult.

[3] *Sermons*, i. p. 311 n. cf. J. R. Parris, *John Wesley's Doctrine of the Sacraments*, p. 56.

Charles Wesley agreed with his brother in this matter, and he made his position clear in two verses on Mark i.10.

1. *Where'er the pure baptismal rite*
   Is duly minister'd below,
   The heavens are open'd in our sight,
   And God His Spirit doth bestow,
   The grace infused invisible,
   Which would with man forever dwell.

2. *But oh, we lost the grace bestow'd,*
   Nor let the Spirit on us remain,
   Made void the ordinance of God,
   By sin shut up the heavens again,
   Who would not keep our garments white,
   Or walk as children of the light.[1]

It is possible that Charles believed that he also had forfeited his baptismal salvation at the age of ten. In April 1736 he wrote from Georgia to his brother Samuel, evidently saying that he 'had lived eighteen years *without God*'.[2] This could refer to the interval between his tenth year and the time of writing, i.e. 1718–1736.

In the absence of any explicit statement of it in John Wesley's writings, it is of interest to find two other Methodists who claimed quite plainly that actual sins have the effect of destroying the filial relationship with God that had been established in infant baptism; and we may feel that here is confirmation of our analysis of Wesley's attitude. The first writer is Charles Perronet, a son of the Vicar of Shoreham and one of Wesley's preachers. He published in 1767 *A Dialogue between the Pulpit and Reading Desk. By a Member of the Church of England.* 'Pulpit' represents formal, legalistic Anglicanism, and 'Reading Desk' speaks for the Evangelicals.

---

[1] v. *infra*, Appendix 2. cf. his hymns for children, which generally stress their sinfulness and the danger of damnation. J. E. Rattenbury said that these hymns 'which threaten their singers with future woes were written not for the pagans of England, but for children; some of them are almost incredibly horrible'. *The Evangelical Doctrines of Charles Wesley's Hymns* (1941) p. 78.

[2] Cit. A. Clarke, *op. cit.* p. 391. cf. *Charles' Journal*, i. p. 376. '... I was, by (harmless diversions), kept dead to God, asleep in the devil's arms, secure in a state of damnation for eighteen years'. v. F. Baker, *Charles Wesley As Revealed by his Letters* (1948) p. 25.

Pulpit.   But surely you would not infer from hence, that all, who are baptized, have had a regular Education, and never been guilty of gross Sin, stand in like need of Pardon, and of this Justification? For in the Office of Baptism, and in the first Homily *On Salvation*, you intimate that the Child is *regenerate;* and what need of any other Justification? As for notorious sinners, I acknowledge it is reasonable.

Reading Desk.
So far I must allow, that Children which are baptized, and die in Infancy, are, by the Sacrifice of *Christ*, made meet for Glory; and such as are not guilty of outward gross sins have not *these* to repent of. But is there *one* that arrives at ten years of Age, without breaking his baptismal Vow, and forfeiting the Favour of God? Who can say *I have not sinned*? Can we find one. ...? I hope, therefore, you see the Good stand in need of Pardon, as well as the Bad.[1]

The other passage is taken from *The Methodist: attempted in Plain Metre*, which was published in 1780 by James Kershaw, one of Wesley's Itinerant Preachers and from time to time his travelling companion.

> But then some say, 'When we're Baptiz'd we rise,
>   'And dying Infants soar above the skies.'
> Allow'd; yet still, when moral agents sin,
>   And more or less do daily live therein;
> Can such be happy, *if not born again*?
>   The thought is foolish, and conclusion vain.
> When we our Vows in Baptism do break,
>   That sacred Covenant quite void we make:
> Each blessing then conferr'd we forfeit still,
>   When we transgress our heavenly Father's will;
> Baptismal grace all wilful sins destroy,
>   And justly damn each sinning girl and boy.[2]

In the light of these confirmatory passages, we may safely conclude that Wesley regarded infant regeneration as being totally lost as a result of actual sin, so that regeneration is once more required, this time on adult terms.

This belief in the total forfeiture of God's favour as received in baptism accounts for two omissions from Wesley's devotional

---

[1] pp. 43 f. cf. his father's statement: '... if you keep not the Laws of *Christ*, we may say of your *Baptism*, as the Apostle says of *Circumcision*, it is made *No-baptism*'. *A Defence of Infant-Baptism*... (1749) p. 63.

[2] p. 47.

writings. The first has to do with the call to adults, as an act of re-dedication, to renew the covenant made at their baptism. W. K. Lowther-Clarke considered this to have been one of the two main devotional thoughts of the eighteenth century,[1] yet Wesley seems not only to have ignored this idea, but deliberately to have avoided any use of it.

Thus in abridging his father's *Discourse* he omitted the final paragraph (which sounded this note), substituting simply an appeal to parents to consecrate their children to God by baptism.[2] Similarly, in revising the *Book of Common Prayer* he erased the rubric giving as reason for the public baptism of infants that 'every Man present may be put in remembrance of his own profession made to God in his Baptism', and nowhere did Wesley recommend such recollection as a profitable spiritual exercise.

Again, Samuel Wesley had taught that both confirmation and the Lord's supper can be regarded as occasions when the baptismal covenant may be renewed,[3] but his sons disregarded confirmation altogether, and in all the rich variety of their teaching about the Lord's supper neither John nor Charles made any use of this understanding of it. Even in Wesley's *Directions for Renewing our Covenant with God*[4]—which might naturally be supposed to be a renewal of the baptismal covenant —baptism is virtually ignored. The only reference to it is in these words:

> There is a two-fold covenanting with God, *In Profession, in Reality*: an entering our names, or an engaging our hearts: the former is done in Baptism, by all that are baptized, who by receiving that Seal of the Covenant, are visibly, or in Profession entered into it: the latter is also two-fold:
> 1. VIRTUAL. Which is done by all those that have sincerely made that closure with God in Christ: those that have chosen the Lord. . . .
> 2. FORMAL. Which is our binding ourselves to the Lord by solemn vow or promise to stand to our choice. And this may be . . . expressed either by words, lifting up of the hands, subscribing the hand, or the like. . . .[5]

It is immediately apparent that this passage, far from being

---

[1] *Eighteenth Century Piety* (1944) p. 10. [2] *Works*, x. p. 200.
[3] *The Pious Communicant* . . . pp. 30 ff. cf. George Whitefield's *Journal*, pp. 194 f.
[4] First published separately in 1780. [5] pp. 16 f.

cast in the mould of Wesley's thought, conforms to the Puritan baptismal outlook of Richard Alleine, whose work Wesley was here reproducing.[1] Furthermore, when this tract is considered as a whole, it is clear that the *Directions* has nothing to do with the renewal of the former baptismal contract. Wesley's aim was to encourage people to make, or to remake (in Alleine's terms) a 'virtual' covenant with God, and to enable them to express this in a 'formal' manner: i.e. to renew that adult self-dedication which is associated with conversion.[2]

Yet we need not be surprised that, in spite of these well-precedented sacramental and devotional opportunities for doing so, Wesley did not urge on his people to renew the covenant which (he taught) had been made at their baptism. His silence is explained by his belief that the baptismal covenant is so irretrievably broken by actual sin that it requires not renewal but complete remaking: and this remaking he looked for in adult regeneration.

The other significant omission is in Wesley's sermon on 'The Means of Grace'.[3] These means are there defined (in a manner exactly befitting baptism) as 'outward signs, words, or actions, ordained of God, and appointed for this end, to be the ordinary channels whereby He might convey to men, preventing, justifying, or sanctifying grace': and yet while prayer, searching the scriptures, and the Lord's supper are listed, baptism is absent. In an editorial note on this, E. H. Sugden said that baptism is 'naturally omitted in this list, because practically all those of whom Wesley was thinking had already been baptised in infancy'[4]: but this is adequate comment only if adult baptism is in mind as a means of grace. Sugden had ignored the other possibility—that infant baptism can be regarded as continuing to be a means of grace over the whole consequent life-time. But Wesley did not accept it as such since

---

[1] v. D. Tripp, *The Renewal of the Covenant in the Methodist Tradition* (1969) pp. 2, 153, 177 ff.
[2] cf. 'I explained the new covenant in the market-place, and many seemed desirous to enter into it.' *Charles' Journal*, i. p. 352.
[3] *Sermons*, i. pp. 238 ff.
[4] *Ibid.* p. 242 n. cf. this same omission from Charles Wesley's poems, 'The Means of Grace' and 'The Bloody Issue' (*IVth Extract from Wesley's Journal*, pp. 115 ff).

he believed that its effectiveness ceases as a result of conscious sin, and therefore he did not mention it in this sermon.

We come now to the last point to be considered in this chapter. Having elicited the way in which Wesley related the two regenerations to one another, we can now see whether he allowed that there is any link between infant baptism and adult regeneration—and the answer must be: 'None at all'. Since actual sin completely destroys the whole effect of infant baptism, the once more unregenerate adult can derive no help whatsoever, in his search for the second re-birth, from his past baptism in infancy.

This being so, Wesley's understanding of infant baptism is very much open to criticism: and it is to a consideration of his doctrine of baptism, both infant and adult, that we turn in the next chapter.

CHAPTER 7

Wesley's Doctrine: 3 An Assessment

A summary of Wesley's teaching about the efficacy of baptism is now possible, and this may be given in the form of six propositions, as follows.

1. Regeneration is signified by baptism, and is offered to all at two stages of life, in infancy and adulthood.
2. The normal channel of infant regeneration is infant baptism, in which the sign and the signification invariably accompany one another.
3. Actual sin (which begins at about the age of nine) completely obliterates the benefits received in infant baptism, and the person, now once more unregenerate, requires the further regeneration of conversion.
4. Conversion is given freely in response to faith in the use of any of the means of grace, and neither in principle nor in practice is it tied particularly to adult baptism.
5. While adult baptism is not the normal channel of conversion, it nevertheless serves as a means of grace in general when received in faith and penitence, and so it may happen that a candidate is born again at the time of baptism—but this is an occasional coincidence.
6. Adult regeneration is thus associated with baptism only as its signification. Otherwise it is wholly unrelated to infant baptism, and only occasionally accompanies adult baptism.

Since various adverse comments[1] must be made on this doctrine, it is good to preface these by noticing that Wesley regarded baptism as being of great positive value. He was not so totally concerned with the efficacy of preaching that this

[1] No comment is made either on Wesley's acceptance of the practice of infant baptism, or on his belief in baptismal regeneration (although both of these positions may be questioned), since in these matters he was merely remaining loyal to his Anglican background. It is only where he made innovations that criticism is called for.

sacrament became for him an effete formality. He considered that infants, born in sin, are re-born in baptism, and that adult baptism is an effective means of grace. This is in strong contrast to the attitude of some later evangelicals—Anglican, Free Church, and Methodist—who have been inclined to regard regeneration as only formally (if at all) associated with the baptism of infants, and to view adult baptism merely as an unrewarding prerequisite for Church membership. Yet if Wesley was emphatic about the effectiveness of baptism, nevertheless his account of it cannot be regarded as adequate.

In the first place, his teaching about infant baptism is unsatisfactory because, no matter how greatly he may have stressed the importance of the ordinance for the child at the time, he said that it is inconsequential for later adult life.

In various Christian traditions where infant baptismal regeneration has been accepted, some continuity has been preserved between the sacrament and later adult religious life. Thus Martin Luther, in times of sin, despair, and doubt, looked to his baptism as an objective pledge that God will not renounce him, that His love will not waver and that He waits with forgiveness for the penitent to turn back. Indeed, the whole consequent life of the Christian was seen by Luther as a working out of what was given and promised in baptism. He said:

Believe the warrant of your baptism. You are grafted into Christ; claim your position. You have the Spirit, you are children of God; do not live as if you belonged to the devil.[1]

But far from encouraging people to say *baptizatus sum* in this way, Wesley urged his hearers to 'Lean no more on the staff of that broken reed, that ye *were* born again in baptism';[2] and he maintained that assurance of God's love is given not by any objective sign, but by the inward witness of the Spirit, who 'beareth witness with our spirit, that we are the children of God'.[3] Writing in 1823, Dr. Van Mildert made the position

---

[1] Cit. J. Baillie, *Baptism and Conversion*, p. 25.
[2] *Sermons*, i. p. 296. cf. *Works*, viii. p. 73.
[3] *Sermons*, i. pp. 202 ff. cf. C. W. Williams, *John Wesley's Theology Today*, p. 112; J. R. Parris, *John Wesley's Doctrine of the Sacraments*, p. 57; B. Citron, *New Birth* (1951) pp. 138 f.

clear (although in overstated terms), when he said of Wesley and Whitefield, that

Regeneration was one of their most frequent and favourite topics; and served, according to *their* acceptance of it, as the groundwork of that delusive scheme of *spiritual experiences*, or *inward perceptible motions of the SPIRIT*, which, in common with some other enthusiastic sects, they strenuously inculcated. The necessity of being *born again*, and made *new creatures*, is, indeed, clearly the doctrine of Scripture. But, separating this *spiritual* regeneration from the *baptismal*, they 'endeavoured to explain away the *outward* part, resolving all into the *inward* part, or thing signified, namely, the grace of the SPIRIT; and thus, while they rendered Baptism, in effect, a nugatory and unavailing ordinance, they necessarily led the believer to seek for some *other* proof that he was actually regenerated. This proof their disciples were taught to expect in the perception of certain divine impulses, or impressions immediately proceeding from the SPIRIT of GOD.[1]

Again, Calvin had said that

at whatever time we are baptized, we are washed and purified once for the whole of life. Wherefore, as often as we fall, we must call up the remembrance of our baptism, so as to feel certain and secure of the remission of our sins;[2]

and one aspect of the Puritan preaching in England had been to plead that people should 'make use of' or 'improve' their baptism 'as a bridle of restraint to keep us in from sin, as a spur of constraint to quicken us to duty'.[3] But Wesley did not accept this way of thinking. For him, baptism cannot be 'improved': it must be replaced by a new reconciliation to God. 'I ask not,' he said, 'whether you *was* born of water and of the Spirit; but are you *now* the temple of the Holy Ghost which dwelleth in you?'[4]

Yet again, one common feature of Anglican devotion in the eighteenth century was the calling to mind and renewal of the vow made at baptism. But, as we have noticed, Wesley made no use of this devotional aid, for he considered that the

---

[1] Cit. *Wesleyan-Methodist Magazine*, 1824, Abridged edition, p. 230.
[2] Cit. J. Baillie, *op. cit.* p. 27.
[3] v. W. F. Flemington, *The New Testament Doctrine of Baptism*, p. 146 n. cf. the Westminster Confession, Question 167 of the larger Catechism.
[4] *Sermons*, i. p. 295.

baptismal covenant is so irreparably broken by sin that what is required is not its renewal but the making of a new covenant: and this he looked for in adult conversion. He maintained that the sinner must make a new start with God, and for this his past baptism is of no consequence.

At this point Wesley's doctrine is surely at fault. If the practice of infant baptism is to be vindicated, one argument in its favour must be that it has relevance over the whole of life, and not just for the first few years. If its importance is limited in this way, the result is to render past baptism a matter of indifference to an adult. If he is a sinner, his baptism will not help him—Wesley said that it may even hinder him—in finding reconciliation to God; and if he is a saint, this is because of his conversion, which has nothing to do with his baptism.

It is a weakness, therefore, in Wesley's scheme of salvation that he should have failed to allow to infant baptism any importance beyond the years of childhood, for by so doing he had emptied the sacrament, very largely, of its meaning. This criticism of Wesley's doctrine is, in fact, the same as that which Martin Luther levelled at the baptismal teaching of the Roman Church, and his words sum up the position exactly:

We must . . . keep clear of the error of those who have reduced the effect of baptism to such small and slender dimensions that, while they say that grace is infused by it, they assert that this grace is afterwards, so to speak, effused by sin; and that we must then go to heaven by some other way, as if baptism had now become absolutely useless. Do not thou judge thus, but understand that the significance of baptism is such that thou mayest live and die in it, and that neither by penitence, nor by any other way, canst thou do aught but return to the effect of baptism, and do afresh what thou wert baptised in order to do and what thy baptism signified. Baptism never loses its effect, unless in desperation thou refuse to return to salvation.[1]

Further criticism of Wesley's doctrine follows on from this, and it can best be set out by asking whether he was right in his insistence that everyone should be regenerated twice. For several reasons—linguistic, scriptural, and experiential—it can be argued that this was an ill-considered demand.

---

[1] *On the Babylonish Captivity of the Church*, in *Luther's Primary Works* (edd. H. Wace and C. A. Buchheim, 1896) p. 352.

First, the very word itself suggests that here is a once for all experience which can hardly be repeated. One of Wesley's own telling expository illustrations was provided by the analogy between regeneration and the physical birth of a baby: 'there is', he said, 'so near a resemblance between the circumstances of the natural and spiritual birth; so that to consider the circumstances of the natural birth, is the most easy way to understand the spiritual'.[1] But the more Wesley pressed this comparison and emphasized that regeneration is the beginning of the Christian life, the more clearly he was delineating an unrepeatable event.

This criticism can be brought home more forcibly still. Wesley's wish was to be *homo unius libri*[2]—what has the Bible to say about regeneration? A full examination of this question is out of place here, but the point to be stressed is that Wesley would have agreed with the opinion of many modern commentators, that regeneration in the New Testament is a baptismal event. W. F. Flemington, for example, writes that baptism

has an outward and an inward aspect which may be separated in thought. The evidence of the New Testament, however, shows that such separation was far less obvious and natural for the early Christians than it is for us.[3]

When considering the early Church, Wesley himself stated that this was so. His comment on Acts XXII.16 reads:

Baptism, administered to real penitents, is both a means and seal of pardon. Nor did God ordinarily in the primitive Church bestow this on any, unless through this means.[4]

If this close association is accepted, then the implication follows from it that, since no one is to be baptised more than once, no one can be regenerated more than once.

Perhaps Wesley would have retorted to this argument: 'that consequence will by no means hold'; and he could point to his repeated distinction between the outward act of baptism and

---

[1] *Sermons*, i. pp. 301 f; ii. pp. 232 f.
[2] *Ibid*, i. p. 32.
[3] *Op. cit.* p. 111. cf. (e.g.) E. G. Selwyn, *The First Epistle of St. Peter* (1958) p. 123; G. R. Beasley-Murray, *Baptism in the New Testament* (1962) pp. 231 f.
[4] v. *Notes*.

its inward signification, and argue that baptism once administered stands as a constant reminder of the need for regeneration however often it may be required—and yet, nevertheless, Wesley seems to have departed from the New Testament use of the word.

Nor is this all. When we consider the place of sin in the life of a baptised person, it may seem from the point of view of experience that Wesley's terminology is not helpful. Number XVI of the Thirty Nine Articles ('Of Sin after Baptism') states that

> the grant of repentance is not to be denied to such as fall into sin after Baptism. After we have received the Holy Ghost, we may depart from grace given, and fall into sin, and by the grace of God we may arise again, and amend our lives.

What is suggested here is that, if the Christian life be likened to the curve of a graph, it has one beginning only, and (unless there is complete apostasy) it rises steadily. There will be more or less frequent downward turns in the line as sin intervenes, but 'repentance' suffices for 'amendment', and the line always recovers its gradual upward tendency. A new start is not required after every sin.

Wesley did not accept this. His belief was that total apostasy invariably occurs at about the age of nine or ten, for in the life of *every* baptised person the beginning of actual sin obliterates past baptismal regeneration.[1] Thus Wesley's view can be represented, in terms of a graph, by *two* distinct lines, one beginning in infant baptism and returning to zero after about nine years, with then, after a longer or shorter unregenerate period, a new and completely separate line beginning at the time of conversion. A little reflection is sufficient, however, to show that such a pattern is not followed in every life. There are Christians who, baptised as infants, have grown progressively into a mature faith without ever making a new start of this kind.[2] On the other hand, there are Christians who, as

---

[1] This is perhaps why Wesley changed the heading of Article XVI in his revised version (Article XII, *Sunday Service*, 1784), to 'Of Sin after Justification': i.e. because he regarded sin after infant baptism as inevitable (and its remedy—conversion—plain), but sin after conversion as being more problematical.

[2] e.g. Wesley's father-in-law, Dr. Samuel Annesley, was 'one that might be said to be sanctified from the womb, for he was early under serious impressions;

adults, have experienced a dramatic new beginning in the faith—but by no means all would confess that this new start was necessitated by their first childhood sins, nor would all agree that the new beginning was so completely independent of their previous devotion as to be a religious 'new birth'.

Our comment on Wesley's insistence upon two re-births is, therefore, that such a demand is inconsistent both with the natural meaning of the word 'regeneration', and with the New Testament and early Church use of it; and that it does not accord with the actual experience of many baptised people.

Of course, such criticism is not new. As soon as they heard reports of his new doctrine, Wesley's family were concerned about its orthodoxy. His brother Samuel wrote to Mrs. Hutton about him on 17 June 1738:

Perhaps it might come into his crown that he was in a state of *mortal sin*, unrepented of; and had long lived in such a course. This I do not believe; however he must answer for himself. But where is the sense of requiring every body else to confess that of themselves in order to commence Christians? Must they confess it, whether it be so or no? *Besides a sinful course is not an abolition of the covenant*, for that very reason because it is a *breach* of it.[1]

A little later, Charles Wesley heard from his mother, who wrote:

I think you are fallen into an odd way of thinking. You say that till within a few months you had no spiritual life, nor any justifying faith.

Now this is as if a man should affirm he was not alive in his infancy, because, when an infant, he did not know he was alive. All then that I can gather from your Letter is, that till a little while ago, you were not so well satisfied of your *being a Christian as you are now*. I heartily rejoice that you have now attained to a strong and lively hope in God's mercy thro' *Christ*. Not that I can think that you were totally without *saving faith* before: but it is one thing to have faith, and another thing to be sensible we have it.[2]

---

so that himself said, he *knew not the time when he was unconverted.*' cit. A. Clarke, *Memoirs of the Wesley Family*, p. 238. v. F. W. B. Bullock, *Evangelical Conversion in Great Britain 1696–1845* (1959) pp. 274 ff, for a summary treatment of this point. He concludes (p. 279): 'Conversion through crisis is essential for some, not for all.'

[1] Cit. A. Clarke, *ibid*. p. 402.

[2] Cit. *ibid*. pp. 347 f. 6 December 1738.

At the same time, others were making the same protest publicly, and, of these, Tristam Land put the point clearly and concisely. The Church of England teaching is, he said, that

> all infants, at the time they are baptized, are sanctified with the Holy Ghost; and that, though they may afterwards depart from the grace given, and fall into sin, they are not to be commanded to be baptized or born again a second time; for to be born more than once, in a spiritual sense, is just as impossible as to be born twice in a natural. All that can be done in this matter is to use the several means of grace; or, in one word, as the Scripture expresses it, they must be renewed again by repentance.[1]

It is of interest to follow up the last suggestion made by Tristam Land, and ask whether Wesley could have used some term other than 'regeneration' to express more fittingly the evangelical experience. As Land proposed, he might have considered 'repentance', or perhaps 'amendment'—both of these words appear in the Article 'Of Sin after Baptism': or he might have used 'confirmed', and thereby linked adult regeneration both to past baptism and to the rite of confirmation as an outward expression of the inner spiritual consecration to God—but all these terms must have seemed too weak to express the traumatic experience which Wesley was trying to describe. Again, the expression 'effectual calling' was used in a comparable way in Calvin's *Institutes* (and recurs in Puritan sources[2]), but this also fails to suggest so great a transformation. Wesley himself used other terms as synonyms for 'adult regeneration'. Leaving aside those that include the idea of re-birth (e.g. 'born again', 'Born anew', 'new birth', 'born of God', 'born of the Spirit') he used 'renewal' and 'conversion'. 'Renewal', while suggesting a new start, allows still for continuity—a person can 'renew' his baptismal covenant—and for

---

[1] Cit. L. Tyerman, *John Wesley*, i. p. 243. cf. Tipping Silvester, University Sermon, 26 February 1738 (cit. *ibid*. i. p. 209); D. Waterland, *Regeneration Stated and Explained* ... (1739); John Andrews, *Of Speaking as the Oracles of God* (1743); *A Letter from a Clergyman* ... (1753) cit. A. M. Lyles, *Methodism Mocked* (1960) p. 103; Alexander Jephson, *A Friendly and Compassionate Address to all Serious and Well Disposed Methodists* ... (1760). Wesley acknowledged that his call for a second regeneration was regarded by some as 'your new doctrine' (*Sermons*, ii. p. 241). For similar charges against Whitefield, published in 1739, v. L. Tyerman, *George Whitefield*, i. pp. 283 ff.

[2] J. Baillie, *op. cit.* pp. 80 f.

this reason it was a suitable word. 'Conversion' occurs in the New Testament with the sense of turning to God, usually for the first time and as a preliminary to baptism;[1] and as such it seems unsuited to Wesley's purpose. But there are two Scriptural places where it is used of a *return* to God after an earlier betrayal of faith,[2] and in this less typical sense it was an apt term to be used of post-baptismal reconciliation to God.

And yet, without doubt, Wesley would have swept all this talk of alternatives aside, saying to us (as he said to his protesting congregations):

let not Satan put it into your heart to cavil at a word, when the thing is clear. Ye have heard what are the marks of the children of God: all ye who have them not on your souls, baptized or unbaptized, must needs receive them;[3]

and the experience of being received in this way as a child of God seemed to him so much like a new birth, that Wesley could only describe it as such.

We can now follow the chain of reasoning which led Wesley to his conclusions. He first became convinced that everyone should make a new spiritual beginning at two stages of life, at birth (in baptism) and in adulthood (by conversion). Both of these he wished to describe as 'regeneration', and in order to lay full stress upon the second re-birth, he stated dogmatically that there is always a lapse into total unregeneracy between the two. The unhappy consequence is, however, that infant baptism thereby becomes largely vitiated, for it is rendered wholly inconsequential for adult regeneration and the mature religious life generally.[4]

Two points arise from the above discussion. The first is this. We have said that Wesley's teaching about infant baptism and re-birth is unsatisfactory: that it is not adequate to speak of two separate regenerations, and thereby to dissociate the second from baptism. But if this is not acceptable, it remains for others to improve upon Wesley's doctrine. He may have

---

[1] v. W. Barclay, *Turning to God* (1963) pp. 14 ff.
[2] Luke xxii. 32; James v. 19 f.   [3] *Sermons*, i. p. 296.
[4] Having pointed this out to Wesley, Gilbert Boyce (a Baptist) concluded that he should 'let (infants) stay (i.e. unbaptised) till they are converted before they are really baptized.' *A Serious Reply* . . . (1770) p. 76.

failed to relate infant baptism adequately to adult religious life, but at least he succeeded in giving due emphasis to the importance of a Christian beginning at two decisive stages of life—at birth and at the point of the adult's own mature decision—and many since have failed even in this. Some have stressed the importance of infant baptism so heavily that adult conversion is under-valued; while others, going to the opposite extreme, have placed so much emphasis upon conversion as the beginning of the Christian life that infant baptism is devalued into mere christening. The difficulty is to give due weight not only to infant baptism as the beginning of a life of discipleship, but also to adult conversion—*and to relate the latter closely to baptism*. If Wesley was not wholly successful in this task, the present widespread ferment over infant baptism may indicate that there are some Churches at least which have not yet succeeded in it to their own satisfaction.

The second consideration is that students of Wesley's theology must take his failure at this point fully into account. Studies of his doctrine are inclined sometimes to dwell upon the neat consistency of his teaching; to stress how adequately Wesley dealt with the facts of sin and the ways of God's grace around such key terms as degeneration, justification, regeneration and sanctification. His baptismal teaching, meanwhile, is commonly either ignored, or referred to only in passing with, in some instances, the admission that here is a minor blemish in his mapping out of the path to perfection. Such a treatment, however, does justice neither to the difficulty Wesley tried to resolve, nor to the inadequacy of his double use of the term 'regeneration'. The place—the awkward place—of infant baptism in Wesley's teaching should be faced squarely whenever his doctrine of conversion comes under consideration.

When we come, in the second place, to an assessment of Wesley's doctrine of adult baptism, approval can be given with scarcely any qualification.

It must be accepted that in departing from the teaching of his Church, Wesley moved away also from what was, on his own admission, the New Testament understanding of adult baptism. He accepted that, Scripturally, regeneration is normally associated with baptism, but he preached that regeneration (or conversion) is generally dissociated from the sacrament. This difference may be readily explained—for, unlike the Apostles, Wesley was preaching mainly to adults who had already been baptised as infants—but, nevertheless, it marks a departure from New Testament teaching.

Yet in a more important respect, Wesley's belief in adult baptism as a means of grace marked not a departure from Scripture but a return to the general spirit in which the sacrament was administered in New Testament times. The Church of England may have maintained that faithful adults are regenerated in the ordinance, but this was scarcely more than a matter of formal definition. Wesley, on the other hand, insisted that adult baptism should be regarded as a real means of grace, effectually used by God to convict, convert or sanctify.

When, in the *Acts of the Apostles*, Peter addressed the Jerusalem crowds, he urged them to 'repent and be baptized ... for the forgiveness of your sins; and you shall receive the gift of the Holy Spirit'.[1] Here was encouragement to approach the sacrament with a sense of expectancy, believing that in its administration God would act: and the accounts of baptisms which follow in the *Acts* are more or less explicit records of men and women who found in the ordinance reconciliation to God and the bestowal of the Holy Ghost. For all its formal correctness, this was very far from the spirit in which Anglican baptism was administered to adults in the eighteenth century. Wesley, however, taught his people to come 'expecting to receive'; and the baptismal experiences of (among many others) Sara Labbe and Anne Gates[2] closely resemble those of Paul and the Ephesian and Samaritan converts in the first age of Christianity.[3]

We conclude that adult baptism was regarded by Wesley as an effective converting and sanctifying ordinance; and our chief criticism of him in this case is, not that his understanding of it at the time was contradictory or confused, but that he failed to ensure that succeeding generations of Methodists should continue to realize the full worth of the sacrament thus administered.[4]

---

[1] Acts, ii. 38.   [2] v. *supra*, pp. 47 ff.
[3] Acts ix. 17 ff; viii. 14 ff; xix. 6.   [4] v. *infra*, Chap 12.

We turn now from this analysis of Wesley's baptismal teaching to the practical aspects of our subject, to examine the way in which baptism was administered to the early Methodists and their children: and our first concern is with the place of this ordinance in the ministry of the Wesley brothers themselves.

CHAPTER 8

Baptism in the Ministry of the Wesleys

There are several features of Wesley's life which have proved difficult to interpret, and of these his conversion experience has been among the more controversial. Some writers have passed it off as being of only secondary importance, but others —notably J. H. Rigg—have seen this as the turning point in Wesley's life at which he changed over from being 'a High Church Ritualist' to become 'an itinerant evangelist',[1] giving up almost immediately those sacramental principles and practices which had shaped his ministry in Georgia.

Dr. J. C. Bowmer, however, has put this whole matter into its correct perspective.[2] He writes:

> Wesley's partiality for certain customs of the Nonjurors was largely a youthful exaggeration of his native Anglicanism which corrected itself as he matured. He discarded many of his early rituals, not altogether as a result of his evangelical conversion, as some biographers have been anxious to prove, but simply as a result of maturity and common sense.

Dr. Bowmer's conclusion is that

> Wesley was no rigid ecclesiastic suddenly turned evangelist, but one who, from boyhood to old age, loved the ordinances of the Christian Church. As he matured, the Lord's Supper became to him more and more a sustaining and satisfying means of grace.

Our purpose now is to discover whether Wesley's life-long regard for the ordinances of his Church extended likewise to baptism.

Shortly after their return to England from America, the Wesleys had an interview with Dr. Gibson, the Bishop of London, which shows that already they had begun to relax their former exclusive views about the sole validity of episcopal

---

[1] *The Churchmanship of John Wesley*, pp. 39 f, 59 f.
[2] *The Sacrament of the Lord's Supper in Early Methodism*, pp. 48 f.

baptism. Charles Wesley gave an account[1] of what passed between them.

Sat., October 21st. (1738) I waited with my brother on the Bishop of London, to answer the complaints he had heard against us. . . (He said) 'But there is a heavy charge against us Bishops, by your bringing the Archbishop's authority for re-baptizing an adult.' My brother answered, 'That he had expressly declared the contrary: yet,' added he, 'if a person dissatisfied with lay-baptism should desire episcopal, I should think it my duty to administer it, after having acquainted the Bishop according to the canon.'[2] 'Well; I am against it myself, where any one has had the Dissenters' baptism.'[3]

A few weeks later, Charles Wesley went again to see the Bishop, this time on his own. Once more the conversation was about the re-baptism of Dissenters.

Tues., November 13th. I had another conference with his Lordship of London. 'I have used your Lordship's permission to wait upon you. A woman desires me to baptize her; not being satisfied with her baptism by a Dissenter: she says sure and unsure is not the same.' He immediately took fire, and interrupted me: 'I wholly disapprove of it: it is irregular.' 'My Lord, I did not expect your approbation. I only came, in obedience, to give you notice of my intention.'

The discussion then turned to Charles Wesley's position as curate to Mr. Stonehouse at Islington without official license; and the interview closed upon a cool note. Charles asked:

'Do you then dispense with my giving you notice of any baptisms for the future?' 'I neither dispense, nor not dispense.' He railed at Lawrence on lay-baptism[4] . . . He concluded the conference with, 'Well, Sir, you knew my judgment before, and you know it now. Good morrow to you.'[5]

---

[1] *Charles' Journal*, i. p. 133. cf. *Journal*, ii. p. 93 n.
[2] v. the rubric preceding the 1661 Order for adult baptism.
[3] Dr. Gibson had expressed this opinion in *Codex Juris Ecclesiastici Anglicani* (1713, 2nd ed. 1761, p. 368); but this was only recognized as authoritative within the Anglican Church in the following century. v. J. S. Simon, *John Wesley and the Religious Societies*, pp. 116 f.
[4] i.e. R. Laurence, *Sacerdotal Powers; or the Necessity of Confession, Penance and Absolution, together with the Nullity of Inauthorised Lay-Baptism*, 1711.
[5] *Charles' Journal*, i. p. 135.

Charles took it that he had the Bishop's assent, and went ahead with the ceremony.

Thur., November 16th. After morning prayers (i.e. at Islington), I baptized Mrs. Bell with hypothetical baptism.[1]

Thus we can see that already, by the end of 1738, the Wesleys' attitude had softened. They now regarded the re-baptism of Dissenters, not as necessary (as they had insisted in Georgia), but as permissible when desired; and Wesley showed remorse at his earlier attitude upon hearing in 1749 from Johann Bolzius, the minister of the Salzburger Community to whom he had refused access to the Lord's table. Reflecting on his past bigotry, Wesley said:

Can any one carry High Church zeal higher than this? And how well have I been since beaten with mine own staff![2]

The reason for this change of opinion is not far to seek. Wesley had begun by believing that only those who had received Anglican episcopal baptism could be saved, for towards the end of his life he wrote:

In my youth I was not only a member of the Church of England, but a bigot to it, believing none but the members of it to be in a state of salvation. I began to abate of this violence in 1729.[3]

By the time of his ministry in Georgia, we have found that this extremism had abated to the point where he would accept any episcopal baptism as sufficient—e.g. that of the Moravians —if it were administered by presbyters or deacons ordained by bishops consecrated within an unbroken line of apostolic succession. But now he learned that people might be converted who had accepted non-episcopal baptism. The Salzburgers and some of the Moravians had received non-episcopal Lutheran baptism, yet Wesley found many among them who were 'in a state of salvation': and, more far reaching still, on his return to England he discovered that some were being converted who had not been baptised at all. It was this observation of the free working of God's Spirit which burst the bubble of his earlier narrow-mindedness. Men and women were born again whether

---

[1] *Ibid.* i. p. 136. i.e. using the formula, 'If thou art not baptized ...'. cf. J. S. Simon, *ibid.* p. 236; Jackson, *Life of Charles Wesley*, i. p. 171.
[2] *Journal*, iii. p. 434.   [3] *Letters*, viii. p. 140 (1789).

they had been baptised at the hands of Roman Catholic or Anglican Priest, Dissenting Minister, Reformed Pastor, or even in spite of their lack of any baptism whatsoever—and in the face of this graciousness on the part of God, Wesley could hardly argue any more for the exclusive necessity of baptism of one particular type.

Yet if Wesley was willing from 1738 onwards to accept Dissenters' baptism as valid, he nevertheless held fast to the position he had put forward in conversation with Dr. Gibson and continued to re-baptise Dissenters when they asked for it. Thus on 25 January 1739, Wesley

baptized John Smith (late an Anabaptist) and four other adults at Islington.[1]

Further light is thrown on the background of these candidates by a letter from Susanna Wesley to her son Samuel, dated 8 March of that year. George Whitefield had visited her and told her that

John had baptized five adult Presbyterians in our own way on St· Paul's day, and he believed would bring over many to our communion.[2]

Whitefield was mistaken about one of the candidates (who had been a Baptist and not a Presbyterian), but the implication of his account is that the others had been baptised Dissenters.

Over the years that followed, Wesley's *Journal* and Diaries frequently mention his baptising adults. Very often the writer was at pains to record that the candidates had been formerly Baptists or Quakers—in which case they would presumably be receiving this sacrament for the first time by his administration. Yet on other occasions no such denominational background is indicated, and while some may have been formerly unbaptised, it is possible that others were Dissenters who were 'dissatisfied with lay-baptism', and who desired 'episcopal'. One probable example of this is found in the *Journal* for 1759. On Wednesday 21 March, Wesley set down that, at Colchester,

I baptized seven adults, two of them by immersion; and in the evening (their own ministers having cast them out for going to hear

[1] *Journal*, ii. p. 135.
[2] A. Clarke, *Memoirs of the Wesley Family*, p. 343.

the Methodists) I administered the Lord's Supper to them, and many others, whom their several teachers had repelled for the same reason.[1]

That he should still be willing to re-baptise is borne out by an introduction inserted by Wesley when he used his *Treatise on Baptism* as a sermon. The manuscript of the *Treatise* is preserved in the Methodist Archives, and the date of its original composition is given as 11 November, 1756. But on some subsequent occasion Wesley crossed out this date and added a scriptural text and introduction, and a concluding peroration. The sermon now begins:

Matthew XXVIII. 19. Baptizing them in the Name of the Father, and of the Son, and of the Holy Ghost.

Before I begin to treat of Baptism, I would just observe, that Three Things are essential to Christian Baptism, 1. An Episcopal Administrator. 2. The Application of Water. 3. That it be administered in Name of the Trinity. The two latter need no Proof: and our Lord's commissioning his Apostles only, and those, who should derive their authority from them, to baptize, proves the former. And if so, it necessarily follows, that the Baptism, I ought to call it, the Dipping of the Anabaptists, as much stress as ever they lay upon it, is no Baptism at all, For they want Episcopal Administrators which are essential to Christian Baptism. And indeed this invalidates the Baptism of all who have formally separated from our Church. But of this I need say no more to you. For there is no great Danger of your employing any of them to baptize either yourselves or your children.

There is something of a mystery here. Had Wesley written these words during his time in Georgia there would be no inconsistency, for at that time he had insisted that baptism other than by 'An Episcopal Administrator' is 'no Baptism at all'. However, since 1738 he had not held so extreme an opinion, and it is surprising that at this later period he should have expressed himself in this way. Nevertheless, that he did so gives us an insight into the strength of Wesley's convictions, and we would fully expect that one who could write these words would indeed be willing to re-baptise Dissenters who asked him to do so.

[1] iv. p. 302.

It seems likely therefore that, for many years after his return from America, Wesley continued to re-baptise Dissenters who requested it. Just when, or whether, he discontinued this practice is uncertain. Probably requests became fewer as his association with the Church of England became less close, for Dissenters desiring *Anglican* baptism would turn for it elsewhere than to Wesley the Methodist.

Because of the itinerant nature of their ministry, it was not always possible for the Wesleys to prepare adults for baptism. There had been ample time on board the *Simmonds*, on the way to America, to prepare the Hird family by 'frequent and careful instruction'[1] for the sacrament; but once the pattern of their ministry in Great Britain was established, rapid movement from place to place generally made any such prolonged preliminaries impossible. Indeed, where men and women who had been converted applied for the sacrament, the brothers evidently felt that insistence upon prior instruction was presumptuous. They followed the example of the Apostle Peter who, in like circumstances, had said 'Can any man forbid water, that these should not be baptized, which have received the Holy Ghost as well as we?', and ordered baptism to take place forthwith.[2]

Yet when there was the opportunity the Wesleys thought it fitting that preparatory training should be given, and in these cases they were able to notify the Bishop in the proper manner. Thus on 30 October 1739, Charles wrote from Bristol to the Bishop as follows:

MY LORD,—Several persons, both Quakers and Baptists, have applied to me for baptism. Their names are, W. Crease, Mary Crease, Mary Gregory, Rebecca Dickenson, Anne Spanin, Eliz. Mills, Eliz. Parsons. It has pleased God to make me instrumental in their conviction. This has given them such a prejudice for me, that they desire to be received into the Church by my ministry. They choose likewise to be baptized by immersion; and have engaged me to give your Lordship notice, as the Church requires.[3]

A few days later, he 'spent the time of conference[4] with the

---

[1] *Journal*, i. p. 117.
[2] Acts x. 47 f. v. *Journal*, iii. p. 171; *Charles' Journal*, i. p. 180.
[3] *Charles' Journal*, i. pp. 192 f. cf. *Letters*, i. p. 358. John's letter was evidently copied from that of Charles.   [4] i.e. 11.0 a.m. to 1.0 p.m.

candidates for baptism. All seem prepared for that Holy ordinance'.[1] Of the ceremony itself we have no record—it must have taken place during a three months gap in Charles' Journal (December 1739 to February 1740): but when he was back in Bristol again in June 1740, Charles 'met several of those whom (he) had baptized, and found them grown in grace';[2] and a week later he once more 'exhorted the last-baptized'.[3]

Again, the nature of their ministry determined the whereabouts of the baptisms performed by the Wesleys. We have noted the general tendency in the eighteenth century for the ordinance to be administered privately at home rather than publicly in Church as the rubric of the Prayer Book requires; and that in Georgia the Wesleys insisted upon following the rubric in this respect. There is evidence to suggest that in England during the early months after their return from America they were anxious to continue this practice. They baptised, or brought people to be baptised, in a church whenever possible, and did so particularly at Islington, where Charles was for a time unofficially curate to the incumbent, Mr. Stonehouse. Thus John Wesley baptised five adults there on 25 January 1739;[4] Charles christened there on at least three occasions;[5] and George Whitefield sent a Quaker 'to be baptized by my dear brother, Mr. Stonehouse' on 16 May and another on 2 June of that same year.[6]

Yet very soon this arrangement was to be disturbed. Relationships between the church officials at Islington and the Methodists became strained, and when on Monday 4 June 1739, Charles Wesley 'walked with a young Quaker to Islington Church', he tells us that 'Satan hindered me; so Mr. Scott baptized him'.[7] The break came in the following year. When, on 9 May 1740, Charles again went to Islington 'intending to baptize Bridget Armstead' he was once more prevented, and this time he withdrew from that church, and on 21 May he 'carried Bridget Armstead to Bloomsbury church where the Minister baptized her.[8]

[1] *Charles' Journal*, i. p. 194.
[2] *Ibid.* i. p. 242.   [3] *Ibid.* i. p. 243. cf. i. p. 262.
[4] *Journal*, ii. p. 315.   [5] *Charles' Journal*, i. pp. 136, 145.
[6] *Whitefield's Journals*, pp. 265, 277.   [7] *Charles' Journal*, i. p. 151.
[8] *Ibid.* i. pp. 227, 234.

After this the Wesleys still from time to time made efforts to administer baptism in the churches,[1] but as their typical 'pulpit' very soon became some convenient place outside church walls, so their 'font' usually was elsewhere than in church. Often they baptized in the homes of the people. Such entries as these occur throughout John Wesley's Diaries:

9th July 1740: 8.30 at Bro. Pattison's; 9 christened h(is) son.
24th July 1740: 1.30 at Mr. Wilkinson's, christened his son.
18th October 1740: 4 at Bro. Windsor's christened his son.
27th October 1740: 11 at Bro. Hobbin's christened L. Sd., prayer.[2]

Charles Wesley's *Journal* instances similar occasions in his ministry.[3]

When in London, Wesley seems to have fixed a regular time for the baptism of adults at the Foundery. The earlier published Diaries, which cover the period July 1740 to June 1741, reveal that in this time (during which he was not continuously in London) he baptised adults at the Foundery on Wednesdays at around 2.0 p.m. on eleven occasions. Thus:

9th July 1740: 2 christened Eliz. Ash, Rebecca Perkins, Susan Smithers.
30th July 1740: 2 christened three women, one man.
13th August 1740: 2.15 christened John Padly and Jos. Paul.
27th August 1740: 2 christened Paul Chamberlain, David Jenkins, Sarah Hunlock, Kezia Smith.
8th April 1741: 2 christened Charles Bean.
6th May 1741: 1.15 the Bands, prayer, . . . christened!

Furthermore, on five of these occasions, Wesley seems to have given communion to the newly-baptised.

15th October 1740: 2 christened three, Sarah Southgate, Eliz.—, and—; 3 communion.
22nd October 1740: 2 christened two; communion.
29th October 1740: 2 christened M.S., communion.
3rd December 1740: 2 christened two! communion.
6th February 1741: 3 christened J. Okey, communion.
3rd June 1741: 2 christened many! 3 communion![4]

---

[1] *Ibid.* i. p. 189. 'I waited with my brother upon a Minister, about baptizing some of his parish.' v. F. C. Gill, *In the Steps of John Wesley* (1963) p. 201. 'Wesley often preached and baptized' in St. Martin's, Haverfordwest.
[2] v. Tyerman, *John Wesley*, i. p. 487 n.   [3] i. pp. 107, 441, 465.
[4] Each of these days was a Wednesday, except that in February, 1741. cf. *Journal*, iv. p. 302.

The Diaries are lost for the years 1741 to 1783, and when they begin again we find that this Wednesday afternoon custom was no longer followed.

During their travels the Wesleys frequently baptised in the Methodist preaching houses during Sunday or weekday services. When Hannah C—received the sacrament on a Saturday in 1756, 'A solemn awe spread over the whole congregation, and many could not refrain from tears';[1] and again, on a similar occasion in Bradford on a Monday in 1758, Wesley tells how 'We all found the power of God was present to heal'.[2] In fact, wherever there was a devotional gathering of Methodist people,[3] wherever it was felt that the word of God could appropriately be preached, there the Wesleys would willingly administer baptism—at Kingswood School,[4] 'among the Leaders',[5] in private homes and preaching houses; and, perhaps most interesting of all, in the open air.[6]

No accounts survive of administrations by the Wesleys in rivers, but there are several references to them. This was a method much used by the Baptists in the eighteenth century, and it may have been that in their Epworth childhood the young John and Charles watched such ceremonies from the banks of the nearby river Torne, which was famous for its dippings.[7] An account of one such Baptist ceremony is preserved.[8] It took place at Whittlesford, near Cambridge, and Dr. Andrew Giffard, minister of Eagle Street Baptist Church, London, officiated. After preliminary hymns, prayers and sermon, the administrator

in a long black gown of fine baize, without a hat, with a small New Testament in his hand, came down to the river side accompanied by several Baptist ministers and deacons of their Churches, and the persons to be baptized. . . . A great multitude of spectators

---

[1] *Ibid.* iv. p. 189.
[2] *Ibid.* iv. p. 286. cf. vii. p. 144; *Charles' Journal*, i. pp. 335, 367; ii. pp. 71, 81.
[3] These references show that baptism was a means of grace to the whole gathering as well as to the candidates themselves. One onlooker in this way 'found a divine proof, that infant baptism is of God.' *Charles' Journal*, i. p. 440.
[4] *Journal*, viii. p. 167 (Diary for 25 May 1740); *Charles' Journal*, ii. p. 16.
[5] *Charles' Journal*, i. p. 396.
[6] Wesley used the open-air font at Manor Farm, Luxulyan, near St. Austell, Cornwall. v. F. C. Gill, *op. cit.* p. 98, illustration opp. p. 144.
[7] W. Le Cato Edwards, *Epworth . . . the Home of the Wesleys* (n.d.) p. 8.
[8] Robert Robinson, *A History of Baptism* (1790), pp. 571 ff.

stood on the banks of the river on both sides: some had climbed and sat in the trees, many sat on horseback and in carriages, and all behaved with a decent seriousness which did honour to the good sense and good manners of the assembly. . . . When (the administrator) came to a sufficient depth he stopped, and with the utmost composure placing himself on the left hand of the man, his face being towards the man's shoulder, he put his right hand between his shoulders behind, gathering into it a little of the gown for hold: the fingers of his left hand he thrusted under the sash before, and the man putting his two thumbs into that hand, he locked all together by closing his hand. Then he deliberately said, I baptize thee in the name of the Father, and of the Son, and of the Holy Ghost, and while he uttered these words, standing wide, he gently leaned him backward and dipped him once. As soon as he had raised him, a person in a boat fastened there for the purpose, took hold of the man's hand, wiped his face with a napkin, and led him a few steps to another attendent, who then gave him his arm, walked with him to the house, and assisted him to dress. There were many such in waiting, who like the primitive susceptors assisted during the whole service.

After the men the women were likewise immersed, and the whole service was concluded with further prayers and exhortation of both the crowd and the newly-baptised. Whether the Wesleys ever staged so elaborate and popular a ceremony is doubtful, but, taking scripture for precedent, it was not unusual for them to baptise adult converts in this manner.

Just where the ceremony took place for the seven candidates of whose desire for baptism by immersion Charles had given notice to the Bishop of Bristol, is not known; but four days before that letter was written his Journal records:

Fri., October 26th. I baptized Mr. Wigginton in the river by Baptist-Mills;[1]

and again, in 1748, another similar entry is found:

Thur., May 5th. I baptized Elis. Cart in the river at Cowley; and she washed away all her sin and sorrow.[2]

One of these out-of-doors occasions at which John Wesley officiated is referred to in *The Progress of Methodism in Bristol; or, the Methodist Unmasked* . . . (1743), which, in part, complains that

[1] *Charles' Journal*, i. p. 191.   [2] *Ibid.* ii. p. 13.

In the midst of a most severe winter, (Wesley) had taken his converts, early in the morning, through frost and snow, to the river Froom, at Baptist Mills, where, on the ice being broken, he and they went into the water, where, with 'limbs shuddering and teeth *hackering,*' he baptized or dipped them.[1]

Yet such open air christenings were the exception rather than the rule and, even when the sacrament was given by immersion, it was usually administered indoors. Probably this was so for the undoubtedly spirited and resilient old lady who figures in Charles Wesley's Journal entry for 18 July 1748:

I baptized good old M. Pearce by immersion at four in the morning.[2]

Certainly the baptism by John Wesley of the group of people at Colchester in 1759 was indoors, and it is of interest that in this one service only some were immersed.

I baptized seven adults, two of them by immersion.[3]

One dipping performed by Wesley took place in a cellar, and this occasioned a good deal of scornful amusement. In his *Remarks on Mr. Hill's 'Review'* (1772), Wesley had answered the charge, that

When Mr. W. baptized Mrs. L.S., he held her so long under water, that her friends screamed out, thinking she had been drowned;

by disclaiming knowledge of the event:

When? Where? I never heard of it before.[4]

A. M. Toplady, therefore, in *A Word Concerning the Bathing-Tub Baptism* (1773), wrote to publish full details of the incident. The account is no doubt overdrawn but, sarcasm aside, it provides the best record we have of a baptism administered privately by Wesley.

An account of the baptism of Mrs. Lydia Sheppard, now living in the borough of Southwark ... from her own lips.
Antecedently to the ceremony, Mr. Wesley told her, that, to satisfy

---

[1] Cit. Tyerman, *John Wesley*, i. pp. 429 f.
[2] *Charles' Journal*, ii. p. 14.   [3] *Journal*, iv. p. 302.
[4] *Works*, x. p. 394. Wesley was presumably denying that there was screaming, not that the baptism itself took place.

weak minds, he had occasionally baptized some persons by immersion, at Bristol, and elsewhere; and would do the same for her to make her easy. The time and place were accordingly appointed. An house in Long Lane, Southwark, was to have been the scene of action; and the water, and other requisite conveyances, were there actually got in readiness. But, the matter having taken air, and the curiosity of various people being excited, Mr. John did not choose to accomplish the business in the presence of so many spectators, as were then and there expected to assemble. Thus, the administration was adjourned, and another place fixed upon: at which place, Mr. John Wesley did, with his own hands, baptize the said Mrs. Lydia Sheppard by plunging her under water. And a fine plunging it had like to have proved.

Does the reader ask, in what font this baptism was administered? The font was a common bathing-tub.—Is it further enquired, in what chapel did the font stand at the time? The chapel was, truly, a chapel in cryptis: to wit, a common cellar.—Am I asked, of what cathedral was this subterraneous chapel a part? The cathedral, or mother church, was neither better nor worse than a cheesemonger's house, in Spitalfields, London.—Who were the witnesses to this under-ground baptism! A select party, it seems, carefully draughted from, what Mr. Wesley calls, his classes and bands.[1]

It is noticeable that in his *Journals* Wesley generally makes no reference to Godparents. Writing in 1744 of his ministries in Wroot and Georgia, he claimed that 'In every parish where I have been Curate yet, I have observed the Rubrics with a scrupulous exactness, not for wrath, but for conscience' sake': and among other things he specified that this care had included obedience to Canon 29:

No person shall be admitted godfather or godmother to any child, before the said person hath received the holy communion.[2]

In view of Wesley's remorse at the memory of his having baptised a child in Georgia with only two sponsors,[3] we may

---

[1] Toplady's *Works* (1825) ii. pp. 358 ff. R. Green, *Anti-Methodist Publications* (1902) No. 459. Green has 'him' instead of 'her'.

[2] *Works*, viii. pp. 32 ff. Just how seriously Wesley considered that Godparents should take their responsibilities may be judged from his refusal, in 1733, to stand in this capacity to a child of his sister's (Mehetabel), because, probably due to his absence, he could not discharge the duties involved. v. A. Clarke, *Memoirs of the Wesley Family*, p. 389. But c.f. *Letters*, i. p. 37.

[3] *Works*, i. p. 57. 'This, I own, was wrong; for I ought, at all hazards, to have refused baptizing it till he had procured a third.'

assume that in general he insisted upon the presence of the three godparents for each candidate that the *Book of Common Prayer* demands. This is borne out, in part, by references elsewhere to sponsors at baptisms performed by Wesley when in his own accounts he is silent about them. Thus Benjamin Ingham records that twice he acted as sponsor in such instances.[1] Furthermore, Charles Wesley does mention sureties from time to time. Thus:

I read prayers at Islington, and baptized an adult; Mr. Stonehouse, M. Sims, and M. Burton, being the witnesses.[2]

And again:

I carried Bridget Armstead to Bloomsbury Church, where the Minister baptized her. She had been bred a Quaker. I was one of the witnesses.[3]

Part of the Puritan dissatisfaction with the Prayer Book expressed at the Savoy Conference in 1661, had been 'to the use of Godfathers or Godmothers in Baptism, to the exclusion of parents': and also to the form of the responses as proposed in the *Book of Common Prayer*.[4] This issue was still very much alive,[5] and Charles Wesley included it in a poetical summary of ecclesiastical debating points, published as an open letter after the 1755 Conference.

> Let Others for the Shape and Colour fight
> Of Garments short or long, or black or white;
> Or fairly match'd, in furious battle join
> For and against the Sponsors and the Sign. . . .[6]

Wesley's own views on this matter can be gleaned from his *Serious Thoughts concerning Godfathers and Godmothers* (1752).

---

[1] Tyerman, *Oxford Methodists*, p. 68 (cf. *Journal*, i. p. 111); pp. 70 f (cf. *Journal*, i. p. 117).
[2] *Charles' Journal*, i. p. 136.   [3] *Ibid.* i. p. 234.
[4] E. Calamy, *Abridgment of Mr. Baxter's History of His Life and Times*, pp. 507–510.
[5] In Thomas Deacon's *Compleat Collection of Devotions*, it is advocated that 'there shall be a Sponsor or Surety for every Child to be baptized, which Sponsor shall be the Father or Mother of the Child, if either of them is to be had'. cit. D. S. Bailey, *Sponsors at Baptism and Confirmation* (1952) p. 63. v. Horton Davies, *Worship and Theology in England . . . 1690–1850*, pp. 87, 104 f. Among Evangelicals who objected to Anglican practice were J. Berridge (*Works* 1838, p. 457) and J. Jones (*Free and Candid Disquisitions Relating to the Church of England*, 1749, pp. 129 ff).
[6] *Poetical Works*, vi. p. 58.

Undoubtedly his reason for issuing this tract was to encourage Methodists to undertake this duty.¹ He wrote:

If it be said, 'But why are those questions inserted, which seem to mean what they really do not?' I answer, I did not insert them, and should not be sorry had they not been inserted at all. I believe the compilers of our Liturgy inserted them because they were used in all the ancient Liturgies. And their deep reverence for the primitive Church made them excuse some impropriety of expression.²

In the tract there is no suggestion that sponsors should not be admitted, nor does Wesley suggest that parents ought to be encouraged to stand as godparents for their own children. Rather, the burden of the *Serious Thoughts* is that sureties should be wisely chosen, and that godly people should be willing to act in this capacity.

If then you that are parents will be so wise and kind to your children as to wave every other consideration, and to choose for their sponsors those persons alone who truly fear and serve God; if some of you who love God, and love one another, agree to perform this office of love for each other's children; and if all you who undertake it perform it faithfully, with all the wisdom and power God hath given you; what a foundation of holiness and happiness may be laid, even to your late posterity! Then it may justly be hoped, that not only you and your house, but also the children which shall be born, shall serve the Lord.³

We conclude, therefore, that although he was dissatisfied with the responses required of the godparents Wesley nevertheless had a firm belief in the value of this office and did not want to abolish so ancient an institution. We are in agreement with C. J. Abbey when he said:

Wesley thought the office a good and expedient one; but regretted, as many other Churchmen before and since have done, the form in which some of the questions are put.⁴

Comment is called for on two facets of the Wesleys' practice; and first, on their continuing willingness to baptise by immersion.

While in Georgia it had been their invariable custom, where

---
¹ v. *Letters*, vii. pp. 64 f. (Repeated vii. p. 271).
² *Works*, x. p. 508.   ³ *Ibid*. x. pp. 508 f.
⁴ *The English Church in the Eighteenth Century*, p. 469.

health permitted, to administer this sacrament by triple immersion, and in Wesley's notes on the *Apostolic Constitutions* (made at some time during the years 1735-42[1]) he had reported it as being his duty, so far as possible, 'To baptize by immersion.' But now, as we look at their practice over the long years of their ministry in Britain, we find that while both brothers sometimes baptised by dipping, this was no longer their general rule.

The reason for this change is not immediately clear.[2] It has been suggested that Wesley was simply falling into line with the customary practice of his Church—but while others less strongly willed may have been ready to conform in this way, Wesley was not the man to sacrifice his principles for such a reason. Nor had his convictions in this matter changed. He had based his practice upon the belief that he was following the custom of the early Church, and his *Notes Upon the New Testament*, written in 1754, show that at that time he still believed baptism by immersion to have been 'the ancient manner'.[3]

We must look elsewhere, therefore, for the explanation of Wesley's more flexible attitude, and the reason is probably this—that looking back behind the procedures of the primitive Church, Wesley now saw that in the New Testament no one method of administration is prescribed, and he was willing to take this as his pattern.

It is not clear just when, or under whose influence, Wesley came to these conclusions. Perhaps it was due to a reading of Isaac Watts' sermon on 'Christian Baptism', for this seems to have been the main source on which he drew for his *Thoughts Upon Infant Baptism*.[4] But by 1751 (the year in which the *Thoughts* was published) he had clearly decided that

> the manner of baptizing (whether by dipping or sprinkling) is not determined in Scripture. There is no command for one rather than the other. There is no example from which we can conclude for dipping rather than sprinkling. There are probable examples of

---

[1] v. J. C. Bowmer, *The Sacrament of the Lord's Supper in Early Methodism*, pp. 233 ff.
[2] cf. the discussion in W.H.S. xxix. p. 19, and L.Q.H.R. Jan. 1966, p. 51.
[3] *Notes* for Rom. vi. 4 and Col. ii. 12.
[4] For full notes, v. *infra*, Appendix 1.

both; and both are equally contained in the natural meaning of the word.[1]

As for the signification of the two modes, Wesley argued that both represent regeneration by different figures—immersion in terms of dying and rising with Christ, and affusion in terms of

the Sprinkling of the Blood of *Christ* on the Conscience, or the Pouring out of the Spirit on the Person baptized, or Sprinkling him with clean Water, as an Emblem of the Influence of the Spirit.[2]

Wesley's procedure seems to have been as follows. In general he baptised infants and adults by affusion or sprinkling; but sometimes, at the request of the adult candidate (as apparently in the case of Mrs. Lydia Sheppard) or of the parents of infants, he used immersion.[3] At the multiple baptism at Colchester in 1759 it seems that, since two of the candidates chose immersion, both methods were employed in the one service.

This conclusion as to Wesley's procedure is borne out by an extract from his *Thoughts Upon Infant-Baptism*.

With regard to the Mode of Baptizing, I would only add, Christ nowhere, as far as I can find, requires *Dipping*, but only *Baptizing*; which Word, many most eminent for Learning and Piety, have declared, signifies to *pour on*, or *sprinkle*, as well as to *dip*. As our LORD has graciously given us a Word of such extensive Meaning, doubtless the Parent, or the Person to be baptized, if he be Adult, ought to choose which way he best approves. What GOD has left *indifferent* it becomes not *Man* to make necessary.[4]

Nevertheless, we must remember that it was not common for Anglican clergy to use immersion, and that, in particular, river baptisms of the type Wesley countenanced were most unusual outside the Baptist Denomination. In spite of his shift to a more accommodating and liberal attitude, Wesley therefore still stood out as eccentric in this matter.

[1] *Works*, x. p. 190.   [2] *Thoughts*, p. 20.
[3] cf. R. Southey, *The Life of Wesley*, 1899 ed., p. 454.
[4] p. 19. There is no evidence to show whether the Wesleys continued to use triple immersion. James Whitehead (*The Life of the Rev. John Wesley*, i. p. 227) said of Charles, that he used trine immersion 'if the persons would submit to it; judging this to be the apostolic mode'—but he instances only the baptism of Mr. Wigginton about which *Charles' Journal* is not so specific. (i. p. 191).

In view of the Wesleys' continued inclination towards immersion, an *Expostulatory Letter* of 1739 was not wholly justified. It was addressed to Whitefield 'and the rest of his brethren, the Methodists of the Church of England' and, while it first commends the Methodist clergy in that when they christen children they do so in Church and during Evening Prayer,[1] it then turns to their '*Mode* and *Manner* of *administering* this *Ordinance*': and here the writer accuses them, of failing

> on a *fundamental Point:* for whereas the *Rubrick* says, the *Minister* shall *dip* the *Child* in *Water* . . . unless the *Child* is weak, . . . nevertheless, you sprinkle *all*, whether they be *healthy* or *sickly*. Thus you *strain at a Gnat and swallow a Camel*, and by a vain, insignificant *Tradition*, render the *Commandment of our Lord Jesus Christ*, of non effect.[2]

So also the short-lived but keenly written *Weekly Miscellany* shows a lack of awareness of Wesley's motives and methods. In its issue for 25 April 1741, it condemns him because he

> rebaptizes adults, on the ground that, *really* they have never been baptized before, the baptism of infants by sprinkling being no true baptism in his esteem.[3]

This accusation—in effect that he shared Baptist views—was compounded of fact and fancy. It was true that Wesley was willing to re-baptise Dissenters, and to baptise by immersion when such requests were made; but he had never re-baptised on the ground that baptism by sprinkling, or paedobaptism itself, was invalid.

The other aspect of Wesley's baptismal practice which requires longer comment is his persistent disregard of confirmation. We have seen how frequently he administered communion to adults after baptising them, and there are two recorded instances when Charles did likewise.

> I baptized a woman in Kingswood, and trembled at the descent of the Holy Ghost. All present were more or less sensible of it, especially the person baptized. We joined in the Lord's supper, and had his never-failing presence.[4]

---

[1] The reference is to the Methodist baptisms at Islington. v. *supra*, p. 90.
[2] pp. 14 f. It is signed 'E.B.'   [3] Cit. Tyerman, *John Wesley*, i. p. 358.
[4] *Charles' Journal*, ii. p. 16. On 12 July 1741, he 'received Jane Sheep into the fold by baptism . . .'. *ibid*. i. p. 286.

I baptized a young Quaker at Kingswood; and then we all joined in the Lord's supper. He was mightily present in both sacraments.[1]

Their letters to the Bishop of Bristol seem therefore to be exact expressions of the attitude of the Wesleys to baptism—that by this means, unaccompanied by confirmation, people are 'received into the Church'.[2]

Wesley made few references to confirmation in his writings and sermons, and what he did say is largely non-committal.[3] He at no time spoke of the 'seal of the Spirit' in association with confirmation, but rather thought of it as one aspect of God's free work in conversion and sanctification.[4] Thus a disregard for confirmation (which in Georgia could be explained and excused on the ground of the absence of Bishops) we find to be a continuing feature of the entire ministry of the Wesleys.

These findings, taken as a whole, reveal that Wesley's entire ministry was marked by a great esteem not only for the Lord's supper but for both of the sacraments. It is true that he soon abandoned the extreme position which he had taken up in Georgia—'maturity and common sense' together with a different view of the biblical evidence led him to lay aside his insistence upon episcopal administration and triple immersion—yet such was still the importance he attached to this ordinance that he was willing to re-baptise Dissenters, or to baptise by immersion, when either was requested; and when we recall that Wesley believed in the baptismal regeneration of infants, and in adult baptism as a means of grace and as the ceremony marking admission into the Church, we are led to see that he regarded this sacrament very highly indeed.

Before we leave this chapter, some points of general interest

---

[1] *Ibid.* ii. p. 83.
[2] cf. *Treatise*, where baptism alone effects entry into the Church (*Works*, x. p. 191); *Serious Thoughts concerning Godfathers and Godmothers*, where the duty of preparing the godchild for confirmation is not mentioned (*Works*, x. pp. 506 ff). Wesley was thus being consistent when he gave communion to (presumably baptised) children. v. *Journal*, v. pp. 291, 525 f; vii p. 23. For his views on the practice of the early Church, v. *Journal*, ii. pp. 360 f.
[3] v. *Works*, x. pp. 116 f; *Letters*, iv. pp. 378 ff. cf. H. J. Cook in *The Doctrine of the Church*, ed. Dow Kirkpatrick, pp. 114 f.
[4] *Notes* for Eph. i. 13, iv. 30; *Works*, xi. pp. 423 f. cf. H. J. Cook, *loc. cit.* pp. 107 f.

may be noticed. We may be surprised, for example, to realize just how frequently Wesley was called upon to administer baptism. During the eleven months detailed in the earlier published Diaries (July 1740 to June 1741) he christened at least fifty people, on twenty-nine recorded occasions; and the later Diary, covering the period 1 December 1782 to 24 February 1791, records his having baptised at least fifty-seven people on forty-seven occasions. Indeed, so commonplace was it for Wesley to administer this sacrament that, detailed as they are, he did not always mention such occasions in his Diaries.[1]

Scanning the *Journals* at large, we find several instances of baptisms of sufficient note to have been included.[2] Thus we are shown Wesley in Glasgow, in June 1757, preaching in the yard of the Poor-House.

After sermon they brought four children to baptize. I was at the kirk in the morning while the minister baptized several immediately after sermon, so I was not at a loss as to their manner of baptizing. I believe this removed much prejudice.[3]

In a curious incident he baptised two foreigners, one in Turkish habit, 'who professed themselves to have been Turks', but who turned out to have been impostors.[4] Wesley baptised on occasion Jews[5] and negroes.[6] Two of these latter belonged to Nathaniel Gilbert, and Wesley wrote:

One of these is deeply convinced of sin, the other rejoices in God her Saviour, and is the first African Christian I have known.[7]

Nearly twenty years later, Charles Wesley had a similar contact with two Africans, although the circumstances were rather different. J. B. Wakeley has gleaned the story for his *Anecdotes of the Wesleys*.

Two African princes were carried off from Old Calabar by a Bristol

---

[1] v. *infra*. Appendix 3; *Journal*, vi. pp. 118 n, 446 n; vii. pp. 181 n, 282 n; W.H.S. xxvii. pp. 16 ff. Charles Wesley's very incomplete surviving Journals record his baptising 10 children on 10 occasions, and 39 adults on 25 occasions, during the period May 1738–November 1756.

[2] Horton Davies (*Worship and Theology in England ... 1690–1850*, p. 205) is misled by the small number of baptisms mentioned in the *Journal*, when he says, 'Wesley himself rarely baptised. . . .'

[3] *Journal*, iv. p. 216.   [4] *Ibid*. iv. p. 540.   [5] *Ibid*. iv. p. 245.
[6] *Ibid*. vii. p. 144.   [7] *Ibid*. iv. p. 292.

captain. ... They were six years in slavery, made their escape to England, and were thrown into irons, but were rescued by Lord Mansfield. For two months Charles Wesley had them under his care and instruction. They professed the Christian faith, and on 22nd of February, 1774, he baptized them. He said they both received the outward visible sign and the inward spiritual grace in a wonderful manner and measure. They were sent back to their brother, the king of Calabar, and Mr. Wesley rejoiced to hear of their safe arrival. The next year he writes, 'My two African children got safe home.'[1]

Thomas Jackson said of Charles Wesley, that

in the administration of . . . baptism, he always used the form contained in the Book of Common Prayer; but he did not confine himself to it. He was often drawn out largely in extempory prayer.[2]

No doubt the same was also true of his elder brother,[3] and it can never have been the case that the evangelical opportunity afforded by a baptism, whether adult or infant, would have been allowed to pass by ungrasped by either of them.[4]

The last recorded occasion on which Wesley baptised was on 6 November 1790, just four months before his death.

1 at Mr. Wolff's, christened.[5]

---

[1] p. 350. In 1778 they appealed for Methodist preachers to be sent out to their country, but Conference declined this call. v. J. Vickers, *Thomas Coke Apostle of Methodism*, (1969) p. 132.
[2] *Life of Charles Wesley*, ii. p. 14.
[3] e.g. *Journal*, vii. pp. 282 f.n. But notice, above, the exception made when in Scotland.
[4] 'I was sent for to baptize a child. It gave me occasion to speak upon faith.' *Charles' Journal*, i. p. 107.
[5] *Journal*, viii. p. 112.

CHAPTER 9

Baptism and the Early Methodists: Practice

No matter how frequently Wesley baptised, he, along with his small number of ordained helpers, could not hope to offer this sacrament to all the Methodist people who might require it; nor was it his intention that Methodists should, in general, be baptised by anyone other than their parish priest or anywhere else than at the font of their parish church.

It must be remembered that Wesley did not design to establish a new Church but, more simply, to promote a Society within the Church of England. It was expected therefore that the members of that Society should attend the parish churches for worship on Sundays and to receive the sacraments, their distinctively Methodist activities being confined to supplementary devotions during the week. Yet this plan failed almost from the start. Almost immediately the Methodists began to be refused communion, and very soon, in many places, they began to be dissatisfied with the preaching of the local incumbents, so that they started to look to the itinerant preachers not only for additional spiritual nourishment but also for their basic diet of the preached word and the sacrament.

Nevertheless, with baptism the case was different. At no time had Wesley to persuade his people to attend the Churches for baptism, as he had to do for communion and worship generally.[1] By and large, the Methodists went willingly to receive Anglican christening for their children. Thus it is significant that although Charles Wesley lived conveniently near to the New Room in Bristol during the years in which his children were born (1757-68), he nevertheless took them all to be baptised at St. James's, his parish church.[2] A letter

---

[1] e.g. *Minutes* (1862 ed.) i. p. 213; *Minutes* for 1786, i. p. 191.

[2] The baptismal entry for the first child reads: 'John Wesley, of Charles & Sarah a Preacher in the Horsfaier.' cf. F. C. Gill, *Charles Wesley the First Methodist* (1964) p. 176. This contrasts strongly with the baptism of George Whitefield's

written in 1787 by Wesley to one of his preachers, William Percival, shows that he also had had no thought but to turn to the Anglican Church for this ordinance:

DEAR BILLY,—You cannot be too watchful against evil speaking or too zealous for the poor Church of England. I commend Sister Percival for having her child baptized there and for returning public thanks. By all means go to church as often as you can, and exhort all Methodists so to do.[1]

There is no record of any Methodists being refused Anglican baptism in England or Wales, whereas, in contrast, they began to be repelled from her communion tables as early as 1740.[2] The reasons for this greater hospitality are threefold: first, that, by the Sixty-eighth Canon, all-comers must be granted baptism who desire it; second, that the great inconvenience of numbers which militated against the Methodist crowds being allowed Anglican communion[3] did not apply in the case of baptism; and last, that, by the Registration Act of 1695, the Anglican registers of baptisms constituted the only official record. For these reasons it must often have happened that Methodist parents brought their children for baptism to Churches in which they had been refused the Lord's supper, and it can be shown that this baptismal link between Methodism and the Parent Church lasted until well into the nineteenth century, and was one of the last to be severed.[4]

One factor which helped to reduce friction in this matter was the absence of baptism from the conditions laid down for membership of the Methodist Society. Joining the Church—in which baptism was an essential feature—and joining the Methodist Society, were altogether distinct processes. Wesley's

---

first child in 1744, which took place in his own London Tabernacle. v. Tyerman, *George Whitefield*, ii. p. 85.

[1] *Letters*, vii. p. 369. Gilbert Boyce tells of a preacher who insisted on having his child baptised by the priest in the parish Church by immersion. *A Serious Reply to the Rev. Mr. John Wesley* . . . (1770) p. 131.

[2] cf. J. C. Bowmer, *The Sacrament of the Lord's Supper in Early Methodism*, pp. 63 f. In Scotland the Episcopal Churches did sometimes refuse this sacrament to Methodists. v. *Works*, xiii. p. 257; T. Coke and H. Moore, *The Life of the Rev. John Wesley* (1792) p. 417. There was thus a greater need to ordain preachers for Scotland than for England.

[3] v. Jackson, *Charles Wesley*, i. p. 231; *Charles' Journal*, i. p. 189.

[4] e.g. William Shrewsbury, *Infant Baptism Scriptural* (1841) pp. 3 f.

Classes and Bands were composed of people who were, by and large, already initiated into their own Churches, and if any applicant belonged to no Church he could still, without taking this step, become a Methodist—for the 'one only condition previously required' for such admission was 'a desire to flee from the wrath to come, and to be saved from their sins.'[1] Baptism was therefore a Church matter, about which Methodism as a Society within the Church was not greatly concerned.

Yet if Wesley had no occasion to request the Methodist people to go to obtain baptism at the Churches, he had from time to time to require his preachers to desist from administering it to them.

He drew a clear distinction between the office of his lay preachers and the ordained office of priests. Wesley's itinerants were 'extraordinary messengers' whose function was to preach.

We believe it would not be right for us to administer either baptism or the Lord's supper unless we had a commission so to do from those bishops whom we apprehend to be in a succession from the Apostles.[2]

he had said in 1745: and even when later Wesley believed Apostolic Succession to be 'a fable',[3] he nevertheless considered at least presbyteral ordination to be necessary before a man could properly administer the sacraments. However, it was not long before the preachers themselves began to think otherwise.

Methodist people living in rural areas, who were unwilling or unable to receive the Lord's supper at their parish churches, had to go without Communion, or else either to receive it in Dissenting Chapels or at the hands of their own preachers. During the seventeen fifties, some of the preachers began to meet this situation by administering the Lord's supper to the people, and once they had begun to give the one sacrament, it would be an easy step for them to give the other also, even though baptism was always to be had in the parish churches.

The Conference of 1754 saw 'the withdrawal from the itinerant work of Samuel Larwood, . . . Charles Skelton, John Whitford, and one or two others, who had become dissatisfied

---

[1] H. W. Williams, *Constitution and Polity of Wesleyan Methodism* (1880) pp. 2, 259 f. No account of people being received On Trial and then into Membership contains any reference to baptism. v. *Letters*, i. pp. 296, 300, 316, etc.

[2] *Letters*, ii. p. 55. cf. iii. pp. 93, 186; *Notes* for 1 Cor. i. 17; *Works*, x. p. 150.

[3] *Letters*, vii. p. 284 (1785).

with the itinerant plan, and with their position as mere evangelists';[1] and what had begun to show itself in 1754 continued to be a point of difference and friction within Methodism until Wesley's death, and even beyond that.

The 1755 Conference had again to deal with this matter, but this time the offending preachers were persuaded not to administer and to remain within the Connexion. Charles Wesley wrote about the situation:

Charles Perronet, you know, has taken upon him to administer the sacrament, for a month together to the preachers, and twice to some of the people. Walsh and three others have followed his vile example.[2]

Once more, in 1760, the smouldering issue was fanned into flame when the preachers at Norwich—Paul Greenwood, Thomas Mitchell, and John Murlin—began to give the sacraments. Murlin, in a letter dated 23 December 1794, refers back to the years 1758 to 1761.

In the infant state of Methodism, the preachers only preached and did not administer the sacrament, but near thirty-six years since, Mr. Wesley sent me to Norwich where I preached, baptized their children and administered the Lord's supper for a great part of three years, till Mr. Charles made a great outcry and put a stop to it for a time.[3]

In the Provinces, the preachers evidently began to administer the sacraments because of a need for them to do so in the case of the Lord's supper. In London and in other large urban centres where churches abounded, this need could never have arisen, for it would normally be a simple matter to find one church at least where Methodists were able to come for Communion. But even so, it appears that at about this same time the Methodists there began to persuade the preachers to baptise their children. So far as London is concerned, this is indicated by the Return made by Thomas Kemp, Rector of St. Michael, Crooked Lane (between Cannon Street and the Thames) at the Archbishop's Visitation of the Diocese in 1758.

Methodists many, & increasing; of the lower sort. They cause their

---

[1] Tyerman, *John Wesley*, ii. p. 187.　　[2] *Ibid.* ii. pp. 201 f.
[3] J. C. Bowmer, *op. cit.* p. 74. Greenwood had already been warned by Wesley, *Letters*, iii. p. 147 (1755).

Teachers to exercise the ministerial Office in their Houses without my Consent, by baptizing their Children, and visiting the Sick.[1]

From this time forward, and in spite of the firm line taken by the Conference and the known wishes of Wesley, some of the preachers in town and country continued to baptise, even if they would not go so far as to administer the Lord's supper. When Wesley heard of such incidents he wrote quickly and sharply to stop the practice, and some of these letters have been preserved.

On 29 March 1764, he wrote to an unnamed preacher:

MY DEAR BROTHER,—Is it true that you have baptized several children since the Conference? If it is, I cannot but interpret it as a clear renunciation of connexion with us. And if this be the case, it will not be proper for you to preach any longer in our Societies.[2]

Similarly, he wrote even more bluntly to Joseph Thompson in 1772:

Whoever among us undertakes to baptize a child is *ipso facto* excluded from our Connexion;[3]

and as late as 1777 he could still write:

I know not that any lay Preachers in connexion with me, either baptize children, or administer the Lord's supper.[4]

However, in spite of his clearly stated principles in the matter, and these outright denunciations of preachers who took it upon themselves to baptise, Wesley was not able to halt this practice, and evidence is forthcoming to show that before the end of his life many preachers had begun to administer baptism quite openly as an accepted and normal aspect of their pastoral function. This is one of the most illuminating facts which emerge from a study of the early Methodist registers of births and baptisms, now kept at the Public Record Office in London.[5]

For the early years of Methodism no such records are to be found, nor are any preserved locally in such historic centres of the Movement as London, Bristol and Newcastle.

---

[1] *Bulletin of the London Branch, Wesley Historical Society*, No. 4, pp. 8 f.
[2] *Letters*, iv. p. 235.   [3] *Ibid.* v. p. 330.   [4] *Works*, x. p. 450.
[5] For a full analysis, v. *infra*. Appendix 3.

Since it is unlikely that such records would all have been lost or destroyed, we may assume that no registers were kept during the middle years of the eighteenth century. The Registration Act of 1695 required that all baptisms should be notified to the Anglican Incumbent of the parish, but it is doubtful whether those performed by Methodist clergy and preachers were very often reported in this manner.[1]

If anywhere we should expect to find this being done in London, where first the Foundery and then the City Road Chapel came within the parish of St. Luke's, Old Street;[2] but an inspection of the St. Luke's registers[3] reveals that no record was made of the baptisms performed by Wesley and others at either of these places. It can only be assumed that such baptisms in London and elsewhere throughout the British Isles, comparatively few in number, generally went unrecorded for many years. This explains why, in some of the early Methodist registers, it is found that baptisms which had been performed earlier on have been entered in from memory—evidently they had not been registered at the time.[4]

Reference to Appendix 3 will show that sixteen Wesleyan Methodist[5] registers of baptisms were started before Wesley's death in 1791. The earliest known is that of Mount Zion Chapel, Ovenden (now called Ogden), Halifax, which was begun in 1778, and others followed after 1784. While most of them originate from Lancashire and Yorkshire, others were begun in Circuits as far afield as Devon and Northumberland.

There are two factors which account for the opening of these baptismal registers. The first is that in 1785 stamp-duty was extended to include registration in Non-Conformist

[1] W.H.S. xxvii. pp. 16 f may provide an example, in the baptism by Wesley of Eleanor Dornford on 21 February 1787. The page is numbered 132, and has been presumably torn from a Church register. It is suggested that the entry may have been initialled by the Rev. Thomas Scott.

[2] Particularly since Wesley took his congregation from the Foundery, and then from the City Road Chapel, to St. Luke's to receive the Lord's supper. v. F. C. Gill, *In the Steps of John Wesley*, p. 46.

[3] At the London County Record Office. Those of this period available for inspection cover the years 1733–42, 1776–1800.

[4] e.g. the registers of Plymouth Dock, Liverpool (Mount Pleasant), and the Taunton, Stourport and Halifax Circuits.

[5] So called to distinguish this part of Methodism from the other branches of the movement in the eighteenth century. v. Appendix 3 for details. This number had grown to 118 by 1800.

registers; and although it was later to be decided that in fact such records were not legally acceptable,[1] it was thought at the time that they were now on an equal footing, in law, with the parish registers. Scrutiny of the List of Non-Conformist Registers in the Public Record Office shows that, in general, very many of these were begun in 1785 and the years immediately following, and it seems that Methodism also was influenced by this external factor.

But it requires more than this legal sanction to explain why such registers were started over so wide an area of the country—and the registers themselves provide the reason. The lay preachers, itinerant and local, had by now begun to baptise regularly. In the days when the vast majority of Methodists received baptism in the parish churches, and only comparatively few obtained the sacrament at the hands of the small number of ordained Methodist clergy, separate registers were as unnecessary as they were unofficial, but by the mid-1780s the situation had changed. The preachers were christening so often that there was a real need for records to be kept, and it is this fact, allied to the change in the law, which accounts for the opening of the first Methodist baptismal registers.

This movement among the preachers must have been gathering momentum for many years, but the records show that from 1785 onwards and at various places throughout the country, twenty-three itinerant preachers were regarding it as part of their task not only to preach but also to baptise. Some names stand out. Charles Atmore and Thomas Taylor appear most frequently in the registers, although it can be assumed that many other preachers baptised as commonly as they did but in Circuits where no records were kept. That the names of Thomas Hanby, Joseph Taylor, and John Pawson are found is interesting because it sheds light on their conduct on returning to England after travelling in Scotland, for which Country (only) they had been ordained by Wesley in 1785. Wesley had ordered that they should not regard themselves as ordained for ministry in England, and that therefore on their coming south they should no longer wear

---

[1] v. *Journal of the Society of Archivists*, ii. No. 9, pp. 411 ff. 'Nonconformist Registers' by E. Welch.

canonicals or administer the sacraments. Thomas Hanby refused to obey this command. Wesley wrote to Peard Dickinson on 11 April 1789:

I wrote a few days since to Mr. Hanby concerning his baptizing and administering the Lord's supper wherever he goes. He answers me, 'He intends to do still, for he believes it to be his duty.' I wish Brother Creighton and Moore and Rankin and you would spend an hour together, as it is a point of the utmost importance, and consider what steps are to be taken in this matter. Can this be connived at? If so, I fear it is a blow at the very root of Methodism.[1]

On 4 June, 1789, having evidently heard from these London preachers, Hanby wrote to Richard Rodda about the disagreement.

I am in the fire, but, like the salamander, I live there. I am up to the chin in deep waters; but not drowned. Mr. Mather sent me a threatening bull; Mr. Wesley a second; and, to complete the work the clergy in London, Mr. Rankin and Mr. Moore, joined their artillery. The last in command is my colleague, Joseph Taylor, who opposes me with the utmost warmth. You will readily conclude 'Poor Hanby will be overpowered by numbers.' True; but I still keep the field, for all that, and mean to die there.[2]

While Hanby was stationed at Bolton, it seems that a local clergyman, who objected to his baptising, wrote in 1790 to tell Wesley so. He received this in reply:[3]

REVD. SIR,—I do not approve of Mr. Hanby's baptizing children. I have wrote to him, and told him my mind. If I can remove any inconvenience from you, it will be a pleasure to, sir, Your affectionate brother.
To the Revd, Mr. G—,
In Bolton, Lancashire.

The registers confirm that Hanby baptised not only at Bolton but elsewhere during the years 1789 to 1791. But what is more surprising is to find the other two names cited. John Pawson, while remonstrating with Wesley, nevertheless ac-

---

[1] *Letters*, viii. p. 129.
[2] Tyerman, *John Wesley*, iii. pp. 575 f. cf. his letter to James Oddie, *ibid*. p. 574.
[3] *Letters*, viii. p. 279.

cepted his command. Writing to his friend Charles Atmore in 1787, he said:

> We are to be just what we were before we came to Scotland—no sacraments, no gowns, no nothing at all of any kind whatsoever. ... What an astonishing degree of power does our aged father and friend exercise! However, I am satisfied, and have nothing but love in my heart toward the good old man. But really it will not bear the light at all.[1]

On this evidence, it has been generally assumed that Pawson no longer administered the sacraments when back in England.[2] The registers reveal, however, that in fact he continued to baptise. Similarly, Tyerman presumed that Joseph Taylor no longer administered when he left Scotland[3]—and certainly Taylor opposed Hanby in the stand he took—but the registers again show that all the time he also was still baptising. From this it becomes plain that while generally the administration of *both* sacraments was said to be under discussion, in fact it was the Lord's supper alone which was at issue: baptism by the preachers was by now too well-established to be quelled.

This suggests that Wesley must have known of what was afoot. The Methodist Conference of 1794 (after Wesley's death) believed that this had been the case. It laid down that

> The Preachers will not perform the office of baptism, except for the desirable ends of love and concord; though baptism, as well as the burial of the dead, was performed by many of the Preachers long before the death of Mr. Wesley, and with his consent.[4]

In contrast to burying,[5] the Conference was mistaken in saying that Wesley went so far as to give his consent for his preachers to baptise, and yet, reading between the lines of his letters written during the years after 1783, it is possible to discern that here was a common practice among the preachers, of which he was well aware, but about which he was able to do nothing.[1]

---

[1] Tyerman, *John Wesley*, iii. pp. 497 f.
[2] e.g. Tyerman, *John Wesley*, iii. p. 574; J. C. Bowmer, *op. cit.* p. 155; H.M.C. p. 279; L. E. Elliott-Binns, *The Early Evangelicals* (1953), p. 224. However, he continued to give communion in private. v. T. M. Morrow, *Early Methodist Women* (1967), p. 55.   [3] *John Wesley*, iii. p. 574.
[4] *Minutes*, i. p. 314 (1862 ed.). Cf. Jackson, *Life of Charles Wesley*, ii. pp. 182 ff.
[5] v. Letter to Joseph Benson, *infra*.

To Joseph Benson, 19 May 1783:

DEAR JOSEPH,—I do not, and never did, consent that any of our preachers should baptize as long as we profess ourselves to be members of the Church of England. Much more may be said for burying the dead; to this I have no objection.[2]

To John Valton, January 6th, 1784:

I shall have no objection to Mr. Taylor if he does not baptize children; but this I dare not suffer. I shall shortly be obliged to drop all the preachers who will not drop this. Christ sent them not to baptize, but to preach the gospel.[3]

To Alexander Suter, 24 November 1787:

As we have not yet made a precedent of any one that was not ordained administering baptism, it is better to go slow and sure.[4]

The early Methodist baptismal registers thus throw new light on the status of the itinerant helpers. Long before Wesley's death, and apart from ordination, they had confidently assumed the ministerial role of baptising, and were thus already far from being merely travelling evangelists. Wesley's ordinations, therefore, were not simply a gracious bestowal in his own good time of the ministerial office upon them, but (in regard to baptism) a belated regularization of what was already accepted practice. Furthermore, we can see that when, after 1791 (the year of Wesley's death), the Conference had to decide on the future of the Methodist Societies, the possibility of creating some *rapprochement* with the Church of England must have been very remote. By then the preachers (whether or not ordained) had been so long accustomed to this presbyterial function, and were so confident in it, that the only real option was to press forward towards the establishment of a new and independent Denomination. It was a significant indication of the future, therefore, that when a Society Steward at Byker began a baptismal register in 1788, he gave the lay preachers who administered the sacrament in the preaching house the title 'Rev. Mr.'[1]

---

[1] Some preachers felt that there was no Scriptural warrant for this restriction. v. H. Moore, *The Life of the Rev. John Wesley* (1824–5) ii. pp. 339 f.
[2] *Letters*, vii. p. 179.   [3] *Letters*, vii. p. 203.
[4] *Ibid.* viii. p. 23.

Nor is this all that the early Methodist registers reveal. They show that people other than the itinerant preachers also undertook to baptise. Since, of course, Wesley regarded his preachers as laymen, he would not have seen any difference in principle between them and other laymen in the matter of their administering the sacraments; and yet, without doubt, if he disapproved of this action among the travelling preachers, he must have been the more outraged that local preachers should over-reach themselves in this way. His reaction is reflected in a letter to William Percival, on 4 March 1784:

DEAR BILLY,—I desire Mr. Murlin, if any of our lay preachers talk either in public or private against the Church or the clergy, or read the Church Prayers, or baptise children, to require a promise from them to do it no more. If they will not promise, let them preach no more. And if they break their promise, let them be expelled the Society.[2]

Previously, no specific examples had come to light of baptism by local laymen,[3] but now some names can be given, for several registers disclose administrators who were not Wesley's itinerants, and who must therefore have been local lay Methodists; and other registers which record baptisms during these early years but without disclosing the names of the officiants,[4] probably provide anonymous testimony to this same practice. Unfortunately, biographical details of the people named in the registers have been discovered in three cases only—George Walkden and William Banning of Blackburn, and James Maden of Bacup—but in these men we have, without doubt, a good impression of the kind of layman who in various parts of the country assumed this ministerial function.

Walkden and Banning had played a prominent part in the

---

[1] v. Appendix 3.   [2] *Letters*, vii. p. 213.
[3] J. C. Bowmer (*op. cit.* p. 155) mentions one reported occasion when Wesley ordained a Mr. Woodhouse as a *local* preacher. This was almost certainly not the case, but Mr. Woodhouse (of Owston, near Epworth) may have administered the sacraments locally without having been either ordained or appointed an itinerant preacher.
[4] e.g. Halifax Circuit (1772 onwards); Mount Zion Chapel, Ovenden (1775 onwards); Pudsey (1789–90). In this connection it is significant that the earliest known Methodist baptismal register is a Class Leader's notebook. v. Appendix 3.

first days of Methodism in Blackburn. When it was proposed to build a preaching house there,

> The chief men in promoting the scheme were Mr. William Banning and Mr. G. Walkden. . . . The money for the chapel was raised almost entirely by Messrs. Banning and Walkden, who visited nearly every house in the town for the purpose.[1]

The building was opened by Wesley on 17 April 1786,[2] and among the trustees are found

William Banning—Breadmaker.
George Walkden—Yeoman.[3]

Both men were Local Preachers, and Banning and his wife entertained Wesley on his visits to their town.[4] Less is known of James Maden. He was not one of the founders of Methodism in Bacup although the Maden family had been prominent in this work from its beginning. However, there are records to show that from December 1786 to January 1799 he was a Class Leader, and that in 1790 he was a Local Preacher in Bacup.[5]

Here then were men who, along with the itinerant preachers, had begun to baptise several years before Wesley's death, and we can assume that in many parts of Methodism others of this kind—Local Preachers, Trustees, Class Leaders—would have been acting in this same manner. Probably this movement among the laymen (travelling preachers and others) was confined to the administration of the one sacrament, for apart from the more isolated and spasmodic occasions when the itinerants administered the Lord's supper, there is no firm evidence to suggest that they had begun to do this customarily before Wesley's death.[6]

The pattern thus emerges of the way in which baptism was given and received among the Wesleyan Methodists of the eighteenth century. In the main they still went for it to the

---

[1] E. Stanley Shelton, *The Centenary Volume of the Wesleyan Methodist Chapel, Clayton Street, Blackburn, 1885*, p. 20.   [2] *Journal*, vii. p. 155.
[3] John Ward, *The Rise and Progress of Wesleyan Methodism in Blackburn and the Neighbourhood* (1871), p. 26.   [4] *Ibid*. p. 37.
[5] William J. H. Ogden, *Centenary Souvenir of Mount Pleasant Methodist Church, Bacup (1841–1941)*, pp. 27, 40.
[6] cf. J. C. Bowmer, *op. cit.* pp. 80 f.

parish churches; but increasingly, and ordinarily by the mid-seventeen eighties, the itinerant preachers and other laymen were baptising.

The question is now raised as to what they considered baptism to mean, and it is to an investigation into the doctrine of this sacrament held by the first Methodists and the early evangelicals generally that we turn in the chapter that follows.

CHAPTER 10

Baptismal Regeneration: The Climate of Evangelical Opinion

It has sometimes been assumed that, whatever his own views may have been, the preachers and people in Wesley's Societies did not believe in baptismal regeneration, and that, more or less silently, they objected to what they regarded as this taint from his Anglican upbringing in their venerable father in God.

J. H. Rigg, writing in the last quarter of the nineteenth century, said:

Many, probably most, of (Wesley's) preachers no less than of his people, during his lifetime rejected altogether the doctrine of baptismal regeneration, and he never required any of them to receive it.[1]

This statement has been repeated from time to time, until it has become almost taken for granted that the

views of Samuel and his son, John, on Baptismal Regeneration were resisted from the first in Methodism.[2]

In particular it has been suggested that there was a most definite and influential reaction by the American Methodists against Wesley's doctrine. Referring to the baptismal office in the *Sunday Service of the Methodists*,[3] Nolan B. Harmon has written, that the American Methodists

went to work on it from the first moment they got hold of it in 1784.

---

[1] *The Churchmanship of John Wesley*, p. 42. cf. *Was John Wesley a High Churchman?* (1882), p. 21.
[2] M. Edwards, *Family Circle* (1949), p. 42. cf. L.Q.H.R. July 1944, p. 217; J. Bishop, *Methodist Worship in Relation to Free Church Worship* (1950), p. 114.
[3] v. *infra*. Appendix 4.

They said that it 'squinted at Baptismal Regeneration' and they didn't like it.[1]

It is necessary therefore to turn to the literature of the period, to test whether in fact such a judgement on early Methodist baptismal opinion can be sustained. The evidence is elusive for references to baptism in the writings of the evangelicals are usually incidental and brief, but what comments are made go to show that there was a far greater willingness among the Methodists to accept a doctrine of sacramental regeneration than the above extracts might lead us to suppose; and furthermore, when Methodist opinion is viewed not in isolation but within the context of the eighteenth century revival at large, it is found that there was a general climate of opinion which was sympathetic towards this doctrine.

In the first place, hardly any clear voice is heard denouncing the whole concept of baptismal regeneration. Nicholas Manners and John Atlay (who had been Wesley's preachers until they became independent ministers in 1784 and 1788 respectively) did so — but only as a consequence of their dismissing the doctrine of original sin; and in this they were so far outside the *milieu* of evangelical opinion that they cannot be regarded as representative of it.[2]

The nearest that has been found to a complete denial of baptismal regeneration by a true evangelical is in *The Mitre, a Poem* (1756). Its author, Edward Perronet, was a preacher first in association with John Wesley and then with Lady Huntingdon, but this poem, a virulent denunciation of the Church of England, far from being approved by either of them, earned him their censure and Wesley suppressed its publication. Edward Perronet eventually became a Dissenting minister. Some of his verses are as follows:

[1] Cit. W.H.S. xxix. p. 15. cf. H.M.C. pp. 160 f, 268 f.
[2] v. Tyerman, *John Wesley*, iii. p. 559; Manners, *An Attempt to Illustrate the Following Subjects: . . . Creation, Degeneration, and Redemption* (1783); and *Remarks on the Writings of the Rev. J.W.* (1788). The same can be said of the anonymous (Methodist) author of *A Defence of the Rev. Mr. Whitfield's Doctrine of Regeneration: In Answer to the Rev. Mr. Land* (1739) who, upon the assumption that babies are born innocent of original sin, says that infant baptism 'must only be looked upon as a kind of *Religious Dedication* made by the Parents.' (p. 8). cf. David Simpson, *A Plea for Religion and the Sacred Writings* (1797) 1812 ed., p. 226. His main objection seems to be to the doctrine of final perseverance rather than to baptismal regeneration.

27. *Taught from the first, nay BID believe,*
   (What none but madmen e'er receive)
   'That BAPTISM was your GRACE:'
   As well they might have said—and true,
   'The chrystal rivulet was blue:
   'The bason was your face.'

28. *From hence your scorn and disregard*
   Of all that ever since ye heard,
   Of being born again!
   Laugh and reject th' important theme,
   As but a fool or madman's dream,
   The oozings of THEIR brain.

29. *Woe worth such PARENTS and such GUIDES!*
   (Not strange the INFIDEL derides,
   So humorous a sight:)
   What know ye not 'tis but a sign
   Of deeper things—not to refine,
   Or wash the AETHIOP white?

30. *No—nor SUCH washing—never will,*
   Had they e'en kept on washing still,
   You'd been but where you are:
   The shackled slave of guilt and sin,
   A foe to God—of FUTURE pain,
   The everlasting heir!

It is said here that baptism is merely a sign of regeneration, and the implication is that this is so whether it is administered to infants or to adults. But such a sweeping judgement is not found elsewhere in evangelical writings of the period. It was frequently asserted that adult regeneration must not be identified with baptism, yet the doctrine of infant baptismal regeneration was not attacked.[1] Two examples are given, chosen almost at random, for similar passages can be found in the works of very many of the eighteenth century evangelicals.

---

[1] v. Tyerman, *John Wesley*, ii. p. 241. There is no evidence to suggest that some of Wesley's preachers opposed this doctrine and that he exercised censorship to silence them. Such private manuscript journals and sermon notes as survive (e.g. those of John Bennet, Henry Moore and Samuel Bradburn) give no indication of this kind.

The first is from an outline sermon on Acts i.5, by John Fletcher of Madeley, which reads:
1. Material water cannot cleanse the soul.
2. It is not saving,—witness Simon Magus. 'You shall be baptized,' etc.
3. The water flows off, dries up; the effect superficial.

Application.
1. Unconverted.—Rest in no baptism, but that of the Holy Ghost and fire. Water baptism will condemn you alone.[1]

The other is a portion of the first sermon that George Whitefield preached.

Now a Person may be said to be *in Christ* in two Ways. First, only by an outward Profession. And in this Sense, every one that is called a Christian, or baptized into Christ's Church, may be said to be *in Christ*. But that this is not the sole Meaning of the Apostle's Phrase now before us, is evident, because then 'every one that names the Name of Christ,' or is baptized into his visible Church, would be a *new Creature*. Which is notoriously false, it being too plain, beyond all Contradiction, that comparatively but few of those that are '*born of Water*,' are '*born of the Spirit*' likewise; or, to use another Scripture Way of speaking, many are baptized with Water, which were never, effectually at least, baptized with the Holy Ghost.[2]

Time and again this sort of argument was used in the preaching and writing of the evangelicals of the period, but it is a mistake to assume (as some have done[3]) that baptismal regeneration was thereby being altogether repudiated. Echoing Wesley's own teaching, these preachers were clearing the ground for their claim that all adults (baptised or not) are unregenerate and need to be converted. They therefore maintained that *past* baptism does not mean a *present* state of salvation; and they insisted that (for adults) regeneration does not always accompany baptism. But they did not go beyond this and deny that *infants* are born again in baptism. Indeed, when they do refer specifically to infant baptism, we find a general belief in its efficacy. Not all used the term 're-

---

[1] Fletcher's *Works* (1800–9) viii. pp. 464 f. cf. *ibid.* p. 384.
[2] *The Christian's Companion* (1738), p. 9. For similar passages, v. *infra*; and Thomas Coke, *Commentary on the New Testament* for John iii. 5, 1 Pet. iii. 21.
[3] e.g. R. Mant, *An Appeal to the Gospel* ... (1812) 5th ed. 1813, pp. 348 ff (of Wesley and Whitefield); J. S. Simon, *The Revival of Religion in England in the Eighteenth Century*, pp. 154 f (of Whitefield).

generation' in connection with infant baptism, but it was almost universally held that some grace accompanies the administration of the ordinance; and the sacrament emerges, not just as the bare sign of re-birth that Edward Perronet wanted it to be, but as a means of grace used by God, in some measure, to justify and sanctify infants.

In what way then did the early evangelicals describe the benefits of infant baptism? A start to the answering of this question can be made with *The Christian World Unmasked*, in which John Berridge, Vicar of Everton, raised with himself this very point. In a dialogue between two men representing the Author and the Reader, Berridge first made the usual negative assertion about baptism.

Much people, who are strangers to the work of regeneration, suppose the new birth is only Christian baptism; and that every one is *born again*, who is baptized. . . . The nature of a baptized child, belonging to a churchman, is still as froward and as evil as the nature of an unbaptized child belonging to a Quaker: which shews that after water-baptism is received, a spiritual birth is wanting still, not merely to moralize the conduct, but to sanctify the heart and devote it to God.

The Reader is then made to ask our question:

Tell me, then, and tell me honestly, whether you mean to revile the church baptism by what you have said concerning it?

To which Berridge gives this answer:

No, Sir, not at all: I only meant to keep you from relying on baptismal water, without the Spirit's baptism. I have no doubt, that infant baptism is attended with the same blessing now, as infant circumcision was formerly. Both the ordinances are of God's appointment, and introductory rites into his visible church on earth. . . . And if Jewish children were received into the church's fold by circumcision, why not Christian children too by baptism? . . . No harm can possibly arise from baptizing an infant; but harm may arise from neglecting baptism. Such neglect may be considered as contempt: so it was considered formerly, and so it may now.[1]

Now this is by no means a warm and wholehearted apology for infant baptism, nor is the word 'regeneration' mentioned in this connexion, yet Berridge points to an understanding

---

[1] Berridge's *Works*, (1838), pp. 343 ff. cf. *ibid.* p. 457.

of baptism, in the light of circumcision, as giving admission into the new covenant. Thus he is indicating that thereby a relative work only is done—the infant, presumably, being forgiven, reconciled to God, and made a member of his Church and an heir of heaven.

This kind of vague covenantal sacramentalism is to be found elsewhere.[1] Howell Harris, the Welsh evangelist, wrote in his *Journal* in 1742:

Then they brought to me a child to be presented to the Lord. . . . I named her and took her in my arms, gave her to the Lord, and exhorted them that stood by that I did not do this by way of baptizing.[2] When Bro. Whitefield or some other minister came here, I thought it their duty to bring her to him to be baptized. I told them that from Abraham's time to the end of the world, 'tis my judgment believers' children (though the Baptism necessary to salvation is that of the Spirit) should be baptized on their parents' faith, because God declared so in His will, and because they'll bring them up in the nurture of the Lord.[3]

There were others who expressed this covenantal view of baptism more clearly and forcibly, making it plain that not only were the infants hereby granted the *relative* aspects of regeneration (reconciliation to God and admission into His covenant and Church) but also, in the bestowal of the Spirit, they were given a *real* benefit.

Two baptismal hymns can first be cited which illustrate this plainly. The first is by George Whitefield.

> *Thus did the Sons of Abr'ham pass*
> *Under the bloody Seal of Grace:*
> *The young Disciples bore the Yoke,*
> *'Till Christ the painful Bondage broke.*
>
> *By milder Ways doth Jesus prove*
> *His Father's Cov'nant and his Love!*
> *He seals to Saints his Glorious Grace*
> *And not forbids their Infant-Race.*

---

[1] e.g. Joseph Benson, *Sermons on Various Occasions* (1802), pp. 27 ff; *The Life of the Rev. Thomas Scott*, by J. Scott (1822), pp. 164 ff. v. Thomas Scott's *Commentary* (1788–1792) for John iii. 5, 1 Pet. iii. 21.   [2] Harris was not ordained.
[3] Cited by Tom Beynon, *Howell Harris, Reformer and Soldier (1714–1773)*, (1958), p. 27.

> *Their seed is sprinkled with his Blood,*
> *Their Children set apart for God;*
> *His Spirit on their Offspring shed,*
> *Like water poured upon the Head.*
>
> *Let every Saint with chearful Voice*
> *In this large Covenant rejoice,*
> *Young Children in their early Days,*
> *Shall give the God of Abr'ham Praise.*[1]

The other hymn is by one of Wesley's preachers, John Dolman, who served as a Local Preacher in Bristol for some years before leaving the Society to become an Independent Minister. His hymn reads:

> *Sing, Sheep of Jesus, for our LORD*
> *Is, as he promis'd, good;*
> *He loves t'accomplish all his Word,*
> *And seal it with his Blood.*
>
> *He said (and now we prove him true)*
> *Ye shall not be alone:*
> *The Spirit shall descend on you,*
> *And lo! the Thing is done.*
>
> *The Spirit brooding, spreads his Wings*
> *On dry and lifeless Bones;*
> *'Tis he the glorious Record brings,*
> *And seals them Abr'hams Sons.*[2]

This covenantal understanding of baptism (which is very much akin to that of the earlier Puritans and of their successors, the orthodox Independents and Presbyterians of the eighteenth century)[3] is found among Evangelical clergymen who stood much closer to the order of their Church than Whitefield and Wesley had done. Samuel Walker of Truro adduced these

---

[1] *A Collection of Hymns for Social Worship* by George Whitefield (10th ed. 1774), No. cxxv. cf. that for Adult Baptism (No. cxxiv) where the real aspect of regeneration is very much more strongly stressed. Whitefield did not like the use of the term 'regeneration' in association with infant baptism. v. his *Journal*, 1965 ed., pp. 252, 458 f; his *Works*, (1772), iv. pp. 162, 241.

[2] *Hymns and Spiritual Songs for the Travellers to Mount Zion* ... (1758). No. cliv. cf. No. clv. 'For the Baptism of infants.'

[3] cf. *supra*. pp. 15 f. v. Horton Davies, *Worship and Theology in England* ... *1690–1850*, pp. 104 ff.

four reasons for practising infant baptism: God's command for it; the children of professing Christians are federally a holy seed and are entitled to receive it; by this they are made members of the visible Church; and they make a profession of true faith by their proxies. Yet he is careful to state that although baptised infants are spoken of as 'true believers and regenerate persons', they are not 'actually' so but have only a 'charter-title' to these covenant privileges. The child should be taught to say that baptism is

God's seal of indenture, as it were, and obligation, whereby he conveys and makes over to me, in full right, all these blessings, engaging himself, by contract and covenant thus sealed and executed, to make them good to me. But I know also, that, if I do not this which (my sponsors) promised and vowed for me, and until I do it, these blessings are not mine; neither had my baptism at the time, simply of itself, force effectually to make and seal me (a) member of Christ, child of God, and inheritor of the kingdom of heaven. So then I see my having a real right to these things, and my being able to look upon them as mine, in virtue of my baptism conveying and sealing them to me, doth depend upon my believing and doing this which my godfathers and godmothers promised for me.[1]

Charles Simeon made this same distinction between the relative re-birth given sacramentally and the real regeneration of adult conversion. Preaching before the University of Cambridge, he said:

We must distinguish between a change of state and a change of nature. Baptism is a change of state: for by it we become entitled to all the blessings of the new covenant; but it is not a change of nature. A change of nature may be communicated at the time the ordinance is administered; but the ordinance itself does not communicate it.[2]

So far we have given examples of evangelicals from different backgrounds who regarded the benefits of infant baptism principally in terms of entry into the new covenant. There were others who, while not denying this insight, yet made less

---

[1] *Fifty-Two Sermons on the Baptismal Covenant, The Creed, The Ten Commandments* ... 1810 ed. i. pp. 7 ff, 15.
[2] H. C. G. Moule, *Charles Simeon* (1892), pp. 102 f; cf. W. H. B. Proby, *Annals of the 'Low-Church' Party* (1888), i. p. 218.

of it in their analysis of the sacrament, stressing most strongly the forgiveness of original sin as being the chief benefit of baptism. Of these, John Wesley wrote most fully and clearly, and we have seen that he considered baptism to convey, not only to the children of Christian parents but to all who receive it, the relative work of God[1] by which the child, born guilty of original sin, is brought into God's favour, admitted into the new covenant and the Church, made a child of God and an heir to the kingdom of heaven.[2]

There were others, however, who while agreeing with all that Wesley had to say about infant regeneration, yet went further. They used the term 'baptismal regeneration' to mean, as well as this relative atonement with God, a real work of sanctification begun in the infant. In baptism, they said, an effective power for good is implanted. Chief among those who held so high a regard for baptismal efficacy was Charles Wesley. A swift reading through of his baptismal hymns[3] shows at once that he accepted infant regeneration in this full sense. All the five benefits enumerated by his brother are present,[4] but in addition Charles gives far greater place to the bestowal of a real sanctifying power in the sacrament than his brother had done. Thus such lines appear as—

> *The seed of endless life impart.*
>
> *Jesus in our children dwell,*
> *Make their heart the house of God.*
>
> *To each the hallowing Spirit give*
> *Even from their infancy.*

Particularly explicit is one of Charles' verses on Mark i.10:

> *Where'er the pure baptismal rite*
> *Is duly ministered below,*
> *The heavens are open'd in our sight,*

---

[1] Wesley also referred to the real benefit of 'a principle of grace'—but attached little importance to this.

[2] Others who appear to have held similar views were—John Fletcher (*Works*, 1859-60, ii. p. 134); A. M. Toplady (*Works*, 1828, v. pp. 98 f); Charles Perronet and James Kershaw (v. *supra*. pp. 67 f).

[3] v. Appendix 2.

[4] Entry into the covenant is implicit but not specified.

> *And God His Spirit doth bestow,*
> *The grace infused invisible,*
> *Which would with man forever dwell.*[1]

John Wesley never spoke so highly of infant baptism, and this contrast confirms the impression formed by Franz Hildebrandt that Charles regarded baptism as more of an effective regenerative instrument than had John. Hildebrandt writes:

It seems—an impression which has yet to be verified—that Charles Wesley goes further than John in the direction away from the Calvinist *significat* towards the Lutheran *est*.[2]

One of the Methodist Itinerant Preachers who shared Charles Wesley's views (and something of his poetic gift) was John Murlin. The better of his two hymns[3] for infant baptism reads:

> *O Lord our humble pray'r attend,*
> *Thine everlasting arms extend,*
> *This infant to embrace:*
> *Which now we offer up to thee,*
> *O make, and keep him ever free*
> *From sin, and sav'd by grace.*
>
> *In mercy grant our hearts desire,*
> *Baptize him with thy holy fire,*
> *And circumcise his heart:*
> *And now adopt him for thy child,*
> *Through his Redeemer reconcil'd,*
> *This blessing now impart.*
>
> *The outward sign we now apply,*
> *But let the spirit sanctify,*
> *And seal him ever thine:*
> *Protect him by thy spirit's might,*
> *And let thy everlasting light*
> *Throughout his nature shine.*

---

[1] In this verse, Charles seems to identify the infused 'principle of grace' (about which John was so vague) as the gift of the Spirit.

[2] *From Luther to Wesley*, p. 68.

[3] *Sacred Hymns on Various Subjects*, 3rd ed., 1788, No. xcix. cf. No. xlii.

And when his pilgrimage shall end,
Then let the sinners only Friend,
Who bought him with his blood;
His happy soul from earth remove,
To join the Choristers above,
To praise the Triune God.

Vincent Perronet was an Anglican clergyman whose sympathies were almost entirely Methodist and who held this same high doctrine. He wrote three books about baptism, and in one of them[1] he presents a dialogue between Philalethes and Eugenius, in which they consider regeneration.

E. I should be glad to be informed, whether our Church calls any thing by the Name of *Regeneration*, or the *New Birth*, excepting *Baptism:* because this is a Point which is sometimes disputed.

P. You will soon be able to judge of such Disputations.

Philalethes goes on to give quotations from the Homilies, *Book of Common Prayer*, and the Bible which show that regeneration is in those places described as an adult change of mind and heart; and continues—

whoever is thus *altered* and *changed*, and, as it were, *new created* by the Spirit of God, though many years *after* his *Baptism*, is surely as much *born of the Spirit*, as the Person who is *regenerated* at the time he is *Baptized*. It is evidently *one* and the *same Spirit* that works; and indeed the *same work* of *that Spirit;* only manifesting his divine Power at different Seasons.

E. .... I find they are evidently mistaken, who suppose our Church calls nothing by the name of *Regeneration*, or *New Birth*, but only *Baptism*.

Vincent Perronet, therefore, for all his loyalty to the Methodist gospel, took it as self-evident that infants are regenerated in baptism in this full and complete sense.

So also did John Cennick. Cennick was one of the first of the laymen in Wesley's Society to preach, but he became

---

[1] *Some Reflections by Way of Dialogue, on the Nature of Original Sin, Baptismal Regeneration, Repentance, The New Birth* ... (6th ed. 1776), pp. 12–16. cf. *A Defence of Infant-Baptism, (In Answer to the Objections of the late learned Mr. Gale.) In a Letter to the Rev. Mr. John Wesley* (1749). p. 63; and *An Affectionate Address to the People called Quakers; with regard to Water-Baptism,* ... *Wherein the Arguments of the late learned Mr. Robert Barclay, are Considered* (1747), p. 22.

Calvinistic in his theology, and after serving Lady Huntingdon finally joined the Moravians. His sacramental outlook is revealed in a sermon preached in Ireland in 1752 and published posthumously in 1786. We note that Cennick, like many of the evangelicals, makes the efficacy of the sacrament conditional upon the faith of the parents.

It would be sinful to ask, What benefit can a newborn babe receive who neither hears nor understands the gospel, nor has a will or power either to believe or disbelieve the doctrine of Christ? For this would be really to think like the disciples, who therefore forbad the people to bring their children to Christ, and for which Jesus was displeased. ... The question therefore must not be, if the infants are able to receive grace and the Holy Spirit. For this is a true doctrine, and clear and confirmed in the scriptures; and if Jesus saw their faith who let down the paralytic through the roof before him, and forgave the man, made him his son, and healed him, he can see their faith now who bring their children to be washed by him, and do the same generous acts, as he certainly does, and will by no means disappoint those who have believed in him. ... This doctrine then of the baptism of Christ is weighty when administered in faith, and brings with it the seal and sign of the regeneration of the Holy Ghost.[1]

Reference could be made to further evangelical writers who held this same full-blooded belief in baptismal efficacy;[2] and much could be made of the fact that both the English Moravians as well as the Countess of Huntingdon's preachers (and later her Connexion), while being committed most strenuously to the gospel of regeneration by faith alone, were content to use the baptismal offices in the *Book of Common Prayer* in their worship[3]—with all their apparent implication of both a relative and real regeneration given with the sacramental water. But enough has been said to show that far from it being typical of eighteenth century evangelicalism to renounce baptismal regeneration in favour of adult conversion, both regenerations were upheld. It was commonplace for

[1] *The First Principles of Christianity* (1786), pp. 21–4.
[2] e.g. L. E. Elliott-Binns, *The Early Evangelicals: A Religious and Social Study*, pp. 315, 393 f.
[3] For the Moravians, v. Tyerman, *Oxford Methodists*, pp. 178 f, 180, 182, 195 (Gambold); 126 f (Ingham). For Lady Huntingdon's Connexion. v. Peaston, *The Prayer Book Tradition in the Free Churches*, pp. 67 ff; Horton Davies, *op. cit.* pp. 212 f.

baptism to be rejected as an alternative to conversion, but this in itself did not constitute a repudiation of baptismal efficacy. There were, it is true, a few who regarded baptism simply as an empty sign of regeneration, but those who maintained this most emphatically were sometimes basically unorthodox in their doctrines, and not one thoroughly representative evangelical has been found who clearly and unambiguously denied that there is any regenerative accompaniment whatsoever to infant baptism.

Almost to a man the evangelicals—Anglican, Methodist, Whitefieldian, Moravian, and those led by Lady Huntingdon—accepted that regeneration in some sense accompanies infant baptism. Many (in the manner of the Puritans) considered this to be primarily a work of reconciliation to God by admission into the new covenant (some saying with, and others without, the infusion of the Spirit); others, in the Anglican tradition represented by Samuel Wesley, regarded the chief benefit of infant baptism as being the forgiveness of original sin (with consequent atonement with God), and here again some thought that a real benefit is bestowed as well as this relative reconciliation. There were, in fact, many shades of meaning, and in some cases it is hard to determine from short or oblique references to baptism how precisely the author understood it. Yet the overwhelming impression is gained that, considered as a whole, the evangelicals of the eighteenth century, for all their stress upon the universal necessity of adult conversion, believed that regeneration is also given in infant baptism.

This conclusion is of some importance. In the first place, we will see (in the chapter that follows) how it is helpful in interpreting Wesley's emendations to the baptismal orders of the *Book of Common Prayer*. But it is valuable also because it indicates that the weaknesses traced in Wesley's devotional doctrine were characteristic of early evangelicalism generally: and here we have the origins of those clashes over baptismal regeneration which shook the Church of England so violently in the nineteenth century.

The first evangelicals did not disbelieve in baptismal regeneration—it has been shown that they accepted this doctrine in one or another of the forms in which it was understood in the Church of their day. What they did was to graft their new doctrine of conversion on to the existing stock of Anglican thought and practice, claiming that each person should be re-born twice, first in baptism and again by conversion. But (as we have seen in the case of Wesley) the grafting was clumsily done, and the resulting devotional system, therefore, was not wholly satisfactory. The unjustifiable assumption was made that spiritual growth should normally follow the pattern of baptismal re-birth, followed by apostasy, and then conversion: the second regeneration (and adult piety generally) was detached from baptism in an unwarrantable manner: and so much stress was laid upon conversion, that baptism was usually only summarily mentioned by evangelical writers,[1] whose chief concern even then was, very often, to exhort people *not* to trust in their baptism for present salvation.

Thus we can see that the disputes between High and Low Churchmen in the nineteenth century had their rise not in the denial of baptismal regeneration by the early evangelicals, but in their insistence upon the necessity for two regenerations: and the conflict must inevitably begin as soon as men of another persuasion protested that regeneration is normally given once only, and then solely in association with the administration of baptism.

---

[1] This criticism is constantly made by W. H. B. Proby, as he reviews the writings of the Evangelicals. v. *Annals of the 'Low-Church' Party in England* (1888), i. pp. 109, 122, 127, 152, 161 f, etc.

CHAPTER II

Baptismal Regeneration and the 'Sunday Service of the Methodists'

One commonly held opinion is that in his last years Wesley came to disbelieve in infant baptismal regeneration; that however plainly he may have stated it in his early and middle life, in his maturity he denied this form of sacramentalism. The implication is that Wesley at last saw infant regeneration to be contrary to Scripture and a contradiction of the evangelical assertion of the need for faith before re-birth can be received, so that, not long before his death, he threw off this Anglican-forged, ritualistic fetter, and finally achieved his evangelical freedom.

This is to be seen (it has been argued) when in 1784 and later, in 1786 he was preparing service books for use by Methodists overseas. Since he was writing for new Churches in new lands, it is suggested that he no longer felt under any obligation to conceal his true convictions out of loyalty to his own Church, and that he freely expressed his baptismal views by striking out of the *Book of Common Prayer* material which implies that regeneration accompanies the administration of the sacrament.

That Wesley at last thus changed his mind about the efficacy of infant baptism was first given wide currency by J. H. Rigg. Writing in 1878,[1] he said of the alterations to the Article 'Of Baptism'—

This article proves, at all events, that Wesley had in 1784 concluded not to insist on the doctrine of baptismal regeneration in any sense.

Others[2] have stated this conclusion even more categorically; but perhaps the most authoritative source is the editorial note

[1] *The Churchmanship of John Wesley*, pp. 42 ff.   [2] v. *supra*. p. 9 n.

by E. H. Sugden in his *Standard Sermons of John Wesley* (1921):[1] it may fairly be argued that Wesley's revision of the service in 1784 proves that in his later life he altered his earlier opinion.

Since in no place other than the *Sunday Service* is there any indication whatsoever that Wesley repudiated his belief in baptismal regeneration, we must now pause to consider this vital piece of evidence. The matter is not altogether straightforward.

In the first place, two variants of the one 1784 edition have emerged—Versions A and B—in which, in the Order for infant baptism, signation after baptism is retained in the first version but omitted from the other.[2] As this feature of the service has no implications for baptismal re-birth it need not concern us further here.[3] In the second place, there has been much discussion as to the authorship of these earliest editions and those of 1786[4] in view of the differences between them.

There is no need to enter fully into the details of this discussion,[5] but the main points are as follows.

In a covering letter written in 1784 to introduce Thomas Coke (and two companions) to the American Methodists, Wesley said:

I have prepared a Liturgy little differing from that of the Church of England ... which I advise all the travelling preachers to use on the Lord's Day in all congregations.[6]

No one has cast any serious doubts upon Wesley's own statement that he himself prepared the 1784 edition of the *Sunday Service* which Coke took to America; but he later entrusted to Coke the printing of the 1786 edition,[7] and at some point—

---

[1] i. p. 282.

[2] This chapter should be read in conjunction with the analysis and notes in Appendix 4.

[3] v. *infra*. p. 182 n.

[4] Three editions were published in 1786, appearing under different titles and exhibiting some small variations in content, yet with the same orders for baptism. v. W.H.S. xxix. pp. 14 f.

[5] v. W.H.S. xxvii. pp. 32 ff; xxix. pp. 12 ff; xxxii. pp. 97 ff.

[6] *Letters*, vii. p. 239.

[7] v. J. Vickers, *Thomas Coke Apostle of Methodism* (1969), p. 88 n. The letter reads: 'Mr. *Wesley* is going soon to print a new Edition of our *American* Prayer-Book, at the printing of which it is indispensably necessary I should be present.'

either by interference with Wesley's 1784 version on the voyage, or by unauthorized modifications in 1786—it appears that Coke made some changes on his own account, for, writing in 1789 (and without specifying the edition to which he was referring) Wesley said:

> Dr. Coke made two or three little alterations in the Prayer-Book without my knowledge. I took particular care throughout to alter nothing merely for altering's sake. In religion I am for as few innovations as possible. I love the old wine best, And if it were only on this account, I prefer *'which'* before *'who* art in heaven.'[1]

We are left in some doubt as to when Coke made these emendations and what they were, but since Wesley says that they were few in number and 'little alterations' (evidently of the very minor kind indicated in the Lord's prayer), we must assume that the more general and important changes in both editions, relating to baptismal regeneration, were made by Wesley himself; and the 1786 version, known indeed as 'Mr. Wesley's Abridgement', was reprinted in following years[2] and became in 1795, with the *Book of Common Prayer*, the standard service book of British Methodism.

Having established with what certainty is possible their authorship, we turn now to the orders of baptism in the *Sunday Service*:[3] and we look first at those for the baptism of infants. A careful examination of the two versions reveals that while both agree in making baptism a sign of regeneration, the 1784 edition clearly suggests also that re-birth is given with the sacrament. This implication has been removed by careful emendation from the later version. Our contention is, therefore, that since Wesley prepared both of these services he himself progressively removed those prayers, sentences and phrases which imply infant baptismal regeneration. Why, then, did he do so?

Various reasons have been adduced. Some commentators, as we have seen, have argued that he did so because he no longer believed in this doctrine and therefore wished to exclude it.[4] Others suggest that the changes were made in

---

[1] *Letters*, viii. pp. 144 f.
[2] For a list of editions, v. W.H.S. xxix. pp. 14 f.   [3] v. *infra*, pp. 178 ff.
[4] Although this argument should be concerned with the 1786 edition, not that of 1784.

response to the strong objections of Methodists (particularly in America) who disliked the notion of infant regeneration, and who swayed Wesley because he himself, if not disabused of this belief, had come to regard it as unimportant.[1] Others again have argued that the changes were made simply in the process of abbreviation, so that no underlying theological motive should be read into them at all.[2]

Yet closer examination suggests that none of these explanations is wholly satisfactory. Of the three, the second can be dismissed immediately. There is no evidence at all to suggest either that the American or the British Methodists clamoured for the expunging of baptismal regeneration from their baptismal office, or even that they disapproved of this doctrine. Indeed, our study of the evangelical attitude to this ordinance at this time shows that the majority of them believed in it in some form. We cannot accept, therefore, that it was the tide of Methodist opinion which swept infant regeneration out of these services.

By a similar argument we can dismiss the first explanation also. Had Wesley definitely changed his mind about infant re-birth he would have been an innovator among the early evangelicals and, if so, he would surely have made some comment elsewhere about his new opinion and have done something to retract or amend the published statements of his former attitude; but no indication of any such kind can be found. On the evidence of the *Sunday Service* alone it is hard to be convinced that Wesley had clearly and decidedly swung round to a denial of infant regeneration.

But if the first two explanations can be rejected as placing too great a significance upon these changes, the third, surely, must be dismissed for treating them too casually. Whole prayers might well have been erased from the *Book of Common Prayer* to shorten the office, but in this instance we are concerned with certain phrases which have been deleted, obviously not because of their inordinate length but owing to their doctrinal implications. Thus, since none of the above seems

[1] cf. *supra*, pp. 117 f. v. W.H.S. xxix. p. 15; H.M.C. pp. 160 f, 268 f.
[2] F. Hildebrandt, *From Luther to Wesley*, pp. 67 f; T. Dearing, *Wesleyan and Tractarian Worship*, p. 113. v. also the view of B. J. N. Galliers, W.H.S. xxxii. p. 124.

adequate, some other explanation must be found to account for these changes, and perhaps this is provided by a fourth theory which is now put forward.

We have noticed that in the main the evangelicals, while still believing in infant re-birth, did not very often make positive statements of this doctrine. Their most characteristic reference to it was negative—i.e. to insist that regeneration in baptism must not be allowed to stand as a substitute for adult conversion. This theme Wesley frequently returned to in his own preaching. The present suggestion is that, in effect, it is this same point that he was reiterating as he prepared the *Sunday Service*.

Wesley had long known that some people trusted in baptismal regeneration too completely. Confident in their regeneration as infants, they could not, or would not, accept that they were in need of a second re-birth as adults. Here was a hindrance to the effective preaching of conversion, and it was this obstacle that Wesley was concerned to remove. By making these significant erasures he was not denying baptismal regeneration, but he was softening its statement in the baptismal orders—being particularly careful to remove the ambiguous word 'regeneration' from this context—so that people should not be able to find here an excuse for ignoring his call for their conversion. Wesley did not exclude baptismal regeneration, as has been suggested, because the converted had come to distrust it, but because the unconverted trusted in it too greatly.[1]

It may seem that, if this was so, Wesley was unwarrantably casual in his treatment of the baptismal Order; but it must be remembered that it was not until some years after his death that the whole issue of the compatibility of baptismal regeneration with evangelical principles was to be raised, and therefore, in dealing with the passages in the *Book of Common Prayer* relating to this doctrine, Wesley would not have been conscious that here were phrases to be handled with special care and delicacy. It would be very different when the Methodist liturgy was next officially revised almost a hundred years later; but at the time it is understandable that Wesley should have

---

[1] This explanation agrees in part with that given by A. Barrett, *Catholic and Evangelical Principles*, pp. 124 f, cit. *supra*, pp. 5 f.

been, to our mind, a little unguarded when making his abridgement.

Yet of deeper significance than any incaution on Wesley's part is the fact that his willingness to remove regeneration from this Service was a result of the inadequacy noted in his doctrine. He had taught that infant regeneration has no bearing upon later adult re-birth, and it was this insistence which made it easy for him to remove regeneration from his baptismal Order. Wesley would surely have retained it had he allowed that infant regeneration has some helpful consequences for adult religious life generally: but he did not. He would certainly not have erased it had he thought that, on being reminded of their past baptismal re-birth, adults would be stirred to seek conversion or encouraged to further devotional seriousness: but he did not. On the contrary, he had found that some people were confirmed in their sinfulness by hearing of their baptismal re-birth, and so—with his mind intent upon the reaction of adult congregations and not upon making a clear statement of his belief in the baptismal grace given to infants—Wesley removed baptismal regeneration from this Order.

Furthermore, it is possible that these erasures are indicative of a shift in emphasis in Wesley's teaching. We have already seen how, in his preaching, Wesley had found it necessary to explain repeatedly that regeneration in baptism has not made adult regeneration superfluous. The reason for this was that people were bewildered by his double use of the term, and needed to be reassured that a second re-birth was really necessary for those who had been baptised and brought up as Christians. Yet in spite of this resultant confusion, and in the face of constant criticism,[1] he was content for many years to persevere with this two-fold use of the word, and he published his *Thoughts* and *Treatise* partly in order to stress the importance of baptismal regeneration.

These changes in the *Sunday Service*, however, suggest that, at last, Wesley had begun to realize that his terminology might never be generally accepted. Determined, therefore, to be unambiguously clear about the more important of the two regenerations—that of adults—he was willing now to be more

[1] v. *supra*, pp. 78 f.

reticent about regeneration in baptism: and so the term was let slip progressively and quietly out of this Service.[1]

We may contrast Wesley's attitude with that of some evangelicals in the following century. Under pressure from the Tractarian claim that a person is regenerated only in baptism, it was to become a matter of principle with many of them to denounce this doctrine as unscriptural and incredible. The early evangelicals might sometimes have allowed belief in baptismal regeneration to wither by neglect: but some of their successors would not be content until they had killed it by argument.

When we turn to the *Sunday Service* Order for adult baptism, we are faced with a straightforward situation. The apparent implication of the *Book of Common Prayer* Order for adult baptism is that regeneration is given with the sacrament, and this impression (in spite of certain modifications[2]) is clearly conveyed by Wesley's 1784 *Sunday Service* Order, which is essentially an abbreviated version of the office in the Prayer Book.

However, we find that the remaining statements implying adult baptismal regeneration are removed from the 1786 version of the *Sunday Service*, so that adult baptism now stands in relation to regeneration purely as its sign. The reason for these changes must have been that Wesley was progressively bringing his office into line with his belief that adult regeneration is conversion—and that conversion is not in any special sense a baptismal gift (although it may sometimes be received at the moment of baptism.)[3] In other words, Wesley did not believe in the baptismal regeneration of adults, and therefore, in preparing his liturgy, he altered the *Book of Common Prayer* service for adult baptism accordingly.

As a result of this study of the *Sunday Service* we have come to the following conclusions. In spite of the uncertainty induced by Wesley's revisions of the *Book of Common Prayer* in his late years, we find that he did not veer from those opinions about infant and adult baptism which he had formed in his earlier

---

[1] This accounts partly, but not wholly, for the differences between the 1784 and 1786 editions. These may have been due also to the speed with which (it is agreed) Wesley worked in 1784 (W.H.S. xxxii. p. 100), so that two years later he thought it wise to improve upon his first over-hasty handiwork.

[2] v. *infra*, p. 224 ff.   [3] v. *supra*, chap. 5.

ministry, viz. that baptism is in both instances a sign of regeneration, but that infant and adult baptism are related very differently to that re-birth which they signify. Infant baptism is unconditionally and invariably accompanied by infant regeneration—that is, Wesley believed still in infant baptismal regeneration. But he did not believe in the baptismal regeneration of adults, and so he removed this implication from his adult order.

Further, we have suggested that Wesley removed the suggestion of baptismal regeneration from the *Sunday Service* Orders for infant baptism not because it conflicted with his evangelical convictions but out of reticence, since it was a hindrance rather than a help to him in his efforts to convince people of their need of conversion.

We have now completed our study of Wesley's baptismal beliefs, and it may be useful at this point to set these down in a summary form.[1]

Wesley believed INFANT BAPTISM to be:

1. A sign of regeneration.
2. The ordinary and unconditional means of infant regeneration, although not a necessary means since infants dying unbaptised have the merits of Christ's death applied to them, and are saved.
3. The ceremony admitting into membership of the Church.
4. The dedication of the child to God by the parents,[2] assisted by sponsors.
5. An occasion of prayer for the future godliness of the infant.

Similarly he considered ADULT BAPTISM to be:

1. A sign of regeneration.
2. A conditional means of grace in general (including adult regeneration); but not a necessary means, since conversion and the other gifts which may be received in baptism can be (and in most cases are) bestowed non-sacramentally in response to faith. Nevertheless, Wesley found adult baptism to be a useful and effective converting and sanctifying ordinance.

---

[1] Reference should also be made to the notes relating to the *Sunday Service* Orders, *infra*, pp. 181 f, 186 f.
[2] v. *Works*, x. pp. 195, 201.

3. The ceremony admitting into membership of the Church.
4. An act of self-dedication to God by public confession of faith.
5. An occasion of prayer for the future godliness of the candidate.

Without doubt we have here a regard for baptism, both infant and adult, of the highest order. It remains now to be seen whether Wesley was able to convey his own strong convictions and high esteem to the Methodists who came after him, and to this we turn in the final chapter.

CHAPTER 12

Wesley and the Methodist Baptismal Tradition

John Wesley died on 2 March 1791, and accompanied by widespread mourning he was laid to rest behind his London Chapel in the City Road. The long course of the venerable father of Methodism had been run to its triumphant end. But while there was much for his preachers and people to remember with thanksgiving, there were also many urgent matters to be resolved for the future.

With the death of Wesley, Methodism lost not only her father but also her mother—for with his passing the strongest bond which had tied the Societies to the Church of England was severed. Methodism now passed out of the hands of an Anglican presbyter into the keeping of the Legal Hundred, almost all of whom were lay preachers with little loyalty to the Established Church.

Successive Conferences met to shape the future of the Movement, and for four years came to no conclusive decisions. In 1792, in despair, sortilege was resorted to. But finally, in 1795, a Plan of Pacification was agreed upon, and the foundations were laid upon which the Methodist Church as we know it today was to be built.

One of the foremost difficulties to be resolved centred upon the administration of the Lord's supper by the preachers, and the pith of the settlement is contained in these words:

Q.30: What direction shall be given concerning the administration of the Lord's Supper?
A: The Lord's Supper shall be administered by the superintendent only, or such of his helpers as are in full connexion, as he shall appoint, provided no preacher be required to give it against his approbation; and should it be granted in any place, where the preachers on the circuit are all unwilling to give it, the superintendent

shall in that case invite a neighbouring preacher, who is properly qualified, to administer it.[1]

By article ten of the Plan, the 1792 edition of the *Sunday Service*[2] was authorized (along with the *Book of Common Prayer*) to be used within British Methodism. Eagerly the Societies 'petitioned for the Lord's Supper', and very quickly the preachers began to administer it to them, within the limits imposed by article seven: i.e. that the administration of the sacraments 'is intended only for members of our own Society'.

T. H. Barrett has shown how grave damage was caused to the Methodist sacramental tradition by these four years of hesitation. From 1791 to 1795 general permission for the preachers to administer the Lord's supper was withheld, and for a year following the 1792 Conference it was forbidden for anyone (with or without either Anglican or Wesley's ordination) to give Communion in the preaching houses.

Those four years of prohibition followed by the restrictions of 1795 created a tradition which went far to annul the teaching and example of John Wesley and sowed seeds of which we reap the harvest even to this day.[3]

Yet if Methodists in some measure lost their regard for the one sacrament during this period, their attitude to the other was not similarly affected. The early baptismal registers show that during these indecisive years the preachers continued to baptise as freely as they had done prior to Wesley's death: and, in any case, it was still possible (and usual) to go to the parish churches for this ordinance. Thus since baptism was at no time withheld from the Methodist people there was no question here of any sacramental antipathy developing, and the practice of baptism passed on uninterrupted into the nineteenth century.

Yet how satisfactory was the understanding of baptism that Wesley left to his spiritual children? How successful was he in

---

[1] Cit. J. C. Bowmer, *The Sacrament of the Lord's Supper in Early Methodism*, pp. 20 f.
[2] The baptismal orders being the same as those in the 1786 editions.
[3] L.Q.R. January 1923; cit. J. C. Bowmer, *op. cit.* p. 22.

passing on the riches of his own sacramental thought to later Methodism?[1]

In one small matter he did give a clear lead. By inserting in the appropriate rubric in both of the *Sunday Service* Orders that dipping, pouring, or sprinkling may be used indifferently in the performance of baptism,[2] Wesley took a liturgical step which, while not at all adventurous or revolutionary, at least gave expression to accepted practice, and this lead was followed in all subsequent Methodist Orders for baptism.[3]

But in general Wesley's alterations did not give such explicit guidance as this. His emendations to the *Book of Common Prayer* were so tentative that his convictions and intentions were not made plain to those who in due course looked to him for direction in baptismal matters.

In regard to adult baptism, there were two points where Wesley's irresolution paved the way for later Methodist indecisiveness. First, the relationship between adult baptism and Church membership was left unsettled. By ignoring confirmation, and by the apparent purpose of the *Sunday Service* Order, Wesley indicated that he considered adults to be made communicant members of the Church by baptism: and yet this conviction was so indefinitely conveyed to later Methodists that before long they had decreed that membership be conferred by the Minister at the quarterly visitation of the Classes,[4] and later still, that this be signified by a Service for the Public Recognition of New Members. Thus it is clear that Wesley had not spelled out his intentions plainly enough.[5]

This position continued unchanged until 1967, when

---

[1] For a survey of baptism in later Methodism, v. *The Church Quarterly*, July 1969, pp. 43 ff. B. G. Holland, 'The Background to the 1967 Methodist Service for Infant Baptism.'

[2] v. *infra*, pp. 180, 185. Note the intermediate position of the 1784 rubric.

[3] Wesley also removed the Signation from the *Sunday Service* Orders for Infant Baptism of 1784 (B version) and 1786, and from both the 1784 and 1786 Services for Adult Baptism. (v. *infra*, pp. 180, 185). This has been replaced in the 1967 Order for Infant Baptism only.

[4] v. H. W. Williams, *The Constitution and Polity of Wesleyan Methodism* (1880), pp. 8, 259 f.

[5] Since in Britain the Methodists still belonged to a Society attached to the Anglican Church, Wesley had no reason to consider any membership other than that of the Society. But his *Sunday Service* was prepared in the first place for the independent Methodist Church he was establishing in America, so that he should have indicated clearly how baptism and Church membership were to be related.

Conference approved new Orders (subject to revision) under the title, *Baptism and Confirmation (or Recognition) Services*. Here it is clearly set down[1] that adult baptism should normally accompany confirmation, so that the sacrament at last is given in Methodism its traditional function of admitting the candidate into membership of the Church.

Secondly, the association between adult baptism and adult regeneration was not stated with sufficient clarity. Wesley did not believe in adult baptismal regeneration, but he did know that adult baptism can be a means of grace. He found that people were sometimes born again in the moment of baptism, and he had seen that other spiritual refreshments and assurances were commonly received in the use of this sacrament. However, there is no hint of this in the *Sunday Service* Order; and in the nineteenth century, adult baptism, far from being grasped as an evangelical opportunity, was only too often regarded as a somewhat embarrassing formality, necessitated by an annoying parental omission in childhood, to be administered (if at all) as a technical requirement prior to admission into Church membership.

Once more, it is only in the 1967 Order that changes have been made which coincide with Wesley's understanding of baptism. The inclusion of Charles Wesley's hymn ('Come, Father, Son and Holy Ghost'), and the address to the candidates,[2] show that here is an attempt to enliven the administration of adult baptism with that spirit of expectancy with which the Wesleys approached such occasions, looking for God to 'witness with the water now'.

When we turn to infant baptism, we find three points at which there was similar uncertainty. In the first place, Wesley gave no clear lead as to the function of sponsors. He had urged his people to undertake this task as a useful and important duty, but he disliked the responses which the *Book of Common Prayer* prescribes for the godparents. In the *Sunday Service* therefore the responses are removed along with such traditional terms as 'sponsor', 'surety', and 'godparents': and the 'friends of the child' appear instead.[3] Yet apart from the naming of the infant at the moment of christening, no duties are suggested for these friends, nor is it made clear whether

---

[1] pp. 22 ff.   [2] pp. 25 f, 27   [3] v. *infra*, p. 180.

parents can act in this capacity. Here then was an office renamed by Wesley but left by him ill-defined as to its functions.

The reaction of Methodism in the nineteenth and twentieth centuries has been to ignore sponsors, and to stress the importance of the place of parents at the baptism of their children and in their consequent upbringing. Once again it has been the 1967 Services which have reminded Methodism of Wesley's intentions. It is now suggested that sponsors as well as parents may have a valuable part to play, at least in some cases, in the baptism and future Christian training both of infants and adults.[1]

Secondly, Wesley gave no clear indication of how he considered that infant baptism should be related to Church membership. Since he had consistently ignored confirmation, and omitted it from the *Sunday Service* without providing any alternative, it might appear that he intended baptism to comprise the complete act of admission into the Church; and his Order for infant baptism reads as though this is indeed its main function. But, plainly, Wesley did not intend to give this impression. He did not believe that the communion table should be open to everyone who had been baptised, without regard to their Christian seriousness;[2] he had not accepted that the mere fact of baptism should be the one necessary and sufficient condition of membership of his Society—and therefore we cannot believe that he would have wished his successors to regard infant baptism so highly that they would make this the one entrance-gate into the Church which they were to construct after his death.

On the other hand, Wesley clearly believed that infants do have some place in the Church, given them by virtue of their baptism, if only for the duration of their childhood. What this place was, how this juvenile membership should be related to adult membership, and upon what conditions and by what ceremony adults (formerly baptised as infants) should be admitted into the Church—all of these matters Wesley left undecided, and, once more, Methodists in later years would have to arrive at solutions to these problems for themselves.

[1] pp. 2, 22.
[2] v. J. C. Bowmer, *The Sacrament of the Lord's Supper in Early Methodism*, pp. 110 ff.

Meanwhile it is significant that a *Careful Observer*, writing in 1804, should say:

The children of the Methodists making no part of the Methodist body, is a great defect in the religious economy of that people, and the grand cause why so few of them are truly pious.[1]

Around the turn of the last century it was realized that here was indeed a serious deficiency in Methodist churchmanship, and the Wesleyan Conference appointed committees to consider the membership of baptised children—but no conclusions could then be reached. The position was, in effect, that children were not regarded as members of the Church in any real sense until their admission as adults. However, Conference statements issued in 1936, 1952 and 1961[2] have clarified this situation, and the 1967 Baptism and Confirmation Services have made it clear[3] that infant baptism and confirmation (or reception) are two integrated stages by which membership is given, at first in an 'incomplete' form, and then fully.

The third deficiency in Wesley's teaching about infant baptism was that he seemed to speak equivocally about infant baptismal regeneration. On the one hand, he had stated in the 1760s a clear doctrine of what is essentially a relative re-birth so given; but, on the other hand, in his preaching he had so constantly warned sinners against any reliance upon past baptism, and he had made such emendations in preparing the *Sunday Service*, as to give the impression that he disregarded infant baptismal regeneration altogether.

We have explained this apparent contradiction by eliciting Wesley's belief in two separate and successive re-births, and by suggesting a reason to account for his later reticence about the benefits of infant baptism: but to the Wesleyans of the following century he seemed to have been in two minds about this matter, and so there grew up the 'riddle' of Wesley's baptismal beliefs.

This lack of clarity had, however, a more important consequence for Methodism. This was most clearly seen in the years

---

[1] *Strictures on Methodism*, by a Careful Observer, cit. *Wesleyan-Methodist Magazine*, 1879, p. 259.
[2] *Memorandum on Infant Baptism* (1936); *Statement on Holy Baptism* (1952); and *Report on Church Membership* (1961). These all stress the duty of the local Church in caring for and training the baptised children. [3] pp. 12, 17 f.

before 1882, when, in Wesleyan Methodism, there were wide discussions about the nature of the grace bestowed in infant baptism. Those who argued in favour of a strong, positive doctrine were unable to point to Wesley's explicit teaching in support of their case: and so the way was open for Conference to approve an Order which made infant baptism little more than a service of naming and dedication.[1] Wesley's ambiguity was thus a factor of some importance in the process by which this sacrament came to be devalued in Methodism.

It is encouraging to find that since 1936 more attention has been paid to the importance of infant baptism. In various respects the value of the ceremony itself, both as a symbol and as a means of grace, has been emphasized,[2] and some writers have even gone so far as to speak of baptismal regeneration—so that something of Wesley's own positive doctrine has reappeared in Methodism, although refined by the fires of the debates between Evangelicals and Tractarians in the last century.

In all these matters, therefore, Wesley's failure to state his beliefs clearly has introduced uncertainty and weakness into the Methodist baptismal tradition, and there can be no doubt that this situation was due in a large measure to the incomplete nature of his revision of the *Book of Common Prayer*. By erasure, he made modifications to the Anglican Services of baptism at several points—particularly regarding sponsors, Church membership, and the use of adult baptism as a means of grace—but he was either unwilling or unready to go further and compose Orders which incorporated fully all his positive convictions about this sacrament. Had he done so, the Services of baptism subsequently issued by Conference might have been more adequate and purposeful, and the administration of the ordinance would have been more meaningful than it has been in Methodism over the years since Wesley's death.

But the weakness in Wesley's teaching which had the most profound adverse consequences for later Methodism has yet to be stressed.

We have seen how the Methodist baptismal tradition was

---

[1] The weak character of this Service is shared by the Order issued in 1936, following Methodist Union.

[2] For a survey, v. *The Church Quarterly*, July 1969, pp. 50 ff.

weakened by a failure to inherit Wesley's *positive* beliefs, but it is apparent, further, that Methodism was even more greatly impoverished by its ready acceptance of his *negative* insistence that infant baptism has no continuing relevance to adult piety.

We have discussed this flaw in Wesley's theology, and shown how it resulted from his belief that two separate regenerations are needed in each life; and we have indicated how this tenet, shared as it was by the evangelicals generally, prepared the way for the baptismal debates of the nineteenth century: but our concern now is with its effects upon Methodism—and the fact is that this fault in Wesley's teaching impoverished the Denomination devotionally and sacramentally for many generations, and the unhappy consequences of it have not even yet been eradicated.

This weakness can be seen, in part, in the nonchalant attitude towards infant baptism which his followers learned from Wesley. Whatever the benefits conferred at the time of the ceremony might be, Wesley taught that these were subsequently lost at an early age, so that the child becomes an unredeemed sinner. In this predicament Wesley focused attention on those means of grace which God could still use to convince and convert, while infant baptism (which he considered to offer no help) was inevitably ignored. Thus the tendency was for this sacrament to be very largely neglected in the thinking of a Church which emphasized so greatly the need for conversion.

Worse still, Wesley's negative insistence encouraged Methodists to adopt a dogmatic and harmful attitude towards the Christian upbringing of their children.

If the assumption is made that, irrespective of baptism or of any signs of childhood faith, every child must be converted, then conscientious parents will necessarily be concerned to prepare their children for this experience. They will lay the greater stress upon the child's sinfulness rather than upon the attempt to ensure that the youngster grows up in a piety initiated at baptism and uninterruptedly fostered by the prayers and training of home and church.

As a result of Wesley's teaching, this assumption was generally made within Methodism, and in consequence the prevalent attitude towards children was to treat them as sinners and religious outcasts. The harm done in many cases must have been considerable.

It was only during the second half of the nineteenth century that protests began to be made about this perfunctory regard for baptism with its allied condemnatory attitude towards children. Writing in 1874 of his own Methodist upbringing, Henry Arthur Smith, for example, made the position clear:

> During all the years in which the foundations of his future manhood were being laid, it was tacitly assumed that a certain amount of progress in iniquity was necessary, and must be looked for as an inevitable preliminary to the conversion of character for which all responsible guardians, as pious people, of course hoped. . . . All the anxiety, all the complicated arrangements, all the prayers, all the significant meaning of the baptismal service had apparently passed into utter oblivion. The subject of them never heard them alluded to. He had seen christenings himself; he assumed that the operation had, at a period anterior to his recollection, been performed upon him, but the only conception he had formed of it was the fixation of a name. . . . During this whole period of the most impressionable portion of his life he was treated as an outsider, the significance and declaration of the first Christian Sacrament was entirely ignored.[1]

In addition, by restricting the significance of infant baptism to the childhood years, Wesley deprived Methodists of a richness that might have run right through the whole range of their liturgical and devotional life. He had been vague as to the relationship between baptism and Church membership, silent about its associations with the Lord's supper and the Renewal of the Covenant, denied that there is any connexion between baptism and conversion, and he had apparently not understood that this sacrament can stand as an objective pledge to the penitent that God is always ready to forgive, and to the dying that He waits at last to save—and in all these things Methodism followed the lead of its founder.

The seeds of this baptismal impotence, with its related dogmatism regarding the salvation of children and allied general devotional impoverishment, were thus sown by Wesley himself. The flaw in his doctrine—i.e. the insistence that

---

[1] 'Essays on Wesleyan-Methodism: its Dangers and Opportunities.' cit. *Wesleyan-Methodist Magazine*, 1879, p. 259.

everyone must be converted—meant that in spite of the richness of his positive baptismal teaching in other respects, his most commonly uttered comment on this sacrament had been negative:

Lean no more on the staff of that broken reed, that ye *were* born again in baptism.[1]

The pity of it was that later Methodism took this only too seriously.

Today, however, the situation is very different.

Without doubt, Methodism is now fully aware of the importance of nurturing children in holiness, and it is no longer insisted that everyone should experience a conversion of one particular type. Thus the root cause of Wesley's unsatisfactory baptismal teaching has been removed.

Furthermore, there are signs that the value of baptism is being more fully appreciated within Methodism. Some of these have already been mentioned—the consideration that is being given to the proper understanding of baptism (infant and adult) as a means of grace; the suggestion that baptismal sponsors may after all be useful in some cases; and the presentation of confirmation as the completion of the process of initiation into membership begun at baptism.

Other hints of this awakening to the significance of the sacrament may also be seen here and there. The Conference *Memorandum* of 1936 asked that conversion should not be dissociated from baptism, for, it says,

Our hope and confidence is that . . . this Sacrament will be inwardly completed and made effective when the child through faith in Christ responds to the grace proclaimed and pledged by the rite.[2]

Again, Jean and David Head include a chapter in their book *Martin is Baptized* (1962) with the sub-heading 'Assurance from Baptism'.[3] Such a view challenges Wesley's contention that assurance comes principally from the inward witness of the Spirit, for it allows baptism to stand as an objective pledge of God's faithful love when the Christian most needs such an

---
[1] *Sermons*, i. p. 296.
[2] *Minutes* (1936), p. 400. cf. *Statement* (1952), p. 4.   [3] pp. 54 ff.

awareness—at those very times of despair when the inward witness is lacking.

A further sign of the deepening regard for baptism is to be found in David Tripp's study of *The Renewal of the Covenant in the Methodist Tradition* (1969), where it is suggested that, in any future revision, this 'renewal of dedication should be (expressed) in terms of (baptism)': that it should be seen as 'the Renewal of Baptismal Vows'.[1]

And yet when these signs of an undoubted revival of interest in baptism have been noticed, the impression remains that this sacrament has still to be given its full place in the life and thought of the Connexion, and this failure may be due not only to any general lack of interest, but to a crucial gap in the sacramental teaching of Methodism. For, while interest is being taken in the meaning of the rite itself, and the parents of the child and the local congregation have been told plainly how baptism concerns them, the strange fact is that the subject of the ceremony has been left uninstructed about the wide implications for himself of his own baptism.

In this respect it makes no difference whether the candidate came to the font as an infant or an adult: he should be shown that from then onwards his whole life is baptismal—but in Methodism this lesson has not been taught. Baptism, with its message of our call to be children of God and of His unfailing love, can speak to us in all conditions of the soul, through every ordinance of the Church, and throughout life. It has a word to say to us when in sin we run away from God, when in conversion we turn back to Him, and when in despondency or grief we lose faith in Him. Nor are its implications ever exhausted (even though baptism is, in one important sense, 'completed' by conversion and confirmation), until it has spoken its last and most gracious word of reassurance at the hour of our death. But such teaching is not to be found either in the general literature of the Connexion or in the various Orders of Service approved by Conference—Baptism itself, the Lord's Supper, the Renewal of the Covenant, and Reception into Membership[2]—from which it is altogether missing.

---

[1] pp. 159 f.
[2] Baptism is mentioned in this Order (both of 1936 and 1967), but only in connexion with membership of the Church.

Here is a treasure of the Church's sacramental devotion which it was not given to Wesley to grasp. Yet since, through the Moravians, it was from Martin Luther that Wesley learned to understand the vital principle of justification by faith alone, perhaps his spiritual children may be willing to receive from the same mentor another great Protestant truth—how much blessedness there can be in leaning upon one's baptism, and finding it to be a staff which throughout life gives unfailing support.

Luther wrote:

The first thing, then, we have to notice in baptism is the Divine promise which says, 'He who believes and is baptised shall be saved.' . . . This doctrine ought to have been studiously inculcated upon the people by preaching; this promise ought to have been perpetually reiterated; men ought to have been constantly reminded of their baptism; faith ought to have been called forth and nourished. When this Divine promise has been once conferred upon us, its truth continues even to the hour of our death. . . . For the truth of the promise once made always abides, and is ready to stretch out the hand and receive us when we return. . . . This truth of God will preserve (the penitent); and even if all other hopes perish, this, if he believes it, will not fail him. Through this truth he will have something to oppose to the insolent adversary; he will have a barrier to throw in the way of the sins which disturb his conscience; he will have an answer to the dread of death and judgment; finally, he will have a consolation under every kind of temptation in being able to say, God is faithful to His promise; and in baptism I received the sign of that promise. If God is for me, who can be against me? . . .

We see then how rich a Christian, or baptised man, is. . . . [1]

[1] *On the Babylonish Captivity of the Church*, edd. H. Wace and C. A. Buchheim pp. 341 ff.

APPENDIX I

Notes on Wesley's Baptismal Writings; and the Text of his Essay, 'Water Baptism is the Baptism of Christ'

Wesley has been accused of saying too little about baptism,[1] but in fact (and particularly in comparison with the other leaders of the evangelical revival) he gave adequate space to it in his writings. Apart from many occasional references to this sacrament in other places, and in addition to his tract *Serious Thoughts Concerning Godfathers and Godmothers* (*Works*, x. pp. 506 ff), he devoted three small books specifically to this subject, two of which were published.

As always, Wesley wrote not out of academic interest alone but to meet some need, and these works were prepared to provide Methodists with a defence against Baptist rigorism on the one hand, and the Quaker denial of the sacrament on the other.

The Baptists seem to have troubled many of the early Methodist people by coming in among them with their characteristic contentions that baptism should properly be administered only to believing adults, and then by no other method than by total immersion.[2] D. M. Himbury says that 'Many Baptists were afraid that the revival led by Wesley might undermine their own position in the eyes of the people and attacked his Paedo-Baptist views.'[3] Two Baptists at least —William Kingsford[4] and Gilbert Boyce[5]—put out publi-

---
[1] Rigg, *The Churchmanship of John Wesley*, p. 40; C. W. Williams, *John Wesley's Theology Today*, p. 116 n.

[2] e.g. *Journal*, iii. pp. 296, 519; iv. p. 470; v. pp. 180, 250.

[3] In *Christian Baptism* (ed. A. Gilmore), p. 298.

[4] *A Vindication of the Baptists from the Criminality of a Charge exhibited against them by the Rev. Mr. Wesley* (1788). v. Tyerman, *John Wesley*, iii. p. 562 n; and *Three Letters to the Rev. Mr. Wesley, containing Remarks on a Piece Lately Published with his Approbation* (1789).

[5] *A Serious Reply to the Rev. Mr. John Wesley in Particular, and to the People Called Methodists in general* (1770) (v. *Journal*, iii. p. 360; *Letters*, iii. pp. 35 ff). The second part of the *Serious Reply* (pp. 134 ff) is an earnest plea to Methodists, especially those 'whom I have converted, and with whom I am acquainted', to be re-baptised.

cations of this kind. It is against this background that we must view the preparation of Wesley's *Thoughts upon Infant Baptism, Extracted from a late Writer* (Bristol 1751), and *A Treatise on Baptism* (1758). Indeed, it is possible that the immediate reason for the production of the *Treatise* was one particular case of Baptism intrusion. Charles Wesley records in his *Journal* his preaching at Gawksholm on 19 October 1756.

I knew not then, that several Baptists were present, a carnal, cavilling, contentious sect, always watching to steal away our children, and make them as dead as themselves. Mr. Allen informed me that they have carried off no less than fifty out of one Society, and that several Baptist meetings are wholly made out of old Methodists. I talked largely with Mr. Grimshaw, how to remedy the evil. We agreed, 1. That nothing can save the Methodists from falling a prey to every seducer but close walking with God...; 2. That the Preachers should be allowed more time in every place, to visit from house to house...; 3. That a small treatise be written, to ground and preserve them against seducers, and lodged in every family.[1]

It may be that Wesley's *Treatise* (which both in name and contents agrees with the foregoing description) was prepared as a direct result of this conversation, at the request of Charles Wesley and William Grimshaw. At any rate, within a month of the above date Wesley had completed the manuscript of his *Treatise*, although it was not published until two years later.

Presumably misled in the first place by the lack of any ascription as to its source, successive editors have included *A Treatise on Baptism* in Wesley's collected *Works*. However, it has long been well known that Wesley was here, once more, simply abridging an earlier work—in this case his father's *A Short Discourse of Baptism* (1700).[2] The manuscript is contained in a volume entitled *J. Wesley's MSS Sermons and Introduction to N. Testament* (to be found at the Methodist Archives, London), which reveals an introduction neither derived from the *Discourse* nor given in Wesley's *Works*.[3] The manuscript is dated 11 November 1756, and as this date is given in the *Works* it is usually assumed that the *Treatise* was published in that year. In fact it did not appear in print

[1] *Charles' Journal*, ii. p. 128.   [2] v. *supra*. pp. 14 f.
[3] v. *supra*. p. 88.

until it was included in *A Preservative against Unsettled Notions in Religion* (1758, 1770, 1839), and then in Wesley's Works (Pine, xix. pp. 275 ff; Jackson, x. pp. 188 ff).

Wesley produced the *Treatise* by omitting much of his father's supplementary material and by rearranging here and there, but almost every sentence in the *Treatise* was written originally by Samuel Wesley.

The *Thoughts Upon Infant Baptism*[1] is acknowledged in its title as being *Extracted from a late Writer*, and for this reason successive editors have omitted the text from Wesley's collected Works. (v. *Works*, xiv. p. 233, No. xlii in the 'List of Works Revised and Abridged from Various Authors'). Once again they have apparently been misled, for probably (as will be shown) the *Thoughts* was partly of Wesley's own composition and it could well have been included in full in the collection of his Works.

Richard Green had traced the origin of the *Thoughts* to William Wall's *History of Infant Baptism*,[2] and this ascription has passed unchallenged.[3] However, a closer examination reveals that the primary source was Isaac Watts' Sermon II, 'Christian Baptism',[4] and that in addition Wesley included material from Wall's *History* as well as from elsewhere. The composition of the *Thoughts* appears to be as follows:

1. pp. 1–6, Sections I–VI (part): From Watts' Sermon, (*Works*, i. pp. 601–3) abbreviated, re-arranged, and with the inclusion of some additional paragraphs.

2. pp. 6–10, Sections VI (part) and VII: From an unacknowledged (and undiscovered) source, or Wesley's own composition.

3. pp. 10–18, Section VIII. The introduction to this section is from Watts' Sermon (*ibid* p. 601): viz.

In the Christian Church from its earliest Ages, and we think from

---

[1] Editions appeared in 1751, 1780, 1791, 1804, 1824, and 1837. Green's *Bibliography* lists only those of 1751, 1780, 1804 and 1837. Copies of the others are now in the Methodist Archives in London.
[2] *Bibliography*, No. 149.
[3] e.g. R. E. Cushman, in *The Doctrine of the Church* (ed. D. Kirkpatrick) p. 81 n.
[4] Watts' *Works* (1800), i. pp. 597 ff. The other possibility—which would conform more closely to the title of the *Thoughts*—is that Wesley extracted it from one source which already incorporated all the varied material detailed below: but no such publication has been traced.

the Apostles' Time, it has been the Custom to baptize the Infant Children of professed Christians.

Wesley has then added supporting evidence ('To prove this, I shall produce a few Witnesses....'), probably extracted from Wall's *History*, since this author is mentioned by name on p. 11.

4. pp. 18 f, Section VIII continued. A quotation from Richard Baxter (not included in Watts' Sermon), introduced by:

This brings to my Remembrance a very clear Proof for the Baptism of Infants, which much satisfied the Mind of the Great and Good Mr. *Baxter*; I shall relate it in his own words.

The Extract which follows was taken from Baxter's *Plain Scripture Proof of Infants' Churchmembership and Baptism* (1651) Pt. iii. p. 266.

5. p. 19. There follows a short paragraph which is presumably of Wesley's own composition, beginning—

With regard to the Mode of Baptizing, I would only add, *Christ* no where, as far as I can find, requires *Dipping*, but only *Baptizing*. ...

6. pp. 19 to end. Material taken, with minor emendations, from Watts' Sermon (*ibid.* pp. 603 f), beginning—

I think it proper in this place to subjoin what Dr. *Watts* has declared concerning the signification of this Word.

It is not necessary to stay long in considering the arguments put forward in the *Thoughts* and *Treatise* in reply to the Baptist case. Wesley was not trying to make any original contribution to this long-continuing debate; all he aimed to do was to put into Methodist hands the arguments on the paedo-baptist side which were already well established. His points can be summarized as follows.

1. *The mode of baptism may be either dipping in, or sprinkling with, water.*

   (a) Jesus commanded water baptism, but did not specify how it should be administered.
   Thoughts, p. 19.   *Treatise*, I. 2, 3.[1]

[1] cf. *Notes* for John, iii. 5; Matt. xxviii. 19.

(b) The etymology of the word βαπτίγω allows any form of washing—sprinkling, pouring, or immersion.
Thoughts, pp. 19 f.   *Treatise*, I. 4.

(c) Both modes of baptism are probably instanced in the New Testament, although sprinkling more definitely than dipping.
Thoughts, pp. 19 f.   *Treatise*, I. 3, 5.[1]

(d) The two outward forms signify regeneration under two different figures: the one, dying and rising with Christ; the other, the outpouring of the Spirit.
Thoughts, p. 20.   *Treatise*, II. 2.[2]

To sum up all, the manner of baptizing (whether by dipping or sprinkling) is not determined in Scripture. There is no command for one rather than the other. There is no example from which we can conclude for dipping rather than sprinkling. There are probable examples of both; and both are equally contained in the natural meaning of the word.[3]

2. *Baptism may be administered either to adults or infants.*

This was for Wesley the 'grand question',[4] and he gives much of his space in both tracts to defending infant baptism.

(a) Christ's command to baptise does not specify at what age this should be done; and in Scripture, while only adult baptism is instanced, infant baptism is not excluded, and is referred to.
Thoughts, pp. 4 f, 7.   *Treatise*, IV. 7, 8.[5]

(b) In the context of Jewish practice this is to be expected, since proselytes, both adult and infant, were baptised.
Treatise, IV. 7.[6]

(c) As Christ replaced the Old Covenant with the New, so He replaced the sign of initiation into the Old (circumcision) with that for the New (baptism): and since God is more, rather than less, gracious in His New Covenant, children

---

[1] cf. *ibid*. Matt. iii. 6; Acts viii. 38; 1 Cor. x. 2; Col. ii. 12.
[2] cf. *ibid*. Matt. iii. 6; Rom. vi. 3, 4; 1 Cor. x. 2; Col. ii. 12.
[3] *Treatise*, i. 5.
[4] *Treatise*, iv. 1.
[5] cf. *Notes* for Acts xvi. 15; Col. ii. 12.
[6] cf. *ibid*. Matt. xxviii. 19.

should still be admitted into the Covenant under its new administration.
Thoughts, pp. 3–6.   *Treatise*, III. 2, IV. 4–7.[1]

(*d*) Infant baptism has been the universal practice of the Church, until the Anabaptists at the Reformation disputed it.
Thoughts, pp. 10–18.   *Treatise*, IV. 7, 9.

(*e*) Infants are guilty of original sin: but the 'ordinary means' appointed for washing away this guilt is baptism; therefore infants are proper subjects for baptism.
Treatise, IV. 2.

(*f*) Infants are capable of making a Covenant: therefore 'they have a right to baptism, which is the entering seal' of the evangelical covenant.
Thoughts, p. 6.   *Treatise*, IV. 3.

(*g*) Infants ought to come to Christ; are capable of admission into the Church, and of solemn dedication to God: thus they are proper subjects for baptism.
Thoughts, p. 5.   *Treatise*, IV. 6.

(*h*) The argument that some adult response of faith and penitence is a necessary prerequisite of baptism (and that therefore infants are *ex hypothesi* excluded from it), is not valid, because this would apply equally to their exclusion from the Old Covenant—and 'as this Argument would prove too much, it must be looked upon as proving Nothing.'[2]
Thoughts, pp. 7 f.   *Treatise*, Objections 1, 2.

Wesley's conclusion is, therefore, that

All these things put together, seem to prove, that Infant-Baptism was practised in the Church of *Christ* from the *Beginning*, and consequently that it is of an *Apostolical* and *Divine* Original.[3]

So much for Wesley's reply to the Baptists. What had he to say, on the other hand, to the Quakers? In their case there had not been the same aggression as had been shown by the Baptists, and it is only occasionally that we find Wesley referring to the Quakers' anti-sacramentalism. In one place he first set out and then answered Robert Barclay's main

---
[1] cf. *ibid*. Matt. xxviii. 19; Acts xvi. 15.
[2] *Thoughts*, p. 7.   [3] *Thoughts*, p. 18.

argument against 'outward baptism'[1], and in another[2] he said:

between me and them is a great gulf fixed. The sacraments of baptism and the Lord's supper keep us at a wide distance from each other; insomuch that, according to the view of things I have now, I should as soon commence Deist as Quaker.

It is this strong conviction which is expressed and explained in a hitherto unpublished essay, in which Wesley dealt at length with the question of the validity of water baptism. The full text is now given, with some explanatory notes.

Notes

1. The essay is written on three pages, which are now contained in a volume entitled *Portraits and Letters of Presidents of the Wesleyan Conference* (Vol. i, p. 14), kept at the Methodist Archives, London.
2. It appears to be an original composition; and is evidently a first draft, for there are several erasures and corrections, as well as unnecessary numbers alongside two paragraphs.
3. No date is given, but the writing is firm and clear, showing that this work does not belong to Wesley's later years.
4. The script is very small, much abbreviated, and at the edges the paper is worn and stained, so that some words and phrases are scarcely decipherable. Doubtful readings, or gaps in legibility, are shown in square brackets.
5. The number 8 opposite the heading may indicate that this essay was intended as part of a longer work.

8. WATER BAPTISM IS THE BAPTISM OF CHRIST

The Words of Christ are these (Matthew 28. 19) 'Go ye therefore and teach all Nations, baptizing them in the Name of the Father and of the Son and of the Holy Ghost.' That the Baptism here enjoined by Christ is Water Baptism appears

From the Significance and Etymology of the Word Baptize:
1. The Word is a Greek word: It signifies To Wash and is applied to this Sacrament because this is an Outward Washing. To wash and to baptize are the very same; and if the word Baptize had been rendered in English instead of 'Go and baptize,' it must have been said, 'Go and wash' instead in the [verse]. So that Water Baptism

---

[1] *Works*, x. pp. 177, 184.   [2] *Works*, xii. p. 78.

is as much here commanded, as if it had been exprest in English Words, or as we can now express it. But because the Word Baptize was a Technical Word in other Languages for this Sacrament of old, therefore Translators did rightly retain it here and elsewhere.

But in other places they translate the Word literally. So Mark 7. 4 'Ἐὰν μὴ βαπτίσουται[1] is translated 'Except they Wash' and in the same [verse] they translate βαπτισμεὶς ποτηρίων[1] 'the washing of Cups.' And so Hebrews 9. 10 ποικίλοις βαπτισμμ̄οις[1] is translated 'Divers Washings': Though the Vulgate Latin retains the Greek Word in all these Texts, 'Sive baptizentur, non comedunt,' 'baptismata Calicum,' and 'Variis Baptismatibus.'[2] So that it is plain that the Word Baptism and the Word Washing, though not the same Word, have yet the Selfsame Meaning.

2. It is true that the Word Baptism is often taken in a figurative Sense, to mean the Washing or Cleansing of the Holy Spirit. But so is the Word Washing as often. And there is scarce a Word in the World but is capable of many figurative meanings. Thus Circumcision is often used for the Inward Circumcision or Purity of Heart. But it is a received Rule for the interpretation of Scripture, and indeed of all other Writings and Words, that the Plain, literal Meaning is always to be taken, when there is no manifest contradiction or absurdity in it (As when we are commanded to Wash or Circumcise our Hearts.) But if a man will take upon himself to understand words in a figurative sense at his own will and pleasure, without such an apparent Necessity [he surely] leaves no certainty in any Words or Expressions in the World. Unless therefore it can be shewn that there is an Apparent contradiction or absurdity in the literal sense of this Text, it must be meant of Water Baptism, because that is the literal Signification of the Word.

And that there is no contradiction or absurdity therein is plain 1. Because Christ did practice water Baptism 2. Because the Apostles did it after him, and 3. Because the Catholic Church has done it after Them.

1. Christ did practice Water Baptism. It is written John 3. 26 'And they came unto John and said unto him, Rabbi, he that was with Thee beyond Jordon, to whom Thou bearest Witness, behold, the same baptizeth, and all men come to him.' That this was Water Baptism, there can be no doubt, because

[1] A. Souter's Greek text gives, ἐὰν μή βαπτίσωνται; βαπτισμοὺς ποτηρίων; and διαφόροις βαπτισμύος in these places.
[2] The Vulgate (Edd. Wordsworth and White, 1920) reads for these phrases: Nisi baptizenter; non comedunt; Baptismata calicum; and Variis baptismis.

1. The Baptism with the Holy Ghost was not yet given; for that was not given till Pentecost. This Spirit Baptism was promised John 14. 16, 26 and 15. 26 and 16. 7. And the Apostles were commanded to tarry in Jerusalem, till it should come upon them. Luke 24. 49.
2. John did baptize with Water, and there is no other sort of Baptism here mentioned with which Christ did baptize: therefore these Baptisms being spoken of both together, there can be no reason to interpret the One to be with water and the other not. Besides, it is said [...'. ...] more Diciples than John.'[1] How could the Pharisees hear of it, if it was not an Outward Baptism? The Outward Effects of the Baptism with the Holy Ghost were not yet. And since it was an Outward it [points] to water Baptism: for there was then no other.

If it be objected from the [verse] 'Jesus himself baptized not, but his Disciples,'[2] we answer

1. Though Jesus himself baptized not, yet it is said in the first verse that He *made and baptized*, i.e. those whom his disciples, by his Order, baptized. If it had not been done by his Order, it could not be said that He had baptized those whom his disciples baptized. But because 'he that do a thing by another is said to do it himself,'[3] therefore Christ himself is said to baptize those whom his Disciples baptized by his Order.
2. We grant, Christ did not baptize himself—at This Time: All that follows therefore is, that at sometimes Christ did baptize himself, and at others, left it to his Disciples. But it is the same thing whether he did it himself or commanded them to do it: for either way it is his Baptism, his only: His Disciples did but administer what he commanded.

2. As Christ himself did baptize with water, and his Disciples while he was upon Earth, so did his Apostles and others commissioned by him, after his Death. For

It is written Acts 10. 47. 'Can any man forbid Water, that these should not be baptized:' and Acts 8. 36 'As they (Philip and the Eunuch) went on their way they came to a certain water and the Eunuch said, See here is Water; what doth hinder me to be baptized? 38. And they went both down in the water, both Philip and the Eunuch, and he baptized him.' [Hereat] it is undeniable, that the Apostles did practice Water Baptism.

---

[1] John iv. 1.   [2] John iv. 2.
[3] Latin proverb: *Qui facit per alium facit per se.*

APPENDIX

Whence I argue thus: the Apostles did practice the Baptism which Christ commanded, Matthew 28. 19: But the Apostles did practice Water Baptism: therefore Water Baptism was the Baptism of Christ, the Baptism which Christ [himself] commanded.

3. And as the Practice of the Apostles is a most Sure Rule, whereby to understand the Meaning of that Command which they executed; so the Practice of those who in turn succeeded the Apostles, who lived with them, and learned the faith from their Mouth is as sure a rule to know what the Practice of the Apostles was. And thus the Practice of the present Age as to Water Baptism, is an undeniable evidence that this was the Practice of the Last Age, Many of the same persons being alive in both. For One Age does not cease all at once, and another succeed, but there are Old Men of the Last Age, and Young Men and Children growing up to Another Age, All alive at the same time. And Mankind being disperst in far distant Countries who know not of one another nor hold any correspondence, it is impossible for any man to deceive us, in what hath been the Universal Practice of the last Age, to which the present Age is so linkt that it is even a part of it: I say, it is impossible, all the Old Men in the World, if willing, should be able to impose upon All Younger than themselves, that they had been All Baptized, that this was an Universal Custom: that Registers were kept in Every Parish of all who had been from time to time baptized, and that such Registers might be recurred to, by all that had a mind to it. And as certainly as the present Age knows the Universal Practice of the last Age, so certainly and by the same Rules, must the last Age know the Practice of the Age before that, and so backward all the way to the first Institution, to the Age of Christ and His Apostles.

Water Baptism being an Outward Matter of fact, of which men's Eyes and Ears are judges, not like Matters of Opinion.[1] [in] which Tares may be privately sown, and long propagated before discovered: and this so Public Matter [. . .] having been universally practiced [at] all the far distant [. . .] Nations of Christianity: I say, these Two Marks make it Impossible for the World to be impos'd upon, in any such matter of Fact so universally practiced. It is therefore undeniably plain, that the Last Age did practice Water Baptism, and that the same was as certainly practiced in the Age before the Last Age, and by the same Rule, in the Age before that, and so onward, to the Age of the Apostles.

[1] cf. *Thoughts*, pp. 15 f. where this argument, here applied to *water* baptism, is used of *infant* baptism, and acknowledged as deriving from Richard Baxter.

In All the Ages from the Apostles, till 1650,[1] no one could be found to bear their Testimony against this Water Baptism, though it was constantly and universally practiced; and that, though Christians were Then so zealous as to contend against the least Variation or Corruption of the Faith, even [with] Death.

[1] Although George Fox began, in fact, to preach in 1647, this date shows that Wesley was addressing this essay to the Quakers.

APPENDIX 2

Baptism in Charles Wesley's Hymns and Verse

1. *HYMNS FOR INFANT BAPTISM*
   Hymns for the Use of Families (1767), No. 112; *A Collection of Hymns for the Use of the People Called Methodists* (1780), No. 740 (with verse 2 omitted, and written throughout for a boy); omitted from the revised hymn book of 1876.

   1. God of eternal truth and love,
        Vouchsafe the promis'd aid we claim,
      Thine own great ordinance approve,
        The child baptized into thy name,
      Partaker of thy nature make,
      And give her all thine image back.

   2. Born in the dregs of sin and time,
        These darkest, last, apostate days,
      Burden'd with Adam's curse and crime,
        Thou in thy mercy's arms embrace,
      And wash out all her guilty load,
      And quench the brand in Jesu's blood.

   3. Father, if such thy sovereign will,
        If Jesus did the rite enjoin,
      Annex thy hallowing Spirit's seal,
        And let the grace attend the sign;
      The seed of endless life impart,
      Take for thine own our infant's heart.

   4. Answer in her they wisdom's end,
        In present and eternal good;
      Whate'er thou did'st for man intend,

Whate'er thou hast on man bestow'd,
Now to this favour'd child be given,
Pardon, and holiness, and heaven.

5. *In presence of thy Heavenly Host*
    Thyself we faithfully require;
Come Father, Son, and Holy Ghost,
    By blood, by water, and by fire,
And fill up all thy human shrine,
And seal our souls for ever thine.

Poetical Works, xi. pp. 119 f, on Luke ii. 22; 1780 *Collection*, No. 742; 1876 Hymn Book, No. 890; 1904 Hymn Book, No. 722; omitted in 1933.

1. *Lord of all, with pure intent,*
    From their tenderest infancy,
In thy temple we present
    Whom we first received from thee:
Through thy well-beloved Son,
    Ours acknowledged for thine own.

2. *Sealed with the baptismal seal,*
    Purchased by th' atoning blood,
Jesus in our children dwell,
    Make their heart the house of God.
Fill thy consecrated shrine,
Father, Son, and Spirit divine.

Poetical Works, x. p. 322; *Hymns on the Four Gospels*, No. 478; No. 893 in the 1876 Hymn Book (the third line of the second verse being altered to—'Into thy holy church receive'); omitted in 1904. Paraphase of Matthew xix. 13.

1. *Jesus, in earth and heaven the same,*
    Accept a parent's vow,
To thee, baptized into thy name,
    I bring my children now;
Thy love permits, invites, commands,
    My offspring to be blessed;
Lay on them Lord, thy gracious hands,
And hide them in thy breast.

2. *To each the hallowing Spirit give*
       Even from their infancy;
   And pure into thy church receive,
       Whom I devote to thee;
   Committed to thy faithful care,
       Protected by thy blood,
   Preserve by thine unceasing prayer,
       And bring them all to God.

Poetical Works, ix. p. 31, versification of Genesis xlviii. 16; Short Scripture Hymns Nos. 98 and 99; No. 894 in the 1876 Hymn Book; omitted in 1904.

1. *The great redeeming Angel, thee,*
       O Jesus, I confess;
   Who hast through life delivered me,
       Thou wilt my offspring bless;
   Thou that hast borne my sins away,
       My children's sins remove,
   And bring them through the evil day,
       To sing thy praise above.

2. *My name be on the children? No!*
       But mark them, Lord, with thine,
   Let all the heavenly offspring know
       By characters divine;
   Partakers of thy nature make,
       Partakers of thy Son,
   And then the heirs of glory take,
       To their eternal throne.

2. HYMNS FOR ADULT BAPTISM

Poetical Works, v. pp. 388 f; Hymns and Sacred Poems (1749), ii. No. 182 (with slight variations in punctuation, etc.); No. 476 in the 1780 and 1876 Hymn Books; omitted in 1904.

1. *Come, Father, Son, and Holy Ghost,*
       Honour the Means Injoin'd by Thee!
   Make good our Apostolic Boast,
       And own thy Glorious Ministry.

2. *We now thy Promised Presence claim,*
   Sent to disciple all Mankind,
   Sent to baptize into thy Name,
   We now the promis'd presence find.

3. *Father! in These reveal thy Son,*
   In These, for whom we seek thy Face,
   The hidden Mystery make known,
   In Inward, Pure, Baptizing Grace.

4. *Jesu, with Us thou always art,*
   Effectuate now the Sacred Sign,
   The Gift Unspeakable impart,
   And bless the Ordinance Divine.

5. *Eternal Spirit! descend from high,*
   Baptizer of our Spirits thou!
   The Sacramental Seal apply,
   And witness with the Water Now!

6. *O! that the Souls baptized therein,*
   May now thy Truth and Mercy feel;
   May rise, and wash away their sin—
   Come, Holy Ghost, their Pardon seal!

Poetical Works, v. p. 389; *Hymns and Sacred Poems* ii. No. 183 (only with a male candidate referred to throughout; and in verse 2, line 4 reads—'The character divine!', and line 6— 'Jesus, all thy name impart!'; with other minor changes in punctuation); No. 477 in the 1780 and 1876 Hymn Books; omitted in 1904.[1]

1. *Father, Son, and Holy Ghost,*
   In solemn Power come down,
   Present with thy Heavenly Host
   Thine Ordinance to crown:
   See a Sinful Worm of Earth!

[1] F. Hildebrandt refers to this hymn as though it has been written for *infant* baptism; and he also incorrectly cites No. 475 (1780 Hymn Book)—'But who sufficient is to lead'—as one of Charles Wesley's baptismal hymns. *From Luther to Wesley*, p. 148.

APPENDIX

> *Bless for her the Laving Flood,*
> *Plunge her, by a second birth*
> *Into the depths of God.*

> 2. *Let the Promis'd Inward Grace*
> *Accompany the Sign;*
> *On her new-born Soul impress*
> *The glorious Name Divine:*
> *Father, all thy name reveal!*
> *Jesus, all thy Mind impart!*
> *Holy Ghost, renew, and dwell,*
> *For ever in her heart.*

3. REFERENCES IN OTHER VERSES

Charles Wesley's best baptismal poetry was used for hymns, but some other of his verses are worth noticing.

Poetical Works, x. pp. 445 f: on Mark i. 5.

> 2. *Bid me step into the pool,*
> *By repentance I obey:*
> *But my filthiness of soul*
> *Cannot thus be purged away:*
> *Tears may wash my actual sin;*
> *Guilt requires a stronger flood:*
> *Purge, and make my spirit clean*
> *In the fountain of Thy blood.*[1]

Poetical Works, x. pp. 445 f: on Mark i. 8.

> 1. *What avails the outward sign,*
> *Without the inward grace?*
> *Lord, I want Thy Spirit Divine*
> *The spark of love to raise.*
> *Straiten'd through intense desire*
> *To feel the pure baptismal flame*
> *Let the Holy Spirit inspire,*
> *And plunge me in Thy name.*

[1] cf. *Poetical Works*, x. p. 148 (on Matt. iii. 14) and xi pp. 127 f (on Luke iii. 16).

2. *Unbaptized, in sin I live,*
   Till I Thy Spirit feel;
   To Thy ransom'd servant give
   That Gift unspeakable,
   Witness, Pledge of joys unseen
   Thy Spirit breathe into my breast:
   Partner of Thy nature then
   And one with Thee I rest.

Poetical Works, x. pp. 446 f: on Mark i. 10.

1. *Where'er the pure baptismal rite*
   Is duly minister'd below,
   The heavens are open'd in our sight,
   And God His Spirit doth bestow,
   The grace infused invisible,
   Which would with man forever dwell.

2. *But oh, we lost the grace bestow'd,*
   Nor let the Spirit on us remain,
   Made void the ordinance of God,
   By sin shut up the heavens again,
   Who would not keep our garments white,
   Or walk as children of the light.

Poetical Works, xi. p. 98: on Mark xvi. 16.

1. *The infidel his doom shall bear,*
   In endless torment cry,
   But never doth our Lord declare
   'The unbaptized shall die:'
   In education's fetters bound
   Who miss the outward way,
   Yet love their God, shall all be found
   His people in that day.

2. *He winks at ignorance sincere*
   In them that know His grace;
   But no unholy souls appear
   Before His glorious face:

Baptized, or unbaptized, they all
Shall die the second death,
And banish'd from His presence fall
Into their place beneath.

Poetical Works, xiii. pp. 114 f: on Titus iii. 4–7.

5. *Our Father, moved by Jesu's prayer,*
Hath sent the indwelling Conforter,
The Spirit of holiness,
To cleanse in the baptismal flood,
Renew our spirits after God,
And perfect us in grace.

APPENDIX 3

Wesleyan Methodist Registers of Births and Baptisms, Begun Before 1791, Held at the Public Record Office, London

The registers are named as they appear in the list of Non-Parochial Registers, with notes where correction is necessary.

Devonshire

Devonport, Morrice Street. 1787.

In fact the register of the Plymouth Dock Society; having at the beginning a few entries subsequently added dating back to 1785; and at the end of the book a few similarly added dating back to 1772.

Lancashire

Blackburn, Clayton Street Chapel. 1784.
  Register for 'Blackburn and Area'.
Bolton, Great, Ridgway Gates. 1789.
  Register for the Bolton Circuit.
(Liverpool, Mount Pleasant Chapel. 1787).
  Started systematically in 1792, with a few subsequent entries dating back to 1787.
Padiham, Whalley. 1785.
  Started in 1786.
Rossendale, Bacup. 1786.
Whalley, Colne, etc. 1788.
  Register of baptisms 'In and Near Colne'.

Northumberland

Newcastle-upon-Tyne, Brunswick Place Chapel, formerly Orphan House Chapel. 1788.
  Register for Byker.

APPENDIX

Nottinghamshire

Nottingham etc. 1787. (*NOTTINGHAM A*)
Register for 'Nottingham and the Adjacent Villages.'
Nottingham, Parliament Street, formerly Hockley Chapel. 1787. (*NOTTINGHAM B*)
Listed under 'Methodist New Connexion', into whose hands the register passed in 1797.

Somerset

(*Ilminster.* 1780)
The early entries are copied from the Taunton Register, below.
(*Taunton, Octagon Chapel and the Temple.* 1785.)
Register of the Taunton Circuit; begun systematically in 1795, but with a few entries subsequently added, dating back to 1785.

Worcestershire

(*Kidderminster.* 1788.)
Begun in 1791. Heading: 'Register of all the Children which have been Baptized by the Methodist Preachers since they Obtained Grant, from the Conference, for the said purpose, and took date the 20th August 1791.'
Stourport. 1788.
Only three entries prior to 1795.

Yorkshire

Delph, Saddleworth. 1786.
(*Greetland, Halifax.* 1788.)
Births only entered until 1795, when baptisms are also recorded.
Halifax, South Parade Chapel. 1772.
Register for the Halifax Circuit, begun systematically in 1785, with a few entries subsequently added of earlier date.
Ovenden, Mount Zion. 1779.
Listed under 'Methodist New Connexion'. The register proper begins in 1785, but bound into the cover are:

(a) A scrap of paper recording baptisms in 1775 (one), 1779 (two) and 1778 (one).
(b) A booklet presumably belonging to a class leader or local preacher (for it contains other jottings), noting baptisms over the years 1779 to 1786: the last 17 entries being copied into the register book.

Holbeck. 1785.
(*Icornshaw.* 1753.)
   Wrongly listed: the register was begun in 1804.
Leeds, the Old Chapel, St. Peter's Street. 1787.
   First entry 1785 or 6 (illegible).
Pudsey, Parish of Calverley. 1787.

NOTES AND COMMENTS

1. *The Earliest Known Methodist Baptismal Register*

Bound inside the front cover of the register of the Mount Zion Chapel, Ovenden, is a small notebook which can claim to be the earliest known Methodist baptismal register. Occasional baptisms of earlier date have been entered *post hoc* into some other registers, but there is no other which was begun systematically before 1779, the year in which entries were first carefully made in this notebook. There is no heading, nor are the names of the administrators given, but there are other jottings and notes in it—e.g. a list of expenses ('Layd out by James Akroyd. . . . '); a table showing attendances of ten people at a Class (?) Meeting; and a list of monies received—which suggest that the owner of the booklet was a Class Leader or other leading layman in the local Society. Perhaps he himself perfomed these christenings (v. Note 4. below). The last seventeen entries have been copied into the register proper, and constitute the first entries in that book.

2. *Baptisms by John Wesley*

Two registers record baptisms by Wesley himself.
(a) *Plymouth Dock.* At the end of the book there is this heading—'Register of Baptism's Prior to any Register Book being kept by the Methodist in this Town. Dock.' Thereunder

Wesley is recorded as having baptised the following: 3 March 1785, Grace Beer; n.d. Thomas Beard; 6 May 1772,[1] Richard Beard; n.d. Alice Beard; 22 September 1779, Elizabeth Launder. None of these occasions is mentioned in Wesley's Journals and Diaries. The register opens with the record of the christening of nine people (at least three of whom were infants) on 1 March 1787 and, as Wesley does note this in his Diary, light is thrown on the entry: 'christened many'. (*Journal*, vii. p. 244). Later on, he baptised two infants at Plymouth Dock on 29 August 1789.

(*b*) *Taunton Society and Circuit Register.* This register opens with the christening by Wesley of three children, Abraham, Isaac, and Mary Crabb, on a date given as 10 September 1795. This is obviously incorrect (Wesley having died in 1791), but the entry is copied into the Ilminster register, and the year is there corrected to 1785. The second entry is of a further infant baptism by Wesley in October 1789. These also do not figure in his *Journal* and Diaries, and it thus seems certain that Wesley baptised even more often than these detailed records of his life have indicated.

3. *Itinerant Preachers who baptised before 1791*

The names of the following twenty-three preachers appear in the registers indicated.

Charles Atmore: (Ordained for Scotland in 1786)
    Blackburn 1784, 1785, 1786: Padiham 1786, 1788: Colne 1788, 1789: Byker 1790.
James Bogie: (Ordained for Scotland in 1788)
    Nottingham A 1787, 1788: Nottingham B 1787.
William Bramwell:
    Blackburn 1788, 1789: Bacup 1789.
Joseph Cownley: (Ordained for Scotland in 1788)
    Byker 1791.
Thomas Hanby: (Ordained for Scotland in 1785)
    Nottingham A 1789: Nottingham B 1789: Bolton 1789, 1790, 1791: Delph 1790, 1791.

---

[1] The date is incorrect since Wesley was in Scotland at this time. These entries were obviously written in from memory.

Jonathan Hern:
  Nottingham A 1787, 1788: Nottingham B 1787, 1788.
George Highfield:
  Nottingham A 1787, 1788: Nottingham B 1788.
Samuel Hodgson:
  Pudsey 1790.
Christopher Hopper:
  Bolton 1791.
William Horner:
  Plymouth Dock 1791.
William Hunter (Senior):
  Byker 1787, 1788.
Lawrence Kane:
  Plymouth Dock 1787, 1788, 1789.
Thomas Lee:
  Delph 1786.
George Lowe:
  Blackburn 1789, 1790.
William Myles:
  Plymouth Dock 1787.
John Nelson:
  Blackburn 1789, 1790: Bacup 1790.
John Pawson: (Ordained for Scotland in 1785)
  Leeds 1788, 1789: Holbeck 1789.
Jeremiah Robertshaw:
  Pudsey 1787.
Richard Rodda:
  Delph 1789, 1790.
Joseph Taylor: (Ordained for Scotland in 1785)
  Stourport 1788, 1791: Nottingham A 1789: Nottingham B 1788, 1789, 1790: Kidderminster 1791.
Thomas Taylor:
  Holbeck 1785, 1786, 1787, 1788, 1789: Leeds 1785, 1786: Delph 1788, 1789.
Thomas Vasey: (Ordained for America in 1784)
  Nottingham A 1789: Nottingham B 1790: Byker 1790.
Thomas Warwick:
  Plymouth Dock 1789, 1790, 1791.

Some registers reveal the growing awareness of the ministerial status of the preachers. At Delph a printed register was used with the name of the administrator entered under the heading: 'Protestant Dissenting Minister'. At Byker, the Steward who filled in the register has given the title 'Revd Mr.' to such preachers as William Hunter (1788), Charles Atmore and Thomas Vasey (1790)—thus anticipating the official use of this form of address by some thirty years.[1]

4. *Names of others who administered Methodist Baptism before 1791*

It is to be expected that the Anglican clergymen who assisted Wesley in his work should have baptised in Methodist Chapels, and the names of James Creighton (Liverpool 1787) and Thomas Coke (Padiham 1788: Plymouth Dock 1776, 1787, 1789) duly appear.[2] But what is surprising is to discover other names, of people who were neither itinerant preachers nor Anglican clergymen, and who most probably were local Methodist laymen. Thus:

Bacup:
  William Atmore (1786); Benjamin Dickenson (1786, 1787); James Maden (1787); Samuel Barrowclough (1787); Richard Bentley (1788).
Blackburn:
  George Walkden (1786, 1787); William Banning (1789, 1790, 1791).
Holbeck:
  Edward Parsons (1789).
Leeds:
  Edward Parsons (1788, 1790).
Nottingham A:
  William Tunney (1787, 1788, 1790, 1791)
Nottingham B:
  William Tunney (1787, 1789, 1790, 1791)

Of these, a good deal is known of George Walkden and William Banning, and a little of James Maden;[3] but concerning the

---

[1] This title first appears in the *Minutes* of 1818.
[2] One baptism at Plymouth Dock in 1785 was by 'Rev. Mr. Collins'. This may have been the Rev. B. B. Collins, an Anglican clergyman who assisted Wesley from time to time. v. Tyerman, *John Wesley*, iii. pp. 335 f.
[3] v. *supra.* pp. 114 f.

rest the relevant local histories are silent. It is possible that William Tunney was the preacher of that name who retired from the itinerancy in 1781.

5. *The Wesleyan and Calvinistic Methodist Registers Compared*

There are many Calvinistic Methodist registers listed in the catalogue of Non-Parochial Registers. Most of them, especially the great majority of those pertaining to Welsh chapels, were begun during the years 1800 to 1835, but some antedate the first Wesleyan registers by some years. For example:

Rodborough, Tabernacle: 1762.
Wotton-under-Edge, Tabernacle: 1762.
Broadstairs, St. Mary's Chapel: 1772.
Bristol, Tabernacle, Penn Street: 1775.

These earlier dates are explained by the greater sense of independency felt by Calvinistic as compared to Wesleyan Methodists,[1] so that baptism was shifted from the parish churches rather earlier in the one case than in the other. The registers show that the administrator was always an ordained minister.

---

[1] 'Almost from the beginning of his career, Whitefield was *practically* a Dissenter' (Tyerman, *George Whitefield*, i. p. 67. cf. ibid. pp. 93 f, 334 n, 347, 480). v. *supra*. p. 104 n.

APPENDIX 4

The Baptismal Material in the 'Sunday Service of the Methodists' and the 'Book of Common Prayer' Compared

The editions of the *Sunday Service* used for this comparison are:
1784: the text as given in *The Rites and Ritual of Episcopal Methodism*, by Nolan B. Harmon[1] (U.S.A. 1926).
1786: *The Sunday Service of the Methodists in His Majesty's Dominions. With other Occasional Services.* Copy in the Methodist Archives, London.

1. *RELEVANT POINTS OF DIFFERENCE IN THE ARTICLES OF RELIGION*

B.C.P.	Sunday Service, 1784 and 1786
XVI. 'Of Sin after Baptism.'	XII. 'Of Sin after Justification.'
XXV. 'Of the Sacraments.' 'Sacraments ... be certain sure witnesses, and effectual signs of grace, and God's good will ...'	XVI. 'Of the Sacraments.' 'Sacraments ... are certain signs of grace, and God's good will ...'
XXVII. 'Of Baptism.' 'Baptism is not only a sign of profession ... but it is also a sign of Regeneration or new Birth, whereby, as by an instrument, they that receive Baptism rightly are grafted into the Church; the promises of foregiveness of sin, and of our adoption to be the sons of God by the Holy Ghost, are visibly signed and sealed ... The Baptism of young Children is in any wise to be retained in the Church, as most agreeable with the institution of Christ.'	XVII. 'Of Baptism.'[2] 'Baptism is not only a sign of profession ... but it is also a sign of Regeneration or the new Birth. The Baptism of young Children is to be retained in the Church.'

---

[1] *The Sunday Service of the Methodists in North America: With Other Occasional Services.* Copy in Drew Theological Seminary Library.
[2] v. F. Hunter, W.H.S. xxiii. p. 131. Wesley has removed 'all reference to any

Notes

1. While stating clearly that baptism is a sign of regeneration, the *Sunday Service* Articles are careful not to imply that this re-birth is effectually conveyed with the sacrament.
2. The change in the heading of Article XVI (to 'Of Sin after Justification') must indicate that, for Wesley, the greater problem was not that of dealing with sin after baptism (for this was to be expected, and its forgiveness is one aspect of conversion), but the difficulty caused by sin after conversion—i.e. backsliding.[1]

2. THE SERVICE OF INFANT BAPTISM

B.C.P.	Sunday Service, 1784	Sunday Service, 1786
The Ministration of Publick Baptism of Infants, To be used in the Church.	The Ministration of Baptism of Infants.	The Ministration of Baptism of Infants.
1. Rubrics concerning time, place, etc; sponsors; notification.	Omitted.	Omitted.
2. And the Priest coming to the Font, (which is then to be filled with pure Water,) and standing there, shall say,	The Minister coming to the Font, which is to be filled with pure Water, shall say,	The Same.
'Hath this Child been already baptized, or no?'	Omitted.	Omitted.
3. 'Dearly beloved, forasmuch as all men . . .'	Unaltered.	Unaltered.
4. Then shall the priest say, 'Let us pray.'	Then shall the Minister say, 'Let us pray.'	Then shall the Minister use as many of the following Prayers, as the Time will permit, saying, 'Let us pray.'

---

importation of grace, and made (this Article) affirm that baptism is a sign of the Christian profession and "a sign of regeneration or the new birth".'

[1] v. J. R. Parris, *John Wesley's Doctrine of the Sacraments*, p. 58.

APPENDIX 179

B.C.P.	Sunday Service, 1784	Sunday Service, 1786
Prayer beginning— 'Almighty and everlasting God, who. . .' . . . didst sanctify Water to the mystical washing away of sin; we beseech . . . . . . that thou wilt mercifully look upon . . . . . . and rooted in charity . . .	. . . didst sanctify Water to the mystical washing away of sin; we beseech . . . . . . that thou wilt look upon . . . . . . and rooted in charity . . .	. . . didst sanctify Water for this holy Sacrament, we beseech . . . . . . that thou wilt look upon . . . . . . and rooted in love . . .
Prayer beginning— 'Almighty and immortal God, the aid . . .'	Unaltered.	Omitted.
5. The Gospel.	Unaltered.	Unaltered.
6. Exhortation.	Omitted.	Omitted.
7. Prayer beginning— 'Almighty and everlasting God, heavenly. . .	Unaltered.	Omitted.
8. Address and questions to sponsors.	Omitted.	Omitted.
9. *Then shall the Priest say,* Four petitions for grace. . . . whosoever is here dedicated . . .	*Then shall the Minister say,* . . . whosoever is dedicated . . .	*Then shall the Minister say,* . . . whosoever is dedicated . . .
10. Prayer beginning— 'Almighty, everliving God, whose most . . .' . . . thy congregation; sanctify this Water to the mystical washing away of sin; and grant that this Child, now to be baptized therein, may receive . . .	. . . thy Congregation, sanctify this Water to the mystical washing away of sin; and grant that this Child now to be baptized, may receive . . .	. . . thy congregation; and grant that this Child, now to be baptized, may receive . . .
11. *Then the Priest shall take the Child into his hands, and shall say to the Godfathers and Godmothers,*	*Then the Minister shall take the Child into his hands, and shall say to the Friends of the Child,*	The same.

B.C.P.	Sunday Service, 1784	Sunday Service, 1786
'Name this Child.'	'Name this Child.'	
And then naming it after them, (if they shall certify him that the Child may well endure it) he shall dip it in the Water discreetly and warily, saying,	*And then, naming it after them, he shall dip it in the Water, or sprinkle it therewith, saying,*	*And then, naming it after them, he shall dip it in the Water, or pour Water upon it, or sprinkle it therewith, saying,*
'N. I baptize the...'	Unaltered.	The Same.
Rubric permitting affusion.	Omitted.	Omitted.
12. Reception (with signation) beginning—		
'We receive this Child...'	VERSION A: Unaltered. VERSION B: Omitted.	Omitted.
13. *Then shall the Priest say,*	*Then shall the Minister say,*	*Then shall the Minister say,*
Call to prayer, beginning— 'Seeing now, dearly beloved...'		
...that this Child is regenerate, and grafted into the body...	...that this Child is grafted into the body...	...that this Child is ...admitted into the body...
...for these benefits...	...for these benefits...	...for this benefit...
...according to this beginning.	...according to this beginning.	...to the glory of God.
14. Lord's Prayer.		
...which art in heaven...	...who art in heaven...	...who art in heaven...
...done in earth...	...done on earth...	...done on earth...
15. Prayer and thanksgiving, beginning— 'We yield thee hearty thanks...'		
...pleased thee to regenerate this Infant with thy Holy Spirit, to	...pleased thee to receive this Infant for thine own Child by adoption, and to in-	...pleased thee to receive this Infant for thine own Child by adoption, and to

APPENDIX 181

B.C.P.	Sunday Service, 1784	Sunday Service, 1786
receive him for thine own Child by adoption, and to incorporate him into thy holy Church ...	corporate him into thy holy Church ...	admit him into thy holy Church ...
16. Exhortations to sponsors.	Omitted.	Omitted.
17. Statements regarding the death of baptized infants, and the signation.	Omitted.	Omitted.
18.		The Minister if he see it expedient, may conclude with a prayer extempore.

Notes on the Orders for Infant Baptism in the 1784 and 1786 Editions of the Sunday Service

1. *Baptismal Regeneration.* While some references to a regenerative washing are removed from the 1784 edition, nevertheless sufficient explicit statements of this benefit remain for it to stand as simply an abridged form of the B.C.P. Order, having as its main function the baptismal regeneration of the infant. (Note particularly sections 3, 4, 7 and 10 above.) However, by further erasures (particularly in sections 4, 7, 10 and 13) the 1786 edition loses this regenerative purpose.[1]

2. *Godparents* are replaced by the 'Friends of the Child'—for whom no duties are specified, save only that of naming the infant during the ceremony.

3. The Order for *'Private Baptism ... in Houses'* is omitted.

4. The Order for *Confirmation* is omitted.

5. *Signation*—which was disliked by some as being an additional confirmatory rite[2]—is omitted from the 1784 Version B, and the 1786 edition.

---

[1] cf. A. R. George in H.M.C. p. 269.
[2] The Puritans had objected to consignation as 'a Sacrament Superadded to those which our Blessed Lord hath instituted'; Calamy, *op. cit.* pp. 511 f. cf. Wheatly, *op. cit.* pp. 356 f; Abbey and Overton, *op. cit.* p. 468; Tyerman, *Samuel Wesley*, p. 174. Wesley himself regarded, the Signation as 'superstitious' v. works x. pp. 8f.

6. The Implied Efficacy of the Sunday Service Order.[1]

(a) (1784 Order only) Baptismal Regeneration. i.e. forgiveness of original sin; adoption as a child of God; reception of the Holy Spirit; and being made an heir to the kingdom of heaven.

(b) The complete act of reception into the Church, since confirmation is discarded.

(c) Prayers are said for the future godliness of the infant.

(d) A sign of regeneration. This is stated clearly in the Articles shown above.

7. *Sprinkling* is included. It has sometimes been asserted that the *Sunday Service* was the first prayer book to specify sprinkling as a permitted method of baptising,[2] but A. E. Peaston has shown that there were precedents for it in the Calvinistic tradition,[3] and these are set within a brief historical survey in Chapter 2 above.

3. THE SERVICE OF ADULT BAPTISM

B.C.P.	Sunday Service, 1784	Sunday Service, 1786
The Ministration of Baptism to such as are of Riper Years, and able to Answer for Themselves.	*The Ministration of Baptism to such as are of Riper Years.*	*The Ministration of Baptism to such as are of Riper Years.*
1. Rubrics concerning notice to the bishop; time and place, and question about former baptism.	Omitted.	Omitted.
2. *then shall the Priest say thus,* 'Dearly beloved, forasmuch as . . .'	*The Minister shall say,* Unaltered.	*The Minister shall say,* Unaltered.
3. *Then shall the Priest say,* 'Let us pray.'	*Then shall the Minister say,* 'Let us pray.'	*Then shall the Minister use as many of the following Prayers as the Time will permit, saying,* 'Let us pray.'
(*And here all the Congregation shall kneel.*)	(*And here all the Congregation shall kneel.*)	(*And here all the Congregation shall kneel.*)

---

[1] cf. *Methodist History*, January 1967, p. 15.
[2] W.H.S. xxix. p. 19; xxxii. p. 154.
[3] L.Q.H.R. January 1966, p. 51.

APPENDIX

B.C.P.	Sunday Service, 1784	Sunday Service, 1786
Prayer beginning—'Almighty and everlasting God, who of . . .' . . . sanctify the element of Water to the mystical washing away of sin; We . . . . . . and rooted in charity . . .	Unaltered.	. . . sanctify the element of water for this holy sacrament; We . . . . . . and rooted in love . . .
4. 'Almighty and immortal God, the aid . . .'	Unaltered.	Unaltered.
5. The Gospel.	Unaltered.	Unaltered.
6. Exhortation.	Omitted.	Omitted.
7. Prayer beginning—'Almighty and everlasting God, heavenly Father, we give thee . . .'	*After which he shall say,* Unaltered.	Omitted.
8. Address to candidates, beginning—'Well-beloved, who are come hither . . .' . . . life. Ye have heard also, that our Lord . . . . . . presence of these your Witnesses, and this whole congregation, that . . .	. . . life. And our Lord . . . . . . presence of this whole Congregation, that . . .	The Same. The Same.
9. *Then shall the Priest demand of each of the persons to be baptized, severally, these Questions following:* Questions beginning—'Dost thou renounce . . .' . . . buried; that he went down into hell, and also did rise again . . .	*Then shall the Minister demand of each of the Persons to be baptized, severally,* . . . buried; that he went down into hell, and also did rise again . . .	*Then shall the Minister demand of the Persons to be baptized,* . . . buried; that he rose again . . .

7—BIEM * *

B.C.P.	Sunday Service, 1784	Sunday Service, 1786
... resurrection of the flesh, and ... ... Wilt thou be baptized in this faith? *Answer.* That is my desire.	... resurrection of the body; and ... ... Wilt thou be baptized in this faith? *Answer* This is my desire.	... resurrection of the body; and ... ... Wilt thou be baptized in this faith? *Answer* This is my desire.
10. Four short petitions.	Unaltered.	Unaltered.
11. Prayer beginning— 'Almighty, everliving God, whose most ...' ... congregation; sanctify this Water to the mystical washing away of sin; and grant ... ... to be baptized therein may receive ...	... congregation; sanctify this Water to the mystical washing away of sin; and grant ... ... to be baptized, may receive ...	... congregation; and grant ... ... to be baptized, may receive ... *The Congregation may here sing a Hymn suitable to the Occasion.*
12. *Then shall the Priest take each person to be baptized by the right hand, and placing him conveniently by the Font, according to his discretion, shall ask the Godfathers and Godmothers the Name; and then shall dip him in the water, or pour water upon him, saying,* 'N. I baptize ...'	*Then shall the Minister take each Person to be baptized by the Right Hand; and placing him conveniently by the Font, according to his Discretion, shall ask the Name; and then shall dip him in the Water, or pour Water upon him saying,* Unaltered.	*Then shall the Minister take each Person to be baptized by the Right Hand; and placing him conveniently by the Font, according to his Discretion, shall ask the Name; and then shall dip him in the Water, or pour Water upon him, or sprinkle him therewith, saying,* Unaltered.
13. Reception with signation.	Omitted.	Omitted.
14. *Then shall the Priest say,* Call to prayer, beginning— 'Seeing now, dearly beloved ...'	*Then shall the Minister say,*	*Then shall the Minister say,*

APPENDIX

B.C.P.	Sunday Service, 1784	Sunday Service, 1786
... these persons are regenerate, and grafted into the body of ...	... these Persons are grafted into the body of ...	... these Persons are admitted into the visible body of ...
... for these benefits ...	... for these benefits ...	... for this benefit ...
15. Lord's Prayer. ... Father, which art ...	... Father, who art ...	... Father, who art ...
... done in earth ...	... done on earth ...	... done on earth ...
16. 'We yield thee humble thanks ...	Unaltered.	We yield thee hearty thanks, most merciful Father, that it hath pleased thee to admit these Persons into thy holy Church. And humbly we beseech thee to grant, that they, being dead unto sin, and living unto righteousness, and being buried with Christ in his death, may crucify the old man, and utterly abolish the whole body of sin; and that being made partakers of the death of thy Son, they may also be partakers of his resurrection; so that finally, with the residue of thy holy Church, they may be inheritors of thine everlasting kingdom, through Christ our Lord. Amen.[1]

---

[1] Taken from the B.C.P. order for *infant* baptism, emended as follows:
a. The underlined words are omitted—
 '... *pleased thee to regenerate this infant with thy Holy Spirit*, to receive him *for thine own Child by adoption, and to incorporate him* into thy ...'
b. Suitable personal pronouns, etc. are substituted, so that the prayer refers to adults rather than a single infant.

B.C.P.	Sunday Service, 1784	Sunday Service, 1786
17. Exhortation to Sponsors.	Omitted.	Omitted.
18. Exhortation to the newly baptized.	Omitted.	Omitted.
19. Rubrics concerning confirmation, and the baptism of older children.	Omitted.	Omitted.

Notes on the Orders for Adult Baptism in the 1784 and 1786 Editions of the Sunday Service

1. *Baptismal Regeneration.* As with the orders for Infant Baptism, the 1784 office, while showing some changes, has still a regenerative implication (v. particularly sections 2, 3, 4, 7, 11 and 16 above); and the 1786 Order, by further emendations (v. sections 3, 7, 11, 14 and 16), loses this regenerative character (retaining only one hint of it in section 4).

2. *Sponsors* are discarded—there being no reference even to 'Friends' of the candidate (cf. the order for infant baptism).

3. All references to *confirmation* are removed.

4. *Signation* is omitted.

5. *The Implied Efficacy of the Orders.*[1]

(*a*) (1784 only) Regeneration. i.e. washing away the guilt of former sin; reception of the Holy Spirit; entering into eternal life; and becoming an heir to the kingdom of heaven.

(*b*) The complete act of reception into the Church (confirmation being discarded).

(*c*) An act of confession of faith.

(*d*) Prayers are said for future Godliness.

6. For the inclusion of *Sprinkling* as a permitted mode, v. *supra* pp. 18 f. 182.

Wesley's Dependence upon the Puritans

It is generally recognized that in revising the *Book of Common*

---

[1] cf. *Methodist History*, January 1967, p. 15.

APPENDIX

Prayer Wesley's alterations were 'in the true Puritan tradition'.[1] In regard to the baptismal offices, A. E. Peaston has pointed to the following emendations which are in conformity with the Puritan mind[2]—the elimination of the godparents' responses; the omission of the closing rubric ('It is certain by God's Word, that children which are baptized, dying before they commit actual sin, are undoubtedly saved'); the removal of phrases regarding the sanctifying of water for sacramental use; the omission of the signation; the removal of the offices for private baptism and confirmation; the elimination of the implication of universal regeneration[3]; and (as Peaston elsewhere adds[4]) the inclusion of sprinkling as a permitted mode of administration.

Thus in many ways Wesley's emendations were of the kind the Puritans had wished to make to the Prayer Book during the previous century, and there is no doubt that in a general sense he was swayed by a sympathy with their outlook.

But can it be said that there was a more direct influence than this? F. Hunter has suggested that there was: that Wesley made his 1784 revision with Calamy's book (*Abridgment of Mr. Baxter's History of his Life and Times*, 1702) before him, and that he proceeded to emend the *Book of Common Prayer* in line with the wishes of the Puritans as set out in this particular source. More specifically, Hunter claims that where Calamy showed that the suggestions made in 1689 met the demands made by the Presbyterians in 1661, Wesley followed them; and where they departed from those demands, Wesley did not follow them.[5] In the absence of any direct evidence, it remains uncertain whether in fact Wesley did work in this

---

[1] A. E. Peaston, *The Prayer Book Tradition in the Free Churches*, p. 40. cf. Nolan B. Harmon, *The Rites and Ritual of Episcopal Methodism*, pp. 33 f, 42, 193; J. A. Newton, *Methodism and the Puritans* (1964), p. 14; Horton Davis, *Worship and Theology in England ... 1690–1850*, pp. 190, 206; R. C. Monk, *John Wesley His Puritan Heritage* (1966), pp. 24 f.

[2] *Op. cit.* p. 40.

[3] We have not accepted that Wesley's alterations carry this implication. Rather they reflect his desire to remove ambiguity concerning the need for adult regeneration—and this concern had been previously expressed by the Puritans. v. *supra*. p. 62 n.

[4] L.Q.H.R. January 1966, p. 51.

[5] W.H.S. xxiii. pp. 125 ff. cf. Nolan B. Harmon, *op. cit.* p. 43.

manner,[1] and it seems more likely that his revision reflects rather a general coincidence of baptismal viewpoint between Wesley and the Puritans than his use of this one precise source.

[1] v. J. E. Rattenbury, W.H.S. xxiii. pp. 173 ff; Wesley Swift, W.H.S. xxix. pp. 14 ff.

APPENDIX 5

Bibliography of Works Cited

1. *PRIMARY SOURCES*

ANON. *A Defence of the Rev. Mr. Whitefield's Doctrine of Regeneration: In Answer to the Rev. Mr. Land.* 1739.
BENSON, JOSEPH. *Sermons on Various Occasions.* 1802.
BERRIDGE, JOHN. *Works.* Ed. R. Whittingham. 1838.
BOYCE, GILBERT. *A Serious Reply to the Rev. Mr. John Wesley in Particular, and to the People Called Methodists in General.* 1770.
CALAMY, EDMUND. *Abridgment of Mr. Baxter's History of his Life and Times.* 1702.
CENNICK, JOHN. *The First Principles of Christianity.* 1786.
COKE, THOMAS. *Commentary on the New Testament.* 1801-3.
DEACON, THOMAS. *Compleat Collection of Devotions.* 1734.
DOLMAN, JOHN. *Hymns and Spiritual Songs for the Travellers to Mount Zion, Partly Composed, and Partly Collected, from Various Authors.* 1758.
E.B. *An Expostulatory Letter to the Reverend Mr. Whitefield, And the rest of his Brethren, The Methodists of the Church of England.* 1739.
FLETCHER, JOHN. *Works.* 9 vols. 1800-9.
GAMBOLD, JOHN. *A Collection of Hymns.* (Translation) 1754.
JONES, J. *Free and Candid Disquisitions Relating to the Church of England, and the Means of Advancing Religion Therein.* 1749.
KERSHAW, JAMES. *The Methodist: attempted in Plain Metre.* 1780.
KINGSFORD, W. *A Vindication of the Baptists from the Criminality of a Charge exhibited against them by the Rev. Mr. Wesley.* 1788.
——*Three Letters to the Rev. Mr. Wesley, containing Remarks on a Piece Lately Published with his Approbation. And Three Challenges to all the Methodists in the Kingdom.* 1789.
MANNERS, N. *An attempt to illustrate the Following Subjects: ...Creation, Degeneration, Redemption.* 1783.
——*Remarks on the Writings of the Rev. J. W.* 1788.
MURLIN, JOHN. *Sacred Hymns on Various Subjects.* 3rd ed. 1788.

PERRONET, CHARLES. *A Dialogue between the Pulpit and Reading Desk. By a member of the Church of England.* 1767.

PERRONET, EDWARD. *The Mitre, a Poem.* 1756.

PERRONET, VINCENT. *A Defence of Infant-Baptism, (In Answer to the Objections of the late learned Mr. Gale). In a Letter to the Rev. Mr. John Wesley.* 1749.

—— *Some Reflections by Way of Dialogue, on the Nature of Original Sin, Baptismal Regeneration, Repentance, The New Birth . . .* c.1745. 6th ed. 1776.

—— *An Affectionate address to the People Called Quakers; with regard to Water-Baptism . . . Wherein the Arguments of the late Learned Mr. Robert Barclay, are Considered.* 1747.

SCOTT, T. *Commentary on the Bible.* 1788–92.

SIMPSON, DAVID. *A Plea for Religion and the Sacred Writings.* 1797. 1812 ed.

TELFORD, J. (ED.) *Wesley's Veterans.* 7 vols. n.d.

TOPLADY, A. M. *Works.* 1825.

WALKER, SAMUEL. *Fifty-two Sermons on the Baptismal Covenant, The Creed, The Ten Commandments . . . .* 2 Vols. 1810 ed.

WALL, WILLIAM. *History of Infant Baptism . . . . Together with M. Gale's Reflections, and Dr. Wall's Defence.* 2 vols. 1862 ed.

WATTS, ISAAC. *Works.* 1800.

WESLEY, CHARLES. *The Journal of Charles Wesley.* Ed. T. Jackson, 2 vols. 1849.

WESLEY, C. and J. *The Poetical Works of John and Charles Wesley.* Ed. G. Osborn, 13 vols. 1868–72.

WESLEY, JOHN. *The Journal of John Wesley.* Ed. N. Curnock, 8 vols. 1909–16.

—— *The Letters of John Wesley.* Ed. J. Telford, 8 vols. 1931.

—— *The Works of John Wesley.* Ed. T. Jackson, 14 vols. 1831.

—— *The Sermons of John Wesley.* Ed. E. H. Sugden, 2 vols. 1921.

—— *Explanatory Notes Upon the New Testament.* 1754. 1950 ed.

—— *Thoughts Upon Infant-Baptism, Extracted from a late Writer.* 1751.

—— *A Treatise on Baptism.* (1758) Included in *Works* vol. x.

—— *Serious Thoughts concerning Godfathers and Godmothers.* (1752) Included in *Works* vol. x.

—— *The Sunday Service of the Methodists.* 1784 and 1786 editions.

—— *Directions for Renewing our Covenant with God.* 1780.

APPENDIX   191

WESLEY, SAMUEL. *A Short Discourse of Baptism.* Included in *The Pious Communicant Rightly Prepar'd.* 1700.
WHITEFIELD, G. *Journals.* Collected ed. 1965.
—— *The Christian's Companion: or Sermons on Several Subjects.* 1738.
—— *A Collection of Hymns for Social Worship.* 1774.
—— *Works.* 6 vols. 1772.
Liturgic Hymns of the United Brethren. 1793.

2. SECONDARY SOURCES

ANON. *Wesley and Modern Methodism.* n.d.
—— *Catechism.* (of the Wesleyan Methodists) 1821.
—— *Wesleyan Tracts for the Times.* 1842.
—— *Remarks upon the 'Wesleyan Tracts for the Times', by a Layman of the Church of England.* 1842.
—— *Wesley on Baptism.* 1885?
ABBEY C. J. and OVERTON J. H. *The English Church in the Eighteenth Century.* 2nd. ed. 1896.
BAILEY, D. S. *Sponsors at Baptism and Confirmation.* 1952.
BAILLIE, JOHN. *Baptism and Conversion.* 1964.
BAKER, C. *A Letter Addressed to the Rev. G. Turner.* . . . 1843.
BAKER, FRANK. *Charles Wesley as Revealed in his Letters.* 1948.
BARCLAY, W. *Turning to God.* 1963.
BARRETT, ALFRED. *Catholic and Evangelical Principles.* 1843.
BEAL, W. *Remarks on Luke xviii. 15, 16, 17; and on the Abrahamic Covenant, Infant Baptism, and Christian Education.* 1824.
BEASLEY-MURRAY, G. R. *Baptism in the New Testament.* 1962.
BECKWITH, R. T. *Priesthood and Sacraments.* 1964.
BENNETT, G. V. and WALSH, J. D. (Edd.) *Essays in Modern English Church History.* 1966.
BENSON, J., CLARKE, A., and COKE, T. *Articles of Religion.* 1806. W.H.S. Publication, 1897.
BEYNON, TOM. *Howell Harris, Reformer and Soldier (1714-1773).* 1958.
BISHOP, J. *Methodist Worship in Relation to Free Church Worship.* 1950.
BOWMER, J. C. *The Sacrament of the Lord's Supper in Early Methodism.* 1951.
BRIGGS, F. W. *Baptism and the Wesleyan Conference.* 1882.

BULLOCK, F. W. B. *Evangelical Conversion in Great Britain 1696-1845.* 1959.
CANNON, W. R. *The Theology of John Wesley.* 1946.
CARTER, H. *The Methodist Heritage.* 1951.
CAVE, WILLIAM. *Primitive Christianity.* 3rd. ed. 1676.
CHURCH, L. F. *More about the Early Methodist People.* 1949.
CITRON, B. *New Birth.* 1951.
CLARKE, A. *Memoirs of the Wesley Family.* 1823.
——*Commentary and Critical Notes on the Holy Bible.* 6 vols. 1857.
COKE, T. and MOORE, H. *The Life of the Rev. John Wesley, A.M.* 1792.
COX, L. G. *John Wesley's Concept of Perfection.* 1964.
CROWTHER, J. *The Methodist Manual.* 1810.
——*A Portraiture of Methodism.* 1810, 2nd. ed. 1815.
DAVIES, HORTON. *Worship and Theology in England from Watts and Wesley to Maurice, 1690-1850.* 1961.
DAVIES, R. E. *Methodism.* 1963.
DAVIES, RUPERT and RUPP, GORDON (Edd.) *A History of the Methodist Church in Great Britain.* vol. 1. 1965.
DEARING, T. *Wesleyan and Tractarian Worship.* 1966.
EDWARDS, M. L. *Family Circle.* 1949.
v. EICKEN, E. *Rechtfertigung und Heiligung bei Wesley.* 1934.
ELLIOTT-BINNS, L. E. *The Early Evangelicals: A Religious and Social Study.* 1953.
FLEMINGTON, W. F. *The New Testament Doctrine of Baptism.* 1948.
GILL, F. C. *In the Steps of John Wesley.* 1962.
——*Charles Wesley the First Methodist.* 1964.
GILMORE, A. (Ed.) *Christian Baptism.* 1959.
GOODE, W. *The Doctrine of the Church of England as to the Effects of Baptism in the Case of Infants.* 1849.
GREEN, R. *The Works of John and Charles Wesley, A Bibliography.* 1896.
——*Anti-Methodist Publications issued during the Eighteenth Century. A Bibliography.* 1902.
——*John Wesley Evangelist.* 1904.
GREEN, V. H. H. *The Young Mr. Wesley.* 1961.
——*John Wesley.* 1964.
GREGORY, B. *Side Lights on the Conflicts of Methodism, 1827-1852.* 1899 ed.
HARMON, N. B. *The Rites and Ritual of Episcopal Methodism.* 1926.

HARRIS, J. *Wesley on Infant Baptism*. 1886.
HARVEY, E. G. *John Wesley, his Principles and his Practice*. n.d.
HEAD, J and D. *Martin is Baptized*. 1962.
HILDEBRANDT, F. *From Luther to Wesley*. 1951.
HOCKIN, F. *John Wesley and Modern Methodism*. 1887.
HODGES, H. A. and ALLCHIN, A. M. *A Rapture of Praise*. 1966.
HOLDEN, W. H. *John Wesley in Company with High Churchmen, by an Old Methodist*. 1870.
HUGHES, P. E. *Theology of the English Reformers*. 1965.
HUNTER, F. *John Wesley and the Coming Comprehensive Church*. 1968.
JACKSON, G. *A Series of Letters on the Subjects and Mode of Christian Baptism*. 1828.
JACKSON, T. *The Life of the Rev. Charles Wesley M.A.* 2 vols. 1841.
KIRKPATRICK, D. (Ed). *The Doctrine of the Church*. 1964.
LATHBURY, F. *History of the Nonjurors*. 1845.
LE CATO EDWARDS, W. *Epworth . . . the Home of the Wesleys*. n.d.
LEGG, J. W. *English Church Life from the Restoration to the Tractarian Movement*. 1914.
LINDSTRÖM, H. *Wesley and Sanctification*. 1950.
LOWTHER-CLARKE, W. K. *Eighteenth-Century Piety*. 1944.
LUCKOCK, H. M. and CARRIER, E. T. *John Wesley's Churchmanship*. 1891.
LYLES, A. M. *Methodism Mocked*. 1960.
MANT, R. *An Appeal to the Gospel, or An Inquiry into the Justice of the Charge, Alleged by Methodists and other Objectors, that The Gospel is not preached by the National Clergy*. 1812. 5th ed. 1813.
MONK, R. C. *John Wesley His Puritan Heritage*. 1966.
MOORE, H. *The Life of the Rev. John Wesley*. 2 vols. 1824, 25.
MORROW, T. M. *Early Methodist Women*. 1967.
MOULE, H. C. G. *Charles Simeon*. 1892.
MOZLEY, J. B. *The Primitive Doctrine of Baptismal Regeneration*. 1856.
——*A Review of the Baptismal Controversy*. 1862. 1895 ed.
NEWTON, J. A. *Methodism and the Puritans*. 1964.
OGDEN, J. H. W. *Centenary Souvenir of Mount Pleasant Methodist Church, Bacup (1841-1941)*. 1941.
OUTLER, A. C. *John Wesley*, 1964.
OVERTON, J. H. *John Wesley*. 1891.
PARRIS, J. R. *John Wesley's Doctrine of the Sacraments*. 1963.
PEASTON, A. E. *The Prayer Book Tradition in the FreeChurches*. 1964.

PROBY, W. H. B. *Annals of the 'Low-Church' Party in England.* 2 vols. 1888.
PROCTOR, F. and FRERE, W. H. *A New History of the Book of Common Prayer.* 1920. 3rd. impression, 1951.
PUSEY, E. B. *Tracts for the Times* No. 67. 'Scriptural Views of Holy Baptism.' 1836. 3rd. ed. 1840.
RACK, H. *The Future of John Wesley's Methodism.* 1965.
RATTENBURY, J. E. *The Conversion of the Wesleys.* 1938.
—— *The Evangelical Doctrines of Charles Wesley's Hymns.* 1941.
—— *The Eucharistic Hymns of John and Charles Wesley.* 1948.
RIGG, J. H. *The Churchmanship of John Wesley.* 1878.
—— *Was John Wesley a High Churchman?* 1882.
—— *The Living Wesley.* 2nd. ed. 1891.
ROBINSON, R. *A History of Baptism.* 1790.
SANGSTER, P. *Pity my Simplicity.* 1963.
SCHMIDT, M. *John Wesley.* vol. 1. 1962.
SCOTT, J. *The Life of the Rev. Thomas Scott.* 1822.
SELWYN, E. G. *The First Epistle of St. Peter.* 1958.
SHELTON, E. S. *The Centenary Volume of the Wesleyan Methodist Chapel, Clayton Street, Blackburn, 1885.* 1885.
SHREWSBURY, W. J. *Infant Baptism Scriptural, Especially as Viewed in Connection with the Scripture Doctrine of General Redemption.* . . . 1841.
SIMON, J. S. *The Revival of Religion in England in the Eighteenth Century.* 1907.
—— *John Wesley and the Religious Societies.* 1921.
SMYTH, C. *Simeon and Church Order.* 1940.
SOUTHEY, R. *The Life of John Wesley.* 1820. 1899 ed.
SYKES, N. *Church and State in England in the Eighteenth Century.* 1934.
TELFORD, J. *The Life of John Wesley.* n.d. 1947 ed.
TOWLSON, C. W. *Moravian and Methodist.* 1957.
TRIPP, D. *The Renewal of the Covenant in the Methodist Tradition.* 1969.
TYERMAN, L. *The Life and Times of the Rev. Samuel Wesley.* 1866.
—— *The Oxford Methodists.* 1873.
—— *The Life of the Rev. George Whitefield.* 2 vols. 1876.
—— *The Life and Times of the Rev. John Wesley M.A.* 3 vols. 1890.

URLIN, R. D. *John Wesley's Place in Church History*. 1870.
—— *A Churchman's Life of Wesley*. 1880.
VICKERS, J. *Thomas Coke Apostle of Methodism*. 1969.
WACE, H. and BUCHHEIM, C. A. (Edd.) *Luther's Primary Works*. 1896.
WAKELEY, J. B. *Anecdotes of the Wesleys*. 1875.
WARD, J. *The Rise and Progress of Wesleyan Methodism in Blackburn and the Neighbourhood*. 1871.
WATERLAND, D. *Works*. Ed. Dr. Van Mildert, 1823.
WATKIN-JONES, H. *Methodist Churchmanship, and its Implications*. 1945.
WATSON, R. *Theological Institutes*. 1823. vols ix–xii in Watson's *Collected Works*, Ed. T. Jackson, 1834.
—— *The Life of the Rev. John Wesley*. 1831.
WEBB, C. C. J. *Religious Thought in the Oxford Movement*. 1927.
WEDGWOOD, Miss J. *John Wesley and the Evangelical Reaction of the Eighteenth Century*. 1870.
WHEATLY, C. *A Rational Illustration of the Book of Common Prayer*. 1710. 1852 ed.
WHEELER, H. *History and Exposition of the Twenty-five Articles of Religion of the Methodist Episcopal Church*. 1908.
WHITEHEAD, J. *The Life of the Rev. John Wesley*. 2 vols. 1793 and 1796.
WILLIAMS, C. W. *John Wesley's Theology Today*. 1960.
WILLIAMS, H. W. *Constitution and Polity of Wesleyan Methodism*. 1880.
WOOD, A. S. *The Burning Heart: John Wesley Evangelist*. 1967.
YATES, A. S. *The Doctrine of Assurance*. 1952.

3. ARTICLES

Journal of the Society of Archivists. vol. ii. No. 9, pp. 411 ff. 'Nonconformist Registers.' Edwin Welch.
Methodist History. January 1967, pp. 11 ff. 'The Sacrament of Baptism According to the Sunday Service of 1784.' John English.
Wesleyan-Methodist Magazine.
1824 (Abridged ed.), pp. 229 ff. 'A Defence of Mr. Wesley and of his Doctrine.' T.J. (Thomas Jackson?)
1879. pp. 54 ff. 'Our Baptized Children.' G. Osborn.

1880. pp. 203 ff. 'On the Need of a Methodist Service-Book.' J. H. Rigg.
1881. pp. 34 ff. 'On the Baptismal Office in the Book of Common Prayer.' J. H. Rigg.

L.Q.H.R.
July 1944. pp. 210 ff. 'The Order of Service for the Baptism of Infants.' K. Grayston.
Jan. 1966. p. 51. 'Sprinkling as a Baptismal Usage.' A. E. Peaston.
Jan. 1968. pp. 51 ff. 'The Need for a Methodist Service for the Admission of Infants to the Catechumenate.' G. Wainwright.

The Christian Advocate. (U.S.A.) May 1962. vol. iv. pp. 11 f. 'Infant Baptism: Dedication.' H. R. Thompson.
Ibid. pp. 10 f. 'Infant Baptism: Entry into Covenant.' F. E. Stoeffler.
The Irish Christian Advocate. Aug. 4–25, 1950. 'The Methodist Doctrine of Baptism.' E. Gallagher.

W.H.S.
xxiii. pp. 123 ff. 'Sources of Wesley's Revision of the Prayer Book in 1784–8.' F. Hunter.
xxvii. pp. 32 ff. 'Methodism and the Book of Common Prayer.' W. F. Swift.
xxix. pp. 12 ff. 'The Sunday Service of the Methodists.' W. F. Swift.
xxxii. pp. 97 ff. 'The Sunday Service of the Methodists.' W. F. Swift and J. H. Barton.
xxxii. pp. 121 ff, 153 ff. 'Baptism in the Writings of John Wesley.' B. J. N. Galliers.

The Bulletin of the London Branch, Wesley Historical Society. No. 4, pp. 5 ff. 'Methodism in the Diocese of Canterbury, 1758.' J. A. Vickers.
The Baptist Quarterly. July 1934, Vol. vii, No. 3. pp. 97 ff. 'Methodism and Baptism.' C. Ryder Smith.
The Church Quarterly. July 1969, Vol. 2, No. 1. pp. 43 ff. 'The Background to the 1967 Methodist Service for Infant Baptism.' B. G. Holland.
Church History. Dec. 1957, pp. 355 ff. 'The Sacraments in Early American Methodism.' P. S. Sanders.

4. CONFERENCE PUBLICATIONS

Minutes of Conference.
Memorandum on Infant Baptism. 1936.
Statement on Holy Baptism. 1952.
Report on Church Membership. 1961.
Baptism and Confirmation (or Recognition) Services. 1967.

Index

Alleine, Richard, 70
Annesley, Samuel, 77n
Atlay, John, 118

Baptism:
  Adult, 43–52, 81f, 182–7
  and Apostolic Succession, 24f, 30, 32, 34, 86ff
  and Church membership, 21, 28, 56, 142, 144f, 182, 187
  Assurance from, 73f, 149ff
  By affusion, 18f, 98f, 155f
  By immersion, 18f, 24f, 28ff, 34, 92ff, 97ff, 155f.
  By sprinkling, 19f, 142, 155f, 182
  In Church, 17f, 27, 90
  Out of doors, 91f
  Preparation for, 89f
  Real benefit of, 2, 56ff
  Relative benefits of, 2, 56ff
Baptists, 53, 87, 99f, 152
Barclay, Robert, 157
Baxter, Richard, 15, 20, 155
Benson, Joseph, 113, 122n
Berridge, John, 121
Böhler, Peter, 37f
Book of Common Prayer, 7, 17, 21f, 24, 33, 42, 55, 69, 103, 128f, 131ff, 141ff, 146, 177ff, 182ff
Boyce, Gilbert, 80n, 105n, 152n

Calvin, John, 18f, 74, 79
Cave, William, 22f
Cennick, John, 127f
Clarke, Adam, 4
Clayton, John, 24, 26, 28n
Coke, Thomas, 4, 120n, 132f
Confirmation, 20f, 28, 56, 100f, 182, 187

Conversion, *see* Regeneration: Adult
Covenant, 15f, 148, 150

Deacon, Thomas, 24
Deaconesses, 29
Delamotte, Charles, 27
Dissenters:
  Re-baptism, 25, 30ff, 34, 87ff
  Wesley refuses to bury, 32f, 34
Dolman, John, 123

Fletcher, John, 61n, 120, 125n

Gambold, John, 38, 40n, 128n
Gilbert, Nathaniel, 102
Grimshaw, William, 53, 153

Hanby, Thomas, 110f, 173
Harris, Howell, 122
Huntingdon, Selina, Countess of, 118, 128f

Ingham, Benjamin, 23, 27, 28n, 57n, 96, 128n

Jackson, Thomas, 4

Kershaw, James, 68, 125n

Land, Tristam, 79
Lord's Supper, 34, 36, 49, 91, 104ff, 112, 115, 140f, 148, 150
Luther, Martin, 40, 42n, 73, 75, 151

Manners, Nicholas, 118
Mant, Richard, 120n
Melanchthon, Philip, 42n
Moravians, 29, 32, 35–42, 45, 50, 62, 86

Morgan, William, 23
Murlin, John, 126

Non-jurors, 21–6, 34

Original Sin, 54f, 56
Oxford Movement, 5, 8, 146

Pawson, John, 110, 112, 174
Percival, William, 105, 114
Perronet, Charles, 67f, 125n
Perronet, Edward, 118f, 121
Perronet, Vincent, 68n, 127
Pietists, 62
Plan of Pacification, 140f
Puritans, 15f, 19, 42n, 55, 62n, 74, 79, 96, 123, 182n, 187f
Pusey, Edward B., 5

Quakers, 87, 152, 157

Regeneration:
  Adult and Infant compared, 58f
  Adult, 1, 35–42
  Baptismal—of adults, 43ff, 53f, 143, 186f
  Baptismal, 1, 14f, 21, 39ff, 117ff, 131ff, 145f, 181f.
  Infant, 1, 53ff
Rigg, James, 7ff, 84, 117, 131

Scott, Thomas, 122n
Signation, 142n, 182, 187

Simeon, Charles, 124
Spangenberg, A. G., 29, 32, 36
Spener, Philipp Jakob, 62
Sponsors, 17f, 95ff, 143ff, 149, 152, 181f, 187
Sunday Service of the Methodists, 7, 117, 132ff, 141ff, 177ff, 182ff

Taylor, Joseph, 110, 112, 174
Taylor, Thomas, 110, 174
Töltschig, John, 50
Toplady, Augustus M., 94f, 125n

Walker, Samuel, 123f
Wall, William, 17ff, 22f, 43f, 154
Waterland, Daniel, 4, 44, 79n
Watson, Richard, 4
Watts, Isaac, 98, 154f
Wesley, Charles, 1n, 24, 27ff, 38n, 39n, 46, 48ff, 53, 67, 69f, 78, 85f, 89ff, 94, 96, 100, 102f, 104f, 107, 125f, 153, 163–9
Wesley, Samuel (Senior), 14–23, 25, 27, 35, 43, 53, 55, 69, 117, 153f
Wesley, Samuel (Junior), 58f, 62f, 78
Wesley, Susanna, 14n, 24, 78
Westminster Confession, 19, 74n
Wheatly, Charles, 19n, 22f, 33
Whitefield, George, 4, 30, 33n, 35n, 69n, 79n, 87, 90, 100, 104n, 120, 122f

DATE DUE

DEC 03 1999			

HIGHSMITH #45230   Printed in USA